THE AMERICANIZATION

OF

EDWARD BOK

EDWARD BOK

COSIMO CLASSICS
NEW YORK

The Americanization of Edward Bok

© 2005 Cosimo, Inc.

All rights reserved. No part of this book may be used or reproduced in any manner whatsoever without prior written permission except in the case of brief quotations embodied in critical articles or reviews.

For information, address:

Cosimo, P.O. Box 416
Old Chelsea Station
New York, NY 10113-0416

or visit our website at:
www.cosimobooks.com

The Americanization of Edward Bok originally published by Charles Scribner's Sons in 1924.

Library of Congress Cataloging-in-Publication Data

A catalog record for this book is available from the Library of Congress

Cover design by www.wiselephant.com

ISBN: 1-59605-073-X

From a photograph by Chandler, Philadelphia

Edward W. Bok

TO THE AMERICAN WOMAN I OWE MUCH
BUT TO TWO WOMEN I OWE MORE

MY MOTHER
AND
MY WIFE

AND TO THEM I DEDICATE THIS ACCOUNT OF THE BOY
TO WHOM ONE GAVE BIRTH AND BROUGHT TO MANHOOD
AND THE OTHER BLESSED WITH ALL THAT A
HOME AND FAMILY MAY MEAN

AN EXPLANATION

THIS book was to have been written in 1914, when I foresaw some leisure to write it, for I then intended to retire from active editorship. But the war came, an entirely new set of duties commanded, and the project was laid aside.

Its title and the form, however, were then chosen. By the form I refer particularly to the use of the third person. I had always felt the most effective method of writing an autobiography, for the sake of a better perspective, was mentally to separate the writer from his subject by this device.

Moreover, this method came to me very naturally in dealing with the Edward Bok, editor and publicist whom I have tried to describe in this book, because, in many respects, he has had and has been a personality apart from my private self. I have again and again found myself watching with intense amusement and interest the Edward Bok of this book at work. I have, in turn, applauded him and criticised him, as I do in this book. Not that I ever considered myself bigger or broader than this Edward Bok: simply that he was different. His tastes, his outlook, his manner of looking at things were totally at variance with my own. In fact, my chief difficulty during Edward Bok's directorship of *The Ladies' Home Journal* was to abstain from breaking through the editor and revealing my real self. Several times I did so, and each time I saw how different was the effect from that when the editorial Edward Bok had been allowed sway. Little by little I learned to subordinate myself and to let him have full rein.

But no relief of my life was so great to me personally as his decision to retire from his editorship. My family and friends were surprised and amused by my intense and obvious relief when he did so. Only to those closest to me could I explain the reason for the sense of absolute freedom and gratitude that I felt.

Since that time my feelings have been an interesting study to myself. There are no longer two personalities. The Edward Bok of whom I have written has passed out of my being as completely as if he had never been there, save for the records and files on my library shelves. It is easy, therefore, for me to write of him as a personality apart: in fact, I could not depict him from any other point of view. To write of him in the first person, as if he were myself, is impossible, for he is not.

The title suggests my principal reason for writing the book. Every life has some interest and significance; mine, perhaps, a special one. Here was a little Dutch boy unceremoniously set down in America unable to make himself understood or even to know what persons were saying; his education was extremely limited, practically negligible; and yet, by some curious decree of fate, he was destined to write, for a period of years, to the largest body of readers ever addressed by an American editor—the circulation of the magazine he edited running into figures previously unheard of in periodical literature. He made no pretense to style or even to composition: his grammar was faulty, as it was natural it should be, in a language not his own. His roots never went deep, for the intellectual soil had not been favorable to their growth;—yet, it must be confessed, he achieved.

But how all this came about, how such a boy, with every disadvantage to overcome, was able, apparently, to "make good"—this possesses an interest and for some, perhaps, a value which, after all, is the only reason for any book.

EDWARD W. BOK

MERION
PENNSYLVANIA
1920

CONTENTS

CONTENTS xiii

ILLUSTRATIONS

AN INTRODUCTION OF TWO PERSONS

IN WHOSE LIVES ARE FOUND THE SOURCE AND MAINSPRING
OF SOME OF THE EFFORTS OF THE AUTHOR OF THIS BOOK
IN HIS LATER YEARS

*Along an island in the North Sea, five miles from the
Dutch Coast, stretches a dangerous ledge of rocks that has
proved the graveyard of many a vessel sailing that turbulent
sea. On this island once lived a group of men who, as
each vessel was wrecked, looted the vessel and murdered
those of the crew who reached shore. The government of
the Netherlands decided to exterminate the island pirates,
and for the job King William selected a young lawyer at
The Hague.*

*"I want you to clean up that island," was the royal
order. It was a formidable job for a young man of twenty-
odd years. By royal proclamation he was made mayor of
the island, and within a year, a court of law being established, the young attorney was appointed judge; and in that
dual capacity he "cleaned up" the island.*

*The young man now decided to settle on the island, and
began to look around for a home. It was a grim place,
barren of tree or living green of any kind; it was as if a
man had been exiled to Siberia. Still, argued the young
mayor, an ugly place is ugly only because it is not beautiful. And beautiful he determined this island should be.*

*One day the young mayor-judge called together his coun-
cil. "We must have trees," he said; "we can make this
island a spot of beauty if we will!" But the practical sea-
faring men demurred; the little money they had was
needed for matters far more urgent than trees.*

*"Very well," was the mayor's decision—and little they
guessed what the words were destined to mean—"I will do
it myself." And that year he planted one hundred trees,
the first the island had ever seen.*

*"Too cold," said the islanders; "the severe north winds
and storms will kill them all."*

*"Then I will plant more," said the unperturbed mayor.
And for the fifty years that he lived on the island he did so.
He planted trees each year; and, moreover, he had deeded to
the island government land which he turned into public
squares and parks, and where each spring he set out shrubs
and plants.*

*Moistened by the salt mist the trees did not wither, but
grew prodigiously. In all that expanse of turbulent sea—
and only those who have seen the North Sea in a storm know
how turbulent it can be—there was not a foot of ground on
which the birds, storm-driven across the water-waste, could
rest in their flight. Hundreds of dead birds often covered
the surface of the sea. Then one day the trees had grown
tall enough to look over the sea, and, spent and driven, the
first birds came and rested in their leafy shelter. And
others came and found protection, and gave their gratitude*

*vent in song. Within a few years so many birds had dis-
covered the trees in this new island home that they attracted
the attention not only of the native islanders but also of the
people on the shore five miles distant, and the island became famous as the home of the rarest and most beautiful
birds. So grateful were the birds for their resting-place
that they chose one end of the island as a special spot for
the laying of their eggs and the raising of their young, and
they fairly peopled it. It was not long before ornithologists
from various parts of the world came to "Eggland," as the
farthermost point of the island came to be known, to see
the marvellous sight, not of thousands but of hundreds of
thousands of bird-eggs. .*

*A pair of storm-driven nightingales had now found the
island and mated there; their wonderful notes thrilled even
the souls of the natives; and as dusk fell upon the seabound
strip of land the women and children would come to "the
square" and listen to the evening notes of the birds of golden
song. The two nightingales soon grew into a colony, and
within a few years so rich was the island in its nightingales
that over to the Dutch coast and throughout the land and into
other countries spread the fame of "The Island of Nightingales."*

*Meantime, the young mayor-judge, grown to manhood,
had kept on planting trees each year, setting out his shrub-
bery and plants, until their verdure now beautifully shaded
the quaint, narrow lanes, and transformed into cool wooded*

*roads what once had been only barren sun-baked wastes.
Artists began to hear of the place and brought their canvases, and on the walls of hundreds of homes throughout
the world hang to-day bits of the beautiful lanes and wooded
spots of "The Island of Nightingales." The American
artist William M. Chase took his pupils there almost
annually. "In all the world to-day," he declared to his
students, as they exclaimed at the natural cool restfulness
of the island, "there is no more beautiful place."*

*The trees are now majestic in their height of forty or
more feet, for it is nearly a hundred years since the young
attorney went to the island and planted the first tree; to-
day the churchyard where he lies is a bower of cool green,
with the trees that he planted dropping their moisture
on the lichen-covered stone on his grave.*

This much did one man do. But he did more.

*After he had been on the barren island two years he
went to the mainland one day, and brought back with him
a bride. It was a bleak place for a bridal home, but the
young wife had the qualities of the husband. "While
you raise your trees," she said, "I will raise our children."
And within a score of years the young bride sent thirteen
happy-faced, well-brought-up children over that island,
and there was reared a home such as is given to few. Said
a man who subsequently married a daughter of that home:
"It was such a home that once you had been in it you felt
you must be of it, and that if you couldn't marry one of the*

daughters you would have been glad to have married the cook."

One day when the children had grown to man's and woman's estate the mother called them all together and said to them, "I want to tell you the story of your father and of this island," and she told them the simple story that is written here.

"And now," she said, "as you go out into the world I want each of you to take with you the spirit of your father's work, and each in your own way and place, to do as he has done: make you the world a bit more beautiful and better because you have been in it.   That is your mother's message to you."

The first son to leave the island home went with a band of hardy men to South Africa, where they settled and became known as "the Boers."   Tirelessly they worked at the colony until towns and cities sprang up and a new nation came into being: The Transvaal Republic.   The son became secretary of state of the new country, and to-day the United States of South Africa bears tribute, in part, to the mother's message to "make the world a bit more beautiful and better."

The second son left home for the Dutch mainland, where he took charge of a small parish; and when he had finished his work he was mourned by king and peasant as one of the leading clergymen of his time and people.

A third son, scorning his own safety, plunged into the

boiling surf on one of those nights of terror so common to that coast, rescued a half-dead sailor, carried him to his father's house, and brought him back to a life of usefulness that gave the world a record of imperishable value. For the half-drowned sailor was Heinrich Schliemann, the famous explorer of the dead cities of Troy.

The first daughter now left the island nest; to her inspiration her husband owed, at his life's close, a shelf of works in philosophy which to-day are among the standard books of their class.

The second daughter worked beside her husband until she brought him to be regarded as one of the ablest preachers of his land, speaking for more than forty years the message of man's betterment.

To another son it was given to sit wisely in the councils of his land; another followed the footsteps of his father. Another daughter, refusing marriage for duty, ministered unto and made a home for one whose eyes could see not.

So they went out into the world, the girls and boys of that island home, each carrying the story of their father's simple but beautiful work and the remembrance of their mother's message. Not one from that home but did well his or her work in the world; some greater, some smaller, but each left behind the traces of a life well spent.

And, as all good work is immortal, so to-day all over the world goes on the influence of this one man and one woman, whose life on that little Dutch island changed its barren rocks to a bower of verdure, a home for the birds and the song of the nightingale.   The grandchildren have gone to the four corners of the globe, and are now the generation of workers—some in the far East Indies; others in Africa; still others in our own land of America.   But each has tried, according to the talents given, to carry out the message of that day, to tell the story of the grandfather's work; just as it is told here by the author of this book, who, in the efforts of his later years, has tried to carry out, so far as opportunity has come to him, the message of his grandmother:

"Make you the world a bit more beautiful and better because you have been in it."

CHAPTER I

THE FIRST DAYS IN AMERICA

THE leviathan of the Atlantic Ocean, in 1870, was *The Queen*, and when she was warped into her dock on September 20 of that year, she discharged, among her passengers, a family of four from the Netherlands who were to make an experiment of Americanization.

The father, a man bearing one of the most respected names in the Netherlands, had acquired wealth and position for himself; unwise investments, however, had swept away his fortune, and in preference to a new start in his own land, he had decided to make the new beginning in the United States, where a favorite brother-in-law had gone several years before. But that, never a simple matter for a man who has reached forty-two, is particularly difficult for a foreigner in a strange land. This fact he and his wife were to find out. The wife, also carefully reared, had been accustomed to a scale of living which she had now to abandon. Her Americanization experiment was to compel her, for the first time in her life, to become a housekeeper without domestic help. There were two boys: the elder, William, was eight and a half years of age; the younger, in nineteen days from his landing-date, was to celebrate his seventh birthday.

This younger boy was Edward William Bok. He had, according to the Dutch custom, two other names, but he had decided to leave those in the Netherlands. And the American public was, in later years, to omit for him the "William."

Edward's first six days in the United States were spent in New York, and then he was taken to Brooklyn, where he was destined to live for nearly twenty years.

Thanks to the linguistic sense inherent in the Dutch, and to an educational system that compels the study of languages, English was already familiar to the father and mother. But to the two sons, who had barely learned the beginnings of their native tongue, the English language was as a closed book. It seemed a cruel decision of the father to put his two boys into a public school in Brooklyn, but he argued that if they were to become Americans, the sooner they became part of the life of the country and learned its language for themselves, the better. And so, without the ability to make known the slightest want or to understand a single word, the morning after their removal to Brooklyn, the two boys were taken by their father to a public school.

The American public-school teacher was perhaps even less well equipped in those days than she is to-day to meet the needs of two Dutch boys who could not understand a word she said, and who could only wonder what it was all about. The brothers did not even have the comfort of each other's company, for, graded by age, they were placed in separate classes.

Nor was the American boy of 1870 a whit less cruel than is the American boy of 1920; and he was none the less loath to show that cruelty. This trait was evident at the first recess of the first day at school. At the dismissal, the brothers naturally sought each other, only to find themselves surrounded by a group of tormentors who were delighted to have such promising objects for their fun. And of this opportunity they made the most. There was no form of petty cruelty boys' minds could devise that was not inflicted upon the two helpless strangers. Edward seemed to look particularly invit- ing, and nicknaming him "Dutchy" they devoted them- selves at each noon recess and after school to inflicting their cruelties upon him.

Louis XIV may have been right when he said that "every new language requires a new soul," but Edward Bok knew that while spoken languages might differ, there is one language understood by boys the world over. And with this language Edward decided to do some ex- perimenting. After a few days at school, he cast his eyes over the group of his tormentors, picked out one who seemed to him the ringleader, and before the boy was aware of what had happened, Edward Bok was in the full swing of his first real experiment with American- ization. Of course the American boy retaliated. But the boy from the Netherlands had not been born and brought up in the muscle-building air of the Dutch dikes for nothing, and after a few moments he found himself looking down on his tormentor and into the eyes of a crowd of very respectful boys and giggling girls who readily made a passageway for his brother and himself when they indicated a desire to leave the schoolyard and go home.

Edward now felt that his Americanization had be- gun; but, always believing that a thing begun must be carried to a finish, he took, or gave—it depends upon the point of view—two or three more lessons in this particular phase of Americanization before he convinced these American schoolboys that it might be best for them to call a halt upon further excursions in torment.

At the best, they were difficult days at school for a boy of six without the language. But the national linguistic gift inherent in the Dutch race came to the boy's rescue, and as the roots of the Anglo-Saxon lie in the Frisian tongue, and thus in the language of his native country, Edward soon found that with a change of vowel here and there the English language was not so difficult of conquest. At all events, he set out to master it.

But his fatal gift of editing, although its possession was unknown to him, began to assert itself when, just as he seemed to be getting along fairly well, he balked at following the Spencerian style of writing in his copy-books. Instinctively he rebelled at the flourishes which embellished that form of handwriting. He seemed to divine somehow that such penmanship could not be useful or practicable for after life, and so, with that Dutch stolidity that, once fixed, knows no altering, he refused to copy his writing lessons. Of course trouble immediately ensued between Edward and his teacher. Finding herself against a literal blank wall—for Edward simply refused, but had not the gift of English with which to explain his refusal—the teacher decided to take the matter to the male principal of the school. She explained that she had kept Edward after school for

EDWARD BOK AT THE AGE OF SIX
Upon his arrival in the United States

as long as two hours to compel him to copy his Spencerian lesson, but that the boy simply sat quiet. He was perfectly well-behaved, she explained, but as to his lesson, he would attempt absolutely nothing.

It was the prevailing custom in the public schools of 1870 to punish boys by making them hold out the palms of their hands, upon which the principal would inflict blows with a rattan. The first time Edward was punished in this way, his hand became so swollen he wondered at a system of punishment which rendered him incapable of writing, particularly as the discerning principal had chosen the boy's right hand upon which to rain the blows. Edward was told to sit down at the principal's own desk and copy the lesson. He sat, but he did not write. He would not for one thing, and he could not if he would. After half an hour of purposeless sitting, the principal ordered Edward again to stand up and hold out his hand; and once more the rattan fell in repeated blows. Of course it did no good, and as it was then five o'clock, and the principal had inflicted all the punishment that the law allowed, and as he probably wanted to go home as much as Edward did, he dismissed the sore-handed but more-than-ever-determined Dutch boy.

Edward went home to his father, exhibited his swollen hand, explained the reason, and showed the penmanship lesson which he had refused to copy. It is a singular fact that even at that age he already understood Americanization enough to realize that to cope successfully with any American institution, one must be constructive as well as destructive. He went to his room, brought out a specimen of Italian handwriting which he had seen in a newspaper, and explained to his father that this simpler penmanship seemed to him better for practical purposes than the curlicue fancifully

SPENCERIAN STYLE IN VOGUE AT THIS PERIOD

embroidered Spencerian style; that if he had to learn penmanship, why not learn the system that was of more possible use in after life?

Now, your Dutchman is nothing if not practical. He is very simple and direct in his nature, and is very likely to be equally so in his mental view. Edward's father was distinctly interested—very much amused, as he confessed to the boy in later years—in his son's discernment of the futility of the Spencerian style of penmanship. He agreed with the boy, and, next morning, accompanied him to school and to the principal. The two men were closeted together, and when they came out Edward was sent to his classroom. For some weeks he was given no penmanship lessons, and then a new copy-book was given him with a much simpler style. He pounced upon it, and within a short time stood at the head of his class in writing.

The same instinct that was so often to lead Edward aright in his future life, at its very beginning served him in a singularly valuable way in directing his attention to the study of penmanship; for it was through his legible handwriting that later, in the absence of the typewriter, he was able to secure and satisfactorily fill three positions which were to lead to his final success.

Years afterward Edward had the satisfaction of seeing

Unbusy Unchary Yearling

SPENCERIAN STYLE NOW IN VOGUE

public-school pupils given a choice of penmanship lessons: one along the flourish lines and the other of a less ornate order. Of course, the boy never associated the incident of his refusal with the change until later when his mother explained to him that the principal of the school, of whom the father had made a warm friend, was so impressed by the boy's simple but correct view, that he took up the matter with the board of education, and a choice of systems was considered and later decided upon.

From this it will be seen that, unconsciously, Edward Bok had started upon his career of editing!

CHAPTER II

THE FIRST JOB: FIFTY CENTS A WEEK

THE elder Bok did not find his "lines cast in pleasant places" in the United States. He found himself, professionally, unable to adjust the methods of his own land and of a lifetime to those of a new country. As a result the fortunes of the transplanted family did not flourish, and Edward soon saw his mother physically failing under burdens to which her nature was not accustomed nor her hands trained. Then he and his brother decided to relieve their mother in the housework by rising early in the morning, building the fire, preparing breakfast, and washing the dishes before they went to school. After school they gave up their play hours, and swept and scrubbed, and helped their mother to prepare the evening meal and wash the dishes afterward. It was a curious coincidence that it should fall upon Edward thus to get a first-hand knowledge of woman's housework which was to stand him in such practical stead in later years.

It was not easy for the parents to see their boys thus forced to do work which only a short while before had been done by a retinue of servants. And the capstone of humiliation seemed to be when Edward and his brother, after having for several mornings found no kindling wood or coal to build the fire, decided to go out of evenings with a basket and pick up what wood they could find in neighboring lots, and the bits of coal spilled from the coal-bin of the grocery-store, or left on the curbs before houses where coal had been delivered. The mother remonstrated with the boys, although in her heart she knew that the necessity was upon them. But Edward had been started upon his Americanization career, and answered: "This is America, where one can do anything if it is honest. So long as we don't steal the wood or coal, why shouldn't we get it?" And, turning away, the saddened mother said nothing.

But while the doing of these homely chores was very effective in relieving the untrained and tired mother, it added little to the family income. Edward looked about and decided that the time had come for him, young as he was, to begin some sort of wage-earning. But how and where? The answer he found one afternoon when standing before the shop-window of a baker in the neighborhood. The owner of the bakery, who had just placed in the window a series of trays filled with buns, tarts, and pies, came outside to look at the display. He found the hungry boy wistfully regarding the tempting-looking wares.

"Look pretty good, don't they?" asked the baker.

"They would," answered the Dutch boy with his national passion for cleanliness, "if your window were clean."

"That's so, too," mused the baker. "Perhaps you'll clean it."

"I will," was the laconic reply. And Edward Bok, there and then, got his first job. He went in, found a step-ladder, and put so much Dutch energy into the cleaning of the large show-window that the baker immediately arranged with him to clean it every Tuesday and Friday afternoon after school. The salary was to be fifty cents per week!

But one day, after he had finished cleaning the window, and the baker was busy in the rear of the store, a customer came in, and Edward ventured to wait on her. Dexterously he wrapped up for another the fragrant currant-buns for which his young soul—and stomach—so hungered! The baker watched him, saw how quickly and smilingly he served the customer, and offered Edward an extra dollar per week if he would come in afternoons and sell behind the counter. He immediately entered into the bargain with the understanding that, in addition to his salary of a dollar and a half per week, he should each afternoon carry home from the good things unsold a moderate something as a present to his mother. The baker agreed, and Edward promised to come each afternoon except Saturday.

"Want to play ball, hey?" said the baker.

"Yes, I want to play ball," replied the boy, but he was not reserving his Saturday afternoons for games, although, boy-like, that might be his preference.

Edward now took on for each Saturday morning—when, of course, there was no school—the delivery route of a weekly paper called the *South Brooklyn Advocate*. He had offered to deliver the entire neighborhood edition of the paper for one dollar, thus increasing his earning capacity to two dollars and a half per week.

Transportation, in those days in Brooklyn, was by horse-cars, and the car-line on Smith Street nearest Edward's home ran to Coney Island. Just around the corner where Edward lived the cars stopped to water the horses on their long haul. The boy noticed that the men jumped from the open cars in summer, ran into the cigar-store before which the watering-trough was placed, and got a drink of water from the ice-cooler placed near the door. But that was not so easily possible for the women, and they, especially the children, were forced to take the long ride without a drink. It was this that he had in mind when he reserved his Saturday afternoon to "play ball."

Here was an opening, and Edward decided to fill it. He bought a shining new pail, screwed three hooks on the edge from which he hung three clean shimmering glasses, and one Saturday afternoon when a car stopped the boy leaped on, tactfully asked the conductor if he did not want a drink, and then proceeded to sell his water, cooled with ice, at a cent a glass to the passengers. A little experience showed that he exhausted a pail with every two cars, and each pail netted him thirty cents. Of course Sunday was a most profitable day; and after going to Sunday-school in the morning, he did a further Sabbath service for the rest of the day by refreshing tired mothers and thirsty children on the Coney Island cars—at a penny a glass!

But the profit of six dollars which Edward was now reaping in his newly found "bonanza" on Saturday and Sunday afternoons became apparent to other boys, and one Saturday the young ice-water boy found that he had a competitor; then two and soon three. Edward immediately met the challenge; he squeezed half a dozen lemons into each pail of water, added some sugar, tripled his charge, and continued his monopoly by selling "Lemonade, three cents a glass." Soon more passengers were asking for lemonade than for plain drinking-water!

One evening Edward went to a party of young people, and his latent journalistic sense whispered to him that his young hostess might like to see her social affair in print. He went home, wrote up the party, being careful to include the name of every boy and girl present, and next morning took the account to the city editor of the *Brooklyn Eagle*, with the sage observation that every name mentioned in that paragraph represented a buyer of the paper, who would like to see his or her name in print, and that if the editor had enough of these reports he might very advantageously strengthen the circulation of *The Eagle*. The editor was not slow to see the point, and offered Edward three dollars a column for such reports. On his way home, Edward calculated how many parties he would have to attend a week to furnish a column, and decided that he would organize a corps of private reporters himself. Forthwith, he saw every girl and boy he knew, got each to promise to write for him an account of each party he or she attended or gave, and laid great stress on a full recital of names. Within a few weeks, Edward was turning in to *The Eagle* from two to three columns a week; his pay was raised to four dollars a column; the editor was pleased in having started a department that no other paper carried, and the "among those present" at the parties all bought the paper and were immensely gratified to see their names.

So everybody was happy, and Edward Bok, as a full-fledged reporter, had begun his journalistic career.

It is curious how deeply embedded in his nature, even in his earliest years, was the inclination toward the publishing business. The word "curious" is used here because Edward is the first journalist in the Bok family in all the centuries through which it extends in Dutch history. On his father's side, there was a succession of jurists. On the mother's side, not a journalist is visible.

Edward attended the Sunday-school of the Carroll Park Methodist Episcopal Church, in Brooklyn, of which a Mr. Elkins was superintendent. One day he learned that Mr. Elkins was associated with the publishing house of Harper and Brothers. Edward had heard his father speak of *Harper's Weekly* and of the great part it had played in the Civil War; his father also brought home an occasional copy of *Harper's Weekly* and of *Harper's Magazine.* He had seen *Harper's Young People;* the name of Harper and Brothers was on some of his school-books; and he pictured in his mind how wonderful it must be for a man to be associated with publishers of periodicals that other people read, and books that other folks studied. The Sunday-school superintendent henceforth became a figure of importance in Edward's eyes; many a morning the boy hastened from home long before the hour for school, and seated himself on the steps of the Elkins house under the pretext of waiting for Mr. Elkins's son to go to school, but really for the secret purpose of seeing Mr. Elkins set forth to engage in the momentous business of making books and periodicals. Edward would look after the superintendent's form until it was lost to view; then, with a sigh, he would go to school, forgetting all about the Elkins boy whom he had told the father he had come to call for!

One day Edward was introduced to a girl whose father, he learned, was editor of the *New York Weekly*. Edward could not quite place this periodical; he had never seen it, he had never heard of it. So he bought a copy, and while its contents seemed strange, and its air unfamiliar in comparison with the magazines he found in his home, still an editor was an editor. He was certainly well worth knowing. So he sought his newly made young lady friend, asked permission to call upon her, and to Edward's joy was introduced to her father. It was enough for Edward to look furtively at the editor upon his first call, and being encouraged to come again, he promptly did so the next evening. The daughter has long since passed away, and so it cannot hurt her feelings now to acknowledge that for years Edward paid court to her only that he might know her father, and have those talks with him about editorial methods that filled him with ever-increasing ambition to tread the path that leads to editorial tribulations.

But what with helping his mother, tending the baker's shop in after-school hours, serving his paper route, plying his street-car trade, and acting as social reporter, it soon became evident to Edward that he had not much time to prepare his school lessons. By a supreme effort, he managed to hold his own in his class, but no more. Instinctively, he felt that he was not getting all that he might from his educational opportunities, yet the need for him to add to the family income was, if anything, becoming greater. The idea of leaving school was broached to his mother, but she rebelled. She told the boy that he was earning something now and helping much. Perhaps the tide with the father would turn and he would find the place to which his unquestioned talents entitled him. Finally the father did. He associated himself with the Western Union Telegraph Company as translator, a position for which his easy command of languages admirably fitted him. Thus, for a time, the strain upon the family exchequer was lessened.

But the American spirit of initiative had entered deep into the soul of Edward Bok. The brother had left school a year before, and found a place as messenger in a lawyer's office; and when one evening Edward heard his father say that the office boy in his department had left, he asked that he be allowed to leave school, apply for the open position, and get the rest of his education in the great world itself. It was not easy for the parents to see the younger son leave school at so early an age, but the earnestness of the boy prevailed.

And so, at the age of thirteen, Edward Bok left school, and on Monday, August 7, 1876, he became office boy in the electricians' department of the Western Union Telegraph Company at six dollars and twenty-five cents per week.

And, as such things will fall out in this curiously

strange world, it happened that as Edward drew up his chair for the first time to his desk to begin his work on that Monday morning, there had been born in Boston, exactly twelve hours before, a girl-baby who was destined to become his wife.   Thus at the earliest possible moment after her birth, Edward Bok started to work for her!

CHAPTER III

THE HUNGER FOR SELF-EDUCATION

WITH school-days ended, the question of self-education became an absorbing thought with Edward Bok. He had mastered a schoolboy's English, but seven years of public-school education was hardly a basis on which to build the work of a lifetime. He saw each day in his duties as office boy some of the foremost men of the time. It was the period of William H. Vanderbilt's ascendancy in Western Union control; and the railroad millionnaire and his companions, Hamilton McK. Twombly, James H. Banker, Samuel F. Barger, Alonzo B. Cornell, Augustus Schell, William Orton, were objects of great interest to the young office boy. Alexander Graham Bell and Thomas A. Edison were also constant visitors to the department. He knew that some of these men, too, had been deprived of the advantage of collegiate training, and yet they had risen to the top. But how? The boy decided to read about these men and others, and find out. He could not, however, afford the separate biographies, so he went to the libraries to find a compendium that would authoritatively tell him of all successful men. He found it in Appleton's *Encyclopædia*, and, determining to have only the best, he saved his luncheon money, walked instead of riding the five miles to his Brooklyn home, and, after a period of saving, had his reward in the first purchase from his own earnings: a set of the *Encyclopædia*. He now read about all the successful men, and was encouraged to find that in many cases their beginnings had been as modest as his own, and their opportunities of education as limited.

One day it occurred to him to test the accuracy of the biographies he was reading. James A. Garfield was then spoken of for the presidency; Edward wondered whether it was true that the man who was likely to be President of the United States had once been a boy on the tow-path, and with a simple directness characteristic of his Dutch training, wrote to General Garfield, asking whether the boyhood episode was true, and explaining why he asked. Of course any public man, no matter how large his correspondence, is pleased to receive an earnest letter from an information-seeking boy. General Garfield answered warmly and fully. Edward showed the letter to his father, who told the boy that it was valuable and he should keep it. This was a new idea. He followed it further: if one such letter was valuable, how much more valuable would be a hundred! If General Garfield answered him, would not other famous men? Why not begin a collection of autograph letters? Everybody collected something.

Edward had collected postage-stamps, and the hobby had, incidentally, helped him wonderfully in his study of geography. Why should not autograph letters from famous persons be of equal service in his struggle for self-education? Not simple autographs—they were meaningless; but actual letters which might tell him something useful. It never occurred to the boy that these men might not answer him.

So he took his *Encyclopædia*—its trustworthiness now established in his mind by General Garfield's letter—and began to study the lives of successful men and women. Then, with boyish frankness, he wrote on some mooted question in one famous person's life; he asked about the date of some important event in another's, not given in the *Encyclopædia;* or he asked one man why he did this or why some other man did that.

Most interesting were, of course, the replies. Thus General Grant sketched on an improvised map the exact spot where General Lee surrendered to him; Longfellow told him how he came to write "Excelsior"; Whittier told the story of "The Barefoot Boy"; Tennyson wrote out a stanza or two of "The Brook," upon condition that Edward would not again use the word "awful," which the poet said "is slang for 'very,'" and "I hate slang."

One day the boy received a letter from the Confederate general Jubal A. Early, giving the real reason why he burned Chambersburg. A friend visiting Edward's father, happening to see the letter, recognized in it a hitherto-missing bit of history, and suggested that it be published in the *New York Tribune.* The letter attracted wide attention and provoked national discussion.

This suggested to the editor of *The Tribune* that Edward might have other equally interesting letters; so he despatched a reporter to the boy's home. This reporter was Ripley Hitchcock, who afterward became literary adviser for the Appletons and Harpers. Of course Hitchcock at once saw a "story" in the boy's letters, and within a few days *The Tribune* appeared with a long article on its principal news page giving an account of the Brooklyn boy's remarkable letters and how he had secured them. The *Brooklyn Eagle* quickly followed with a request for an interview; the *Boston Globe* followed suit; the *Philadelphia Public Ledger* sent its New York correspondent; and before Edward was aware of it, newspapers in different parts of the country were writing about "the well-known Brooklyn autograph collector."

Edward Bok was quick to see the value of the publicity which had so suddenly come to him. He received letters from other autograph collectors all over the country who sought to "exchange" with him. References began to creep into letters from famous persons to whom he had written, saying they had read about his wonderful collection and were proud to be included in it. George W. Childs, of Philadelphia, himself the possessor of probably one of the finest collections of autograph letters in the country, asked Edward to come to Philadelphia and bring his collection with him—which he did, on the following Sunday, and brought it back greatly enriched.

Several of the writers felt an interest in a boy who frankly told them that he wanted to educate himself, and asked Edward to come and see them. Accordingly, when they lived in New York or Brooklyn, or came to these cities on a visit, he was quick to avail himself of their invitations. He began to note each day in the newspapers the "distinguished arrivals" at the New York hotels; and when any one with whom he had corresponded arrived, Edward would, after business hours, go up-town, pay his respects, and thank him in person for his letters. No person was too high for Edward's boyish approach; President Garfield, General Grant, General Sherman, President Hayes—all were called upon, and all received the boy graciously and were interested in the problem of his self-education. It was a veritable case of making friends on every hand; friends who were to be of the greatest help and value to the boy in his after-years, although he had no conception of it at the time.

The Fifth Avenue Hotel, in those days the stopping-place of the majority of the famous men and women visiting New York, represented to the young boy who came to see these celebrities the very pinnacle of opulence. Often while waiting to be received by some dignitary, he wondered how one could acquire enough means to live at a place of such luxury. The main dining-room, to the boy's mind, was an object of special interest. He would purposely sneak up-stairs and sit on one of the soft sofas in the foyer simply to see the well-dressed diners go in and come out. Edward would speculate on whether the time would ever come when he could dine in that wonderful room just once!

One evening he called, after the close of business, upon General and Mrs. Grant, whom he had met before, and who had expressed a desire to see his collection. It can readily be imagined what a red-letter day it made in the boy's life to have General Grant say: "It might be better for us all to go down to dinner first and see the collection afterward." Edward had purposely killed time between five and seven o'clock, thinking that the general's dinner-hour, like his own, was at six. He had allowed an hour for the general to eat his dinner, only to find that he was still to begin it. The boy could hardly believe his ears, and unable to find his voice, he failed to apologize for his modest suit or his general after-business appearance.

As in a dream he went down in the elevator with his host and hostess, and when the party of three faced toward the dining-room entrance, so familiar to the boy, he felt as if his legs must give way under him. There have since been other red-letter days in Edward Bok's life, but the moment that still stands out pre-eminent is that when two colored head waiters at the dining-room entrance, whom he had so often watched, bowed low and escorted the party to their table. At last, he was in that sumptuous dining-hall. The entire room took on the picture of one great eye, and that eye centred on the party of three—as, in fact, it naturally would. But Edward felt that the eye was on him, wondering why he should be there.

What he ate and what he said he does not recall. General Grant, not a voluble talker himself, gently drew the boy out, and Mrs. Grant seconded him, until toward the close of the dinner he heard himself talking. He remembers that he heard his voice, but what that voice said is all dim to him. One act stamped itself on his mind. The dinner ended with a wonderful dish of nuts and raisins, and just before the party rose from the table Mrs. Grant asked the waiter to bring her a paper bag. Into this she emptied the entire dish, and at the close of the evening she gave it to Edward "to eat on the way home." It was a wonderful evening, afterward up-stairs, General Grant smoking the inevitable cigar, and telling stories as he read the letters of different celebrities. Over those of Confederate generals he grew reminiscent; and when he came to a letter from General Sherman, Edward remembers that he chuckled audibly, reread it, and then turning to Mrs. Grant, said: "Julia, listen to this from Sherman. Not bad." The letter he read was this:

DEAR MR. BOK:—

I prefer not to make scraps of sentimental writing. When I write anything I want it to be real and connected in form, as, for instance, in your quotation from Lord Lytton's play of "Richelieu," "The pen is mightier than the sword." Lord Lytton would never have put his signature to so naked a sentiment. Surely I will not.

In the text there was a prefix or qualification:

Beneath the rule of men entirely great
The pen is mightier than the sword.

Now, this world does not often present the condition of facts herein described. Men entirely great are very rare indeed, and even Washington, who approached greatness as near as any mortal, found good use for the sword and the pen, each in its proper sphere.

You and I have seen the day when a great and good man ruled this country (Lincoln) who wielded a powerful and prolific pen, and yet had to call to his assistance a million of flaming swords.

No, I cannot subscribe to your sentiment, "The pen is mightier than the sword," which you ask me to write, because it is not true.

Rather, in the providence of God, there is a time for all things; a time when the sword may cut the Gordian knot, and set free the principles of right and justice, bound up in the meshes of hatred, revenge, and tyranny, that the pens of mighty men like Clay, Webster, Crittenden, and Lincoln were unable to disentangle. Wishing you all success, I am, with respect, your friend,

W. T. SHERMAN.

Mrs. Grant had asked Edward to send her a photograph of himself, and after one had been taken, the boy took it to the Fifth Avenue Hotel, intending to ask the clerk to send it to her room. Instead, he met General and Mrs. Grant just coming from the elevator, going out to dinner. The boy told them his errand, and said he would have the photograph sent up-stairs.

"I am so sorry we are just going out to dinner," said Mrs. Grant, "for the general had some excellent photographs just taken of himself, and he signed one for you, and put it aside, intending to send it to you when yours came." Then, turning to the general, she said: "Ulysses, send up for it. We have a few moments."

"I'll go and get it. I know just where it is," returned the general. "Let me have yours," he said, turning to Edward. "I am glad to exchange photographs with you, boy."

To Edward's surprise, when the general returned he brought with him, not a duplicate of the small *carte-de-visite* size which he had given the general—all that he could afford—but a large, full cabinet size.

"They make 'em too big," said the general, as he handed it to Edward.

But the boy didn't think so!

That evening was one that the boy was long to remember. It suddenly came to him that he had read a few days before of Mrs. Abraham Lincoln's arrival in New York at Doctor Holbrook's sanitarium. Thither Edward went; and within half an hour from the time

Mrs Abraham Lincoln
October. 13.ᵗʰ 1881.

he had been talking with General Grant he was sitting at the bedside of Mrs. Lincoln, showing her the wonderful photograph just presented to him. Edward saw that the widow of the great Lincoln did not mentally respond to his pleasure in his possession. It was apparent even to the boy that mental and physical illness had done their work with the frail frame. But he had the memory, at least, of having got that close to the great President.

The eventful evening, however, was not yet over. Edward had boarded a Broadway stage to take him to his Brooklyn home when, glancing at the newspaper of a man sitting next to him, he saw the headline: "Jefferson Davis arrives in New York." He read enough to see that the Confederate President was stopping at the Metropolitan Hotel, in lower Broadway, and as he looked out of the stage-window the sign "Metropolitan

Hotel" stared him in the face.   In a moment he was out of the stage; he wrote a little note, asked the clerk to send it to Mr. Davis, and within five minutes was talking to the Confederate President and telling of his remarkable evening.

Mr. Davis was keenly interested in the coincidence and in the boy before him.   He asked about the famous collection, and promised to secure for Edward a letter written by each member of the Confederate Cabinet. This he subsequently did.   Edward remained with Mr. Davis until ten o'clock, and that evening brought about an interchange of letters between the Brooklyn boy and Mr. Davis at Beauvoir, Mississippi, that lasted until the latter passed away.

Edward was fast absorbing a tremendous quantity of biographical information about the most famous men and women of his time, and he was compiling a collection of autograph letters that the newspapers had made famous throughout the country.   He was ruminating over his possessions one day, and wondering to what practical use he could put his collection; for while it was proving educative to a wonderful degree, it was, after all, a hobby, and a hobby means expense.   His autograph quest cost him stationery, postage, car-fare—all outgo. But it had brought him no income, save a rich mental revenue.   And the boy and his family needed money. He did not know, then, the value of a background.

He was thinking along this line in a restaurant when a man sitting next to him opened a box of cigarettes, and taking a picture out of it threw it on the floor.   Edward picked it up, thinking it might be a "prospect" for his collection of autograph letters. It was the picture of a well-known actress. He then recalled an advertisement announcing that this particular brand of cigarettes contained, in each package, a lithographed portrait of some famous actor or actress, and that if the purchaser would collect these he would, in the end, have a valuable album of the greatest actors and actresses of the day. Edward turned the picture over, only to find a blank reverse side. "All very well," he thought, "but what does a purchaser have, after all, in the end, but a lot of pictures? Why don't they use the back of each picture, and tell what each did: a little biography? Then it would be worth keeping." With his passion for self-education, the idea appealed very strongly to him; and believing firmly that there were others possessed of the same thirst, he set out the next day, in his luncheon hour, to find out who made the picture.

At the office of the cigarette company he learned that the making of the pictures was in the hands of the Knapp Lithographic Company. The following luncheon hour, Edward sought the offices of the company, and explained his idea to Mr. Joseph P. Knapp, now the president of the American Lithograph Company.

"I'll give you ten dollars apiece if you will write me a one-hundred-word biography of one hundred famous Americans," was Mr. Knapp's instant reply. "Send me a list, and group them, as, for instance: presidents and vice-presidents, famous soldiers, actors, authors, etc."

"And thus," says Mr. Knapp, as he tells the tale today, "I gave Edward Bok his first literary commission, and started him off on his literary career."

And it is true.

But Edward soon found the Lithograph Company calling for "copy," and, write as he might, he could not supply the biographies fast enough. He, at last, completed the first hundred, and so instantaneous was their success that Mr. Knapp called for a second hundred, and then for a third. Finding that one hand was not equal to the task, Edward offered his brother five dollars for each biography; he made the same offer to one or two journalists whom he knew and whose accuracy he could trust; and he was speedily convinced that merely to edit biographies written by others, at one-half the price paid to him, was more profitable than to write himself.

So with five journalists working at top speed to supply the hungry lithograph presses, Mr. Knapp was likewise responsible for Edward Bok's first adventure as an editor. It was commercial, if you will, but it was a commercial editing that had a distinct educational value to a large public.

The important point is that Edward Bok was being led more and more to writing and to editorship.

CHAPTER IV

A PRESIDENTIAL FRIEND AND A BOSTON PILGRIMAGE

EDWARD BOK had not been office boy long before he realized that if he learned shorthand he would stand a better chance for advancement. So he joined the Young Men's Christian Association in Brooklyn, and entered the class in stenography. But as this class met only twice a week, Edward, impatient to learn the art of "pothooks" as quickly as possible, supplemented this instruction by a course given on two other evenings at moderate cost by a Brooklyn business college. As the system taught in both classes was the same, more rapid progress was possible, and the two teachers were constantly surprised that he acquired the art so much more quickly than the other students.

Before many weeks Edward could "stenograph" fairly well, and as the typewriter had not then come into its own, he was ready to put his knowledge to practical use.

An opportunity offered itself when the city editor of the *Brooklyn Eagle* asked him to report two speeches at a New England Society dinner. The speakers were to be the President of the United States, General Grant, General Sherman, Mr. Evarts, and General Sheridan. Edward was to report what General Grant and the

President said, and was instructed to give the President's speech verbatim.

At the close of the dinner, the reporters came in and Edward was seated directly in front of the President. In those days when a public dinner included several kinds of wine, it was the custom to serve the reporters with wine, and as the glasses were placed before Edward's plate he realized that he had to make a decision then and there. He had, of course, constantly seen wine on his father's table, as is the European custom, but the boy had never tasted it. He decided he would not begin then, when he needed a clear head. So, in order to get more room for his note-book, he asked the waiter to remove the glasses.

It was the first time he had ever attempted to report a public address. General Grant's remarks were few, as usual, and as he spoke slowly, he gave the young reporter no trouble. But alas for his stenographic knowledge, when President Hayes began to speak! Edward worked hard, but the President was too rapid for him; he did not get the speech, and he noticed that the reporters for the other papers fared no better. Nothing daunted, however, after the speechmaking, Edward resolutely sought the President, and as the latter turned to him, he told him his plight, explained it was his first important "assignment," and asked if he could possibly be given a copy of the speech so that he could "beat" the other papers.

The President looked at him curiously for a moment, and then said: "Can you wait a few minutes?"

Edward assured him that he could.

After fifteen minutes or so the President came up to where the boy was waiting, and said abruptly:

"Tell me, my boy, why did you have the wine-glasses removed from your place?"

Edward was completely taken aback at the question, but he explained his resolution as well as he could.

"Did you make that decision this evening?" the President asked.

He had.

"What is your name?" the President next inquired.

He was told.

"And you live, where?"

Edward told him.

"Suppose you write your name and address on this card for me," said the President, reaching for one of the place-cards on the table.

The boy did so.

"Now, I am stopping with Mr. A. A. Low, on Columbia Heights. Is that in the direction of your home?"

It was.

"Suppose you go with me, then, in my carriage," said the President, "and I will give you my speech."

Edward was not quite sure now whether he was on his head or his feet.

As he drove along with the President and his host, the President asked the boy about himself, what he was doing, etc. On arriving at Mr. Low's house, the President went up-stairs, and in a few moments came down with his speech in full, written in his own hand. Edward assured him he would copy it, and return the manuscript in the morning.

The President took out his watch.   It was then after midnight.   Musing a moment, he said: "You say you are an office boy; what time must you be at your office?"

"Half past eight, sir."

"Well, good night," he said, and then, as if it were a second thought: "By the way, I can get another copy of the speech.   Just turn that in as it is, if they can read it."

Afterward, Edward found out that, as a matter of fact, it was the President's only copy.   Though the boy did not then appreciate this act of consideration, his instinct fortunately led him to copy the speech and leave the original at the President's stopping-place in the morning.

And for all his trouble, the young reporter was amply repaid by seeing that *The Eagle* was the only paper which had a verbatim report of the President's speech.

But the day was not yet done!

That evening, upon reaching home, what was the boy's astonishment to find the following note:

MY DEAR YOUNG FRIEND:—
I have been telling Mrs. Hayes this morning of what you told me at the dinner last evening, and she was very much interested.   She would like to see you, and joins me in asking if you will call upon us this evening at eight-thirty.
Very faithfully yours,
RUTHERFORD B. HAYES.

Edward had not risen to the possession of a suit of evening clothes, and distinctly felt its lack for this occasion. But, dressed in the best he had, he set out, at eight o'clock, to call on the President of the United States and his wife!

He had no sooner handed his card to the butler than that dignitary, looking at it, announced: "The President and Mrs. Hayes are waiting for you!" The ring of those magic words still sounds in Edward's ears: "The President and Mrs. Hayes are waiting for you!"— and he a boy of sixteen!

Edward had not been in the room ten minutes before he was made to feel as thoroughly at ease as if he were sitting in his own home before an open fire with his father and mother. Skilfully the President drew from him the story of his youthful hopes and ambitions, and before the boy knew it he was telling the President and his wife all about his precious *Encyclopædia*, his evening with General Grant, and his efforts to become something more than an office boy. No boy had ever so gracious a listener before; no mother could have been more tenderly motherly than the woman who sat opposite him and seemed so honestly interested in all that he told. Not for a moment during all those two hours was he allowed to remember that his host and hostess were the President of the United States and the first lady of the land!

That evening was the first of many thus spent as the years rolled by; unexpected little courtesies came from the White House, and later from "Spiegel Grove"; a constant and unflagging interest followed each undertaking on which the boy embarked. Opportunities were opened to him; acquaintances were made possible;

a letter came almost every month until that last little
note, late in 1892:

My Dear Friend;
                    I would write you more fully
if I could. You are always thoughtful
& kind. Thankfully your friend
                    Ruth Fred B. Hayes
Thanks — Thanks for your steady friendship.

The simple act of turning down his wine-glasses had
won for Edward Bok two gracious friends.

The passion for autograph collecting was now leading Edward to read the authors whom he read about.
He had become attached to the works of the New England group: Longfellow, Holmes, and, particularly,
of Emerson.   The philosophy of the Concord sage made
a peculiarly strong appeal to the young mind, and a
small copy of Emerson's essays was always in Edward's
pocket on his long stage or horse-car rides to his office
and back.

He noticed that these New England authors rarely
visited New York, or, if they did, their presence was not
heralded by the newspapers among the "distinguished
arrivals."   He had a great desire personally to meet
these writers; and, having saved a little money, he decided to take his week's summer vacation in the winter,
when he knew he should be more likely to find the peo-

ple of his quest at home, and to spend his savings on a trip to Boston. He had never been away from home, so this trip was a momentous affair.

He arrived in Boston on Sunday evening; and the first thing he did was to despatch a note, by messenger, to Doctor Oliver Wendell Holmes, announcing the important fact that he was there, and what his errand was, and asking whether he might come up and see Doctor Holmes any time the next day. Edward naïvely told him that he could come as early as Doctor Holmes liked—by breakfast-time, he was assured, as Edward was all alone! Doctor Holmes's amusement at this ingenuous note may be imagined.

Within the hour the boy brought back this answer:

MY DEAR BOY:
I shall certainly look for you to-morrow morning at eight o'clock to have a piece of pie with me. That is real New England, you know.
Very cordially yours,
OLIVER WENDELL HOLMES.

Edward was there at eight o'clock. Strictly speaking, he was there at seven-thirty, and found the author already at his desk in that room overlooking the Charles River, which he learned in after years to know better.

"Well," was the cheery greeting, "you couldn't wait until eight for your breakfast, could you? Neither could I when I was a boy. I used to have my breakfast at seven," and then telling the boy all about his boyhood, the cheery poet led him to the dining-room, and for the first time he breakfasted away from home and ate pie—and that with "The Autocrat" at his own breakfast-table!

A cosier time no boy could have had. Just the two were there, and the smiling face that looked out over the plates and cups gave the boy courage to tell all that this trip was going to mean to him.

"And you have come on just to see us, have you?" chuckled the poet. "Now, tell me, what good do you think you will get out of it?"

He was told what the idea was: that every successful man had something to tell a boy, that would be likely to help him, and that Edward wanted to see the men who had written the books that people enjoyed. Doctor Holmes could not conceal his amusement at all this.

When breakfast was finished, Doctor Holmes said: "Do you know that I am a full-fledged carpenter? No? Well, I am. Come into my carpenter-shop."

And he led the way into a front-basement room where was a complete carpenter's outfit.

"You know I am a doctor," he explained, "and this shop is my medicine. I believe that every man must have a hobby that is as different from his regular work as it is possible to be. It is not good for a man to work all the time at one thing. So this is my hobby. This is my change. I like to putter away at these things. Every day I try to come down here for an hour or so. It rests me because it gives my mind a complete change. For, whether you believe it or not," he added with his inimitable chuckle, "to make a poem and to make a chair are two very different things."

"Now," he continued, "if you think you can learn something from me, learn that and remember it when you are a man. Don't keep always at your business, whatever it may be. It makes no difference how much you like it. The more you like it, the more dangerous it is. When you grow up you will understand what I mean by an 'outlet'—a hobby, that is—in your life, and it must be so different from your regular work that it will take your thoughts into an entirely different direction. We doctors call it a safety-valve, and it is. I would much rather," concluded the poet, "you would forget all that I have ever written than that you should forget what I tell you about having a safety-valve."

"And now do you know," smilingly said the poet, "about the Charles River here?" as they returned to his study and stood before the large bay window. "I love this river," he said. "Yes, I love it," he repeated; "love it in summer or in winter." And then he was quiet for a minute or so.

Edward asked him which of his poems were his favorites.

"Well," he said musingly, "I think 'The Chambered Nautilus' is my most finished piece of work, and I suppose it is my favorite. But there are also 'The Voiceless,' 'My Aviary,' written at this window, 'The Battle of Bunker Hill,' and 'Dorothy Q,' written to the portrait of my great-grandmother which you see on the wall there. All these I have a liking for, and when I speak of the poems I like best there are two others that ought to be included—'The Silent Melody' and 'The Last Leaf.' I think these are among my best."

"What is the history of 'The Chambered Nautilus'?" Edward asked.

"It has none," came the reply, "it wrote itself. So, too, did 'The One-Hoss Shay.' That was one of those random conceptions that gallop through the brain, and that you catch by the bridle. I caught it and reined it. That is all."

Just then a maid brought in a parcel, and as Doctor Holmes opened it on his desk he smiled over at the boy and said:

"Well, I declare, if you haven't come just at the right time. See those little books? Aren't they wee?" and he handed the boy a set of three little books, six inches by four in size, beautifully bound in half levant. They were his "Autocrat" in one volume, and his better-known poems in two volumes.

"This is a little fancy of mine," he said. "My publishers, to please me, have gotten out this tiny wee set. And here," as he counted the little sets, "they have sent me six sets. Are they not exquisite little things?" and he fondled them with loving glee. "Lucky, too, for me that they should happen to come now, for I have been wondering what I could give you as a souvenir of your visit to me, and here it is, sure enough! My publishers must have guessed you were here and my mind at the same time. Now, if you would like it, you shall carry home one of these little sets, and I'll just write a piece from one of my poems and your name on the fly-leaf of each volume. You say you like that little verse:

"'A few can touch the magic string.'

Then I'll write those four lines in this volume." And he did.

As each little volume went under the poet's pen Edward said, as his heart swelled in gratitude:

"Doctor Holmes, you are a man of the rarest sort to be so good to a boy."

The pen stopped, the poet looked out on the Charles

A few can touch the magic string,
And noisy Fame is proud to win them,—
Alas for those who never sing,
But die with all their music in them!

Oliver Wendell Holmes.

a moment, and then, turning to the boy with a little moisture in his eye, he said:

"No, my boy, I am not; but it does an old man's heart good to hear you say it. It means much to those on the down-hill side to be well thought of by the young who are coming up."

As he wiped his gold pen, with its swan-quill holder, and laid it down, he said:

"That's the pen with which I wrote 'Elsie Venner' and the 'Autocrat' papers. I try to take care of it."

"You say you are going from me over to see Longfellow?" he continued, as he reached out once more for the pen. "Well, then, would you mind if I gave you a letter for him? I have something to send him."

Sly but kindly old gentleman! The "something" he had to send Longfellow was Edward himself, although the boy did not see through the subterfuge at that time.

"And now, if you are going, I'll walk along with you

if you don't mind, for I'm going down to Park Street to thank my publishers for these little books, and that lies along your way to the Cambridge car."

As the two walked along Beacon Street, Doctor Holmes pointed out the residences where lived people of interest, and when they reached the Public Garden he said:

"You must come over in the spring some time, and see the tulips and croci and hyacinths here. They are so beautiful.

"Now, here is your car," he said as he hailed a coming horse-car. "Before you go back you must come and see me and tell me all the people you have seen; will you? I should like to hear about them. I may not have more books coming in, but I might have a very good-looking photograph of a very old-looking little man," he said as his eyes twinkled. "Give my love to Longfellow when you see him, and don't forget to give him my letter, you know. It is about a very important matter."

And when the boy had ridden a mile or so with his fare in his hand he held it out to the conductor, who grinned and said:

"That's all right. Doctor Holmes paid me your fare, and I'm going to keep that nickel if I lose my job for it."

CHAPTER V

GOING TO THE THEATRE WITH LONGFELLOW

WHEN Edward Bok stood before the home of Long-fellow, he realized that he was to see the man around whose head the boy's youthful reading had cast a sort of halo. And when he saw the head itself he had a feeling that he could see the halo. No kindlier pair of eyes ever looked at a boy, as, with a smile, "the white Mr. Longfellow," as Mr. Howells had called him, held out his hand.

"I am very glad to see you, my boy," were his first words, and with them he won the boy. Edward smiled back at the poet, and immediately the two were friends.

"I have been taking a walk this beautiful morning," he said next, "and am a little late getting at my mail. Suppose you come in and sit at my desk with me, and we will see what the postman has brought. He brings me so many good things, you know."

"Now, here is a little girl," he said, as he sat down at the desk with the boy beside him, "who wants my autograph and a 'sentiment.' What sentiment, I wonder, shall I send her?"

"Why not send her 'Let us, then, be up and doing'?" suggested the boy. "That's what I should like if I were she."

"Should you, indeed?" said Longfellow. "That is a good suggestion. Now, suppose you recite it off to me,

41

so that I shall not have to look it up in my books, and I will write as you recite. But slowly; you know I am an old man, and write slowly."

Edward thought it strange that Longfellow himself should not know his own great words without looking them up. But he recited the four lines, so familiar to every schoolboy, and when the poet had finished writing them, he said:

"Good! I see you have a memory. Now, suppose I copy these lines once more for the little girl, and give you this copy? Then you can say, you know, that you dictated my own poetry to me."

Of course Edward was delighted, and Longfellow gave him the sheet as it is here:

Let us, then, be up and doing,
  With a heart for any fate;
Still achieving, still pursuing,
  Learn to labor and to wait.
            Henry W. Longfellow.

Then, as the fine head bent down to copy the lines once more, Edward ventured to say to him:

"I should think it would keep you busy if you did this for every one who asked you."

"Well," said the poet, "you see, I am not so busy a man as I was some years ago, and I shouldn't like to disappoint a little girl; should you?"

As he took up his letters again, he discovered five

more requests for his autograph. At each one he reached into a drawer in his desk, took a card, and wrote his name on it.

"There are a good many of these every day," said Longfellow, "but I always like to do this little favor. It is so little to do, to write your name on a card; and if I didn't do it some boy or girl might be looking, day by day, for the postman and be disappointed. I only wish I could write my name better for them. You see how I break my letters? That's because I never took pains with my writing when I was a boy. I don't think I should get a high mark for penmanship if I were at school, do you?"

"I see you get letters from Europe," said the boy, as Longfellow opened an envelope with a foreign stamp on it.

"Yes, from all over the world," said the poet. Then, looking at the boy quickly, he said: "Do you collect postage-stamps?"

Edward said he did.

"Well, I have some right here, then," and going to a drawer in a desk he took out a bundle of letters, and cut out the postage-stamps and gave them to the boy.

"There's one from the Netherlands. There's where I was born," Edward ventured to say.

"In the Netherlands? Then you are a real Dutchman. Well! Well!" he said, laying down his pen. "Can you read Dutch?"

The boy said he could.

"Then," said the poet, "you are just the boy I am looking for." And going to a bookcase behind him he brought out a book, and handing it to the boy, he said, his eyes laughing: "Can you read that?"

It was an edition of Longfellow's poems in Dutch.

"Yes, indeed," said Edward. "These are your poems in Dutch."

"That's right," he said. "Now, this is delightful. I am so glad you came. I received this book last week, and although I have been in the Netherlands, I cannot speak or read Dutch. I wonder whether you would read a poem to me and let me hear how it sounds."

So Edward took "The Old Clock on the Stairs," and read it to him.

The poet's face beamed with delight. "That's beautiful," he said, and then quickly added: "I mean the language, not the poem."

"Now," he went on, "I'll tell you what we'll do: we'll strike a bargain. We Yankees are great for bargains, you know. If you will read me 'The Village Blacksmith' you can sit in that chair there made out of the wood of the old spreading chestnut-tree, and I'll take you out and show you where the old shop stood. Is that a bargain?"

Edward assured him it was. He sat in the chair of wood and leather, and read to the poet several of his own poems in a language in which, when he wrote them, he never dreamed they would ever be printed. He was very quiet. Finally he said: "It seems so odd, so very odd, to hear something you know so well sound so strange."

"It's a great compliment. though, isn't it, sir?" asked the boy.

"Ye-es," said the poet slowly. "Yes, yes," he added quickly. "It is, my boy, a very great compliment."

"Ah," he said, rousing himself, as a maid appeared, "that means luncheon, or rather," he added, "it means dinner, for we have dinner in the old New England fashion, in the middle of the day. I am all alone to-day, and you must keep me company; will you? Then afterward we'll go and take a walk, and I'll show you Cambridge. It is such a beautiful old town, even more beautiful, I sometimes think, when the leaves are off the trees.

"Come," he said, "I'll take you up-stairs, and you can wash your hands in the room where George Washington slept. And comb your hair, too, if you want to," he added; "only it isn't the same comb that he used."

To the boyish mind it was an historic breaking of bread, that midday meal with Longfellow.

"Can you say grace in Dutch?" he asked, as they sat down; and the boy did.

"Well," the poet declared, "I never expected to hear that at my table. I like the sound of it."

Then while the boy told all that he knew about the Netherlands, the poet told the boy all about his poems. Edward said he liked "Hiawatha."

"So do I," he said. "But I think I like 'Evangeline' better. Still," he added, "neither one is as good as it should be. But those are the things you see afterward so much better than you do at the time."

It was a great event for Edward when, with the poet nodding and smiling to every boy and man he met, and lifting his hat to every woman and little girl, he walked through the fine old streets of Cambridge with Long-fellow. At one point of the walk they came to a the-atrical bill-board announcing an attraction that evening at the Boston Theatre. Skilfully the old poet drew out from Edward that sometimes he went to the theatre with his parents. As they returned to the gate of "Craigie House" Edward said he thought he would go back to Boston.

"And what have you on hand for this evening?" asked Longfellow.

Edward told him he was going to his hotel to think over the day's events.

The poet laughed and said:

"Now, listen to my plan. Boston is strange to you. Now we're going to the theatre this evening, and my plan is that you come in now, have a little supper with us, and then go with us to see the play. It is a funny play, and a good laugh will do you more good than to sit in a hotel all by yourself. Now, what do you think?"

Of course the boy thought as Longfellow did, and it was a very happy boy that evening who, in full view of the large audience in the immense theatre, sat in that box. It was, as Longfellow had said, a play of laughter, and just who laughed louder, the poet or the boy, neither ever knew.

Between the acts there came into the box a man of courtly presence, dignified and yet gently courteous.

"Ah! Phillips," said the poet, "how are you? You must know my young friend here. This is Wendell Phillips, my boy. Here is a young man who told me to-day that he was going to call on you and on Phillips

Brooks to-morrow. Now you know him before he comes to you."

"I shall be glad to see you, my boy," said Mr. Phillips. "And so you are going to see Phillips Brooks? Let me tell you something about Brooks. He has a great many books in his library which are full of his marks and comments. Now, when you go to see him you ask him to let you see some of those books, and then, when he isn't looking, you put a couple of them in your pocket. They would make splendid souvenirs, and he has so many he would never miss them. You do it, and then when you come to see me tell me all about it."

And he and Longfellow smiled broadly.

An hour later, when Longfellow dropped Edward at his hotel, he had not only a wonderful day to think over but another wonderful day to look forward to as well!

He had breakfasted with Oliver Wendell Holmes; dined, supped, and been to the theatre with Longfellow; and to-morrow he was to spend with Phillips Brooks.

Boston was a great place, Edward Bok thought, as he fell asleep.

CHAPTER VI

PHILLIPS BROOKS'S BOOKS AND EMERSON'S MENTAL MIST

No one who called at Phillips Brooks's house was ever told that the master of the house was out when he was in. That was a rule laid down by Doctor Brooks: a maid was not to perjure herself for her master's comfort or convenience. Therefore, when Edward was told that Doctor Brooks was out, he knew he *was* out. The boy waited, and as he waited he had a chance to look around the library and into the books. The rector's faithful housekeeper said he might when he repeated what Wendell Phillips had told him of the interest that was to be found in her master's books. Edward did not tell her of Mr. Phillips's advice to "borrow" a couple of books. He reserved that bit of information for the rector of Trinity when he came in, an hour later.

"Oh! did he?" laughingly said Doctor Brooks. "That is nice advice for a man to give a boy. I am surprised at Wendell Phillips. He needs a little talk: a ministerial visit. And have you followed his shameless advice?" smilingly asked the huge man as he towered above the boy. "No? And to think of the opportunity you had, too. Well, I am glad you had such respect for my dumb friends. For they are my friends, each one of them," he continued, as he looked fondly at the filled shelves. "Yes, I know them all, and love each for its own sake. Take this little volume," and he picked up a little volume of Shakespeare. "Why, we are the best of friends: we have travelled miles together —all over the world, as a matter of fact. It knows me in all my moods, and responds to each, no matter how irritable I am. Yes, it is pretty badly marked up now, for a fact, isn't it? Black; I never thought of that before that it doesn't make a book look any better to the eye. But it means more to me because of all that pencilling.

"Now, some folks dislike my use of my books in this way. They love their books so much that they think it nothing short of sacrilege to mark up a book. But to me that's like having a child so prettily dressed that you can't romp and play with it. What is the good of a book, I say, if it is too pretty for use? I like to have my books speak to me, and then I like to talk back to them.

"Take my Bible, here," he continued, as he took up an old and much-worn copy of the book. "I have a number of copies of the Great Book: one copy I preach from; another I minister from; but this is my own personal copy, and into it I talk and talk. See how I talk," and he opened the Book and showed interleaved pages full of comments in his handwriting. "There's where St. Paul and I had an argument one day. Yes, it was a long argument, and I don't know now who won," he added smilingly. "But then, no one ever wins in an argument, anyway; do you think so?

"You see," went on the preacher, "I put into these books what other men put into articles and essays for magazines and papers. I never write for publications. I always think of my church when something comes to me to say. There is always danger of a man spreading himself out thin if he attempts too much, you know."

Doctor Brooks must have caught the boy's eye, which, as he said this, naturally surveyed his great frame, for he regarded him in an amused way, and putting his hands on his girth, he said laughingly: "You are thinking I would have to do a great deal to spread myself out thin, aren't you?"

The boy confessed he was, and the preacher laughed one of those deep laughs of his that were so infectious.

"But here I am talking about myself. Tell me something about *yourself?*"

And when the boy told his object in coming to Boston, the rector of Trinity Church was immensely amused.

"Just to see us fellows! Well, and how do you like us so far?"

And in the most comfortable way this true gentleman went on until the boy mentioned that he must be keeping him from his work.

"Not at all; not at all," was the quick and hearty response. "Not a thing to do. I cleaned up all my mail before I had my breakfast this morning.

"These letters, you mean?" he said, as the boy pointed to some letters on his desk unopened. "Oh, yes! Well, they must have come in a later mail. Well, if it will make you feel any better I'll go through them, and you can go through my books if you like. I'll trust you," he added laughingly, as Wendell Phillips's advice occurred to him.

"You like books, you say?" he went on, as he opened his letters. "Well, then, you must come into my library here at any time you are in Boston, and spend a morning reading anything I have that you like. Young men do that, you know, and I like to have them. What's the use of good friends if you don't share them? There's where the pleasure comes in."

He asked the boy then about his newspaper work: how much it paid him, and whether he felt it helped him in an educational way. The boy told him he thought it did; that it furnished good lessons in the study of human nature.

"Yes," he said, "I can believe that, so long as it is good journalism."

Edward told him that he sometimes wrote for the Sunday paper, and asked the preacher what he thought of that.

"Well," he said, "that is not a crime."

The boy asked him if he, then, favored the Sunday paper more than did some other clergymen.

"There is always good in everything, I think," replied Phillips Brooks. "A thing must be pretty bad that hasn't some good in it." Then he stopped, and after a moment went on: "My idea is that the fate of Sunday newspapers rests very much with Sunday editors. There is a Sunday newspaper conceivable in

which we should all rejoice—all, that is, who do not hold
that a Sunday newspaper is always and *per se* wrong.
But some cause has, in many instances, brought it about
that the Sunday paper is below, and not above, the
standard of its weekday brethren.   I mean it is apt to
be more gossipy, more personal, more sensational, more
frivolous; less serious and thoughtful and suggestive.
Taking for granted the fact of special leisure on the
part of its readers, it is apt to appeal to the lower
and not to the higher part of them, which the Sunday
leisure has set free.   Let the Sunday newspaper be
worthy of the day, and the day will not reject it.   So
I say its fate is in the hands of its editor.   He can give
it such a character as will make all good men its cham-
pions and friends, or he can preserve for it the suspicion
and dislike in which it stands at present."

Edward's journalistic instinct here got into full play;
and although, as he assured his host, he had had no such
thought in coming, he asked whether Doctor Brooks
would object if he tried his reportorial wings by experi-
menting as to whether he could report the talk.

"I do not like the papers to talk about me," was the
answer; "but if it will help you, go ahead and practise
on me.   You haven't stolen my books when you were
told to do so, and I don't think you'll steal my name."

The boy went back to his hotel, and wrote an article
much as this account is here written, which he sent to
Doctor Brooks.   "Let me keep it by me," the doctor
wrote, "and I will return it to you presently."

And he did, with his comment on the Sunday newspaper, just as it is given here, and with this note:

If I must go into the Newspapers at all — which I should always pretty prefer to avoid — no words could have been more kind than those of your article. You were very good to send it to me. I am ever

Sincerely Your friend

Phillips Brooks

As he let the boy out of his house, at the end of that first meeting, he said to him:

"And you're going from me now to see Emerson? I don't know," he added reflectively, "whether you will see him at his best. Still, you may. And even if you do not, to have seen him, even as you may see him, is better, in a way, than not to have seen him at all."

Edward did not know what Phillips Brooks meant. But he was, sadly, to find out the next day.

A boy of sixteen was pretty sure of a welcome from Louisa Alcott, and his greeting from her was spontaneous and sincere.

"Why, you good boy," she said, "to come all the way to Concord to see us," quite for all the world as if she were the one favored. "Now take your coat off, and come right in by the fire."

"Do tell me all about your visit," she continued.

Before that cosey fire they chatted. It was pleasant to the boy to sit there with that sweet-faced woman with those kindly eyes! After a while she said: "Now I shall put on my coat and hat, and we shall walk over to Emerson's house. I am almost afraid to promise that you will see him. He sees scarcely any one now. He is feeble, and—" She did not finish the sentence. "But we'll walk over there, at any rate."

She spoke mostly of her father as the two walked along, and it was easy to see that his condition was now the one thought of her life. Presently they reached Emerson's house, and Miss Emerson welcomed them at the door. After a brief chat Miss Alcott told of the boy's hope. Miss Emerson shook her head.

"Father sees no one now," she said, "and I fear it might not be a pleasure if you did see him."

Then Edward told her what Phillips Brooks had said.

"Well," she said, "I'll see."

She had scarcely left the room when Miss Alcott rose and followed her, saying to the boy: "You shall see Mr. Emerson if it is at all possible."

In a few minutes Miss Alcott returned, her eyes moistened, and simply said: "Come."

The boy followed her through two rooms, and at the threshold of the third Miss Emerson stood, also with moistened eyes.

"Father," she said simply, and there, at his desk, sat Emerson—the man whose words had already won Edward Bok's boyish interest, and who was destined to impress himself upon his life more deeply than any other writer.

Slowly, at the daughter's spoken word, Emerson rose with a wonderful quiet dignity, extended his hand, and as the boy's hand rested in his, looked him full in the eyes.

No light of welcome came from those sad yet tender eyes. The boy closed upon the hand in his with a loving pressure, and for a single moment the eyelids rose, a different look came into those eyes, and Edward felt a slight, perceptible response of the hand. But that was all!

Quietly he motioned the boy to a chair beside the desk. Edward sat down and was about to say something, when, instead of seating himself, Emerson walked away to the window and stood there softly whistling and looking out as if there were no one in the room. Edward's eyes had followed Emerson's every footstep, when the boy was aroused by hearing a suppressed sob, and as he looked around he saw that it came from Miss Emerson. Slowly she walked out of the room. The boy looked at Miss Alcott, and she put her finger to her mouth, indicating silence. He was nonplussed.

Edward looked toward Emerson standing in that window, and wondered what it all meant. Presently Emerson left the window and, crossing the room, came to his desk, bowing to the boy as he passed, and seated himself, not speaking a word and ignoring the presence of the two persons in the room.

Suddenly the boy heard Miss Alcott say: "Have you read this new book by Ruskin yet?"

Slowly the great master of thought lifted his eyes from his desk, turned toward the speaker, rose with stately courtesy from his chair, and, bowing to Miss Alcott, said with great deliberation: "Did you speak to me, madam?"

The boy was dumfounded! Louisa Alcott, his Louisa! And he did not know her! Suddenly the whole sad truth flashed upon the boy. Tears sprang into Miss Alcott's eyes, and she walked to the other side of the room. The boy did not know what to say or do, so he sat silent. With a deliberate movement Emerson resumed his seat, and slowly his eyes roamed over the boy sitting at the side of the desk. He felt he should say something.

"I thought, perhaps, Mr. Emerson," he said, "that you might be able to favor me with a letter from Carlyle."

At the mention of the name Carlyle his eyes lifted, and he asked: "Carlyle, did you say, sir, Carlyle?"

"Yes," said the boy, "Thomas Carlyle."

"Ye-es," Emerson answered slowly. "To be sure, Carlyle. Yes, he was here this morning. He will be here again to-morrow morning," he added gleefully, almost like a child.

Then suddenly: "You were saying——"

Edward repeated his request.

"Oh, I think so, I think so," said Emerson, to the boy's astonishment. "Let me see. Yes, here in this drawer I have many letters from Carlyle."

At these words Miss Alcott came from the other part of the room, her wet eyes dancing with pleasure and her face wreathed in smiles.

"I think we can help this young man; do you not think so, Louisa?" said Emerson, smiling toward Miss Alcott. The whole atmosphere of the room had changed. How different the expression of his eyes as now Emerson looked at the boy! "And you have come all the way from New York to ask me that!" he said smilingly as the boy told him of his trip. "Now, let us see," he said, as he delved in a drawer full of letters.

For a moment he groped among letters and papers, and then, softly closing the drawer, he began that ominous low whistle once more, looked inquiringly at each, and dropped his eyes straightway to the papers before him on his desk. It was to be only for a few moments, then! Miss Alcott turned away.

The boy felt the interview could not last much longer. So, anxious to have some personal souvenir of the meeting, he said: "Mr. Emerson, will you be so good as to write your name in this book for me?" and he brought out an album he had in his pocket.

"Name?" he asked vaguely.

"Yes, please," said the boy, "your name: Ralph Waldo Emerson."

But the sound of the name brought no response from the eyes.

"Please write out the name you want," he said finally, "and I will copy it for you if I can."

It was hard for the boy to believe his own senses. But picking up a pen he wrote: "Ralph Waldo Emerson, Concord; November 22, 1881."

Emerson looked at it, and said mournfully: "Thank you." Then he picked up the pen, and writing the single letter "R" stopped, followed his finger until it reached the "W" of Waldo, and studiously copied letter by letter! At the word "Concord" he seemed to hesitate, as if the task were too great, but finally copied again, letter by letter, until the second "c" was reached. "Another 'o,'" he said, and interpolated an extra letter in the name of the town which he had done so much to make famous the world over. When he had finished he handed back the book, in which there was written:

R. Waldo Emerson

Conocord
November 22, 1881

The boy put the book into his pocket; and as he did so Emerson's eye caught the slip on his desk, in the boy's handwriting, and, with a smile of absolute enlightenment, he turned and said:

"You wish me to write my name? With pleasure. Have you a book with you?"

Overcome with astonishment, Edward mechanically

handed him the album once more from his pocket. Quickly turning over the leaves, Emerson picked up the pen, and pushing aside the slip, wrote without a moment's hesitation:

Ralph Waldo Emerson
Concord

The boy was almost dazed at the instantaneous transformation in the man!

Miss Alcott now grasped this moment to say: "Well, we must be going!"

"So soon?" said Emerson, rising and smiling. Then turning to Miss Alcott he said: "It was very kind of you, Louisa, to run over this morning and bring your young friend."

Then turning to the boy he said: "Thank you so much for coming to see me. You must come over again while you are with the Alcotts. Good morning! Isn't it a beautiful day out?" he said, and as he shook the boy's hand there was a warm grasp in it, the fingers closed around those of the boy, and as Edward looked into those deep eyes they twinkled and smiled back.

The going was all so different from the coming. The boy was grateful that his last impression was of a moment when the eye kindled and the hand pulsated.

The two walked back to the Alcott home in an almost unbroken silence. Once Edward ventured to remark:

"You can have no idea, Miss Alcott, how grateful I am to you."

"Well, my boy," she answered, "Phillips Brooks may

be right: that it is something to have seen him even so, than not to have seen him at all. But to us it is so *sad*, so very sad. The twilight is gently closing in."

And so it proved—just five months afterward.

Eventful day after eventful day followed in Edward's Boston visit. The following morning he spent with Wendell Phillips, who presented him with letters from William Lloyd Garrison, Lucretia Mott, and other famous persons; and then, writing a letter of introduction to Charles Francis Adams, whom he enjoined to give the boy autograph letters from his two presidential forbears, John Adams and John Quincy Adams, sent Edward on his way rejoicing. Mr. Adams received the boy with equal graciousness and liberality. Wonderful letters from the two Adamses were his when he left.

And then, taking the train for New York, Edward Bok went home, sitting up all night in a day-coach for the double purpose of saving the cost of a sleeping-berth and of having a chance to classify and clarify the events of the most wonderful week in his life!

CHAPTER VII

A PLUNGE INTO WALL STREET

THE father of Edward Bok passed away when Edward was eighteen years of age, and it was found that the amount of the small insurance left behind would barely cover the funeral expenses. Hence the two boys faced the problem of supporting the mother on their meagre income. They determined to have but one goal: to put their mother back to that life of comfort to which she had been brought up and was formerly accustomed. But that was not possible on their income. It was evident that other employment must be taken on during the evenings.

The city editor of the *Brooklyn Eagle* had given Edward the assignment of covering the news of the theatres; he was to ascertain "coming attractions" and any other dramatic items of news interest. One Monday evening, when a multiplicity of events crowded the reportorial corps, Edward was delegated to "cover" the Grand Opera House, where Rose Coghlan was to appear in a play that had already been seen in Brooklyn, and called, therefore, for no special dramatic criticism. Yet *The Eagle* wanted to cover it. It so happened that Edward had made another appointment for that evening which he considered more important, and yet not wishing to disappoint his editor he accepted the assignment. He had seen Miss Coghlan in the play;

so he kept his other engagement, and without approaching the theatre he wrote a notice to the effect that Miss Coghlan acted her part, if anything, with greater power than on her previous Brooklyn visit, and so forth, and handed it in to his city editor the next morning on his way to business.

Unfortunately, however, Miss Coghlan had been taken ill just before the raising of the curtain, and, there being no understudy, no performance had been given and the audience dismissed. All this was duly commented upon by the New York morning newspapers. Edward read this bit of news on the ferry-boat, but his notice was in the hands of the city editor.

On reaching home that evening he found a summons from *The Eagle*, and the next morning he received a rebuke, and was informed that his chances with the paper were over. The ready acknowledgment and evident regret of the crestfallen boy, however, appealed to the editor, and before the end of the week he called the boy to him and promised him another chance, provided the lesson had sunk in. It had, and it left a lasting impression. It was always a cause of profound gratitude with Edward Bok that his first attempt at "faking" occurred so early in his journalistic career that he could take the experience to heart and profit by it.

One evening when Edward was attending a theatrical performance, he noticed the restlessness of the women in the audience between the acts. In those days it was, even more than at present, the custom for the men to go out between the acts, leaving the women alone. Edward looked at the programme in his hands. It was a large eleven-by-nine sheet, four pages, badly printed, with nothing in it save the cast, a few advertisements, and an announcement of some coming attraction. The boy mechanically folded the programme, turned it long side up and wondered whether a programme of this smaller size, easier to handle, with an attractive cover and some reading-matter, would not be profitable.

When he reached home he made up an eight-page "dummy," pasted an attractive picture on the cover, indicated the material to go inside, and the next morning showed it to the manager of the theatre. The programme as issued was an item of considerable expense to the management; Edward offered to supply his new programme without cost, provided he was given the exclusive right, and the manager at once accepted the offer. Edward then sought a friend, Frederic L. Colver, who had a larger experience in publishing and advertising, with whom he formed a partnership. Deciding that immediately upon the issuance of their first programme the idea was likely to be taken up by the other theatres, Edward proceeded to secure the exclusive rights to them all. The two young publishers solicited their advertisements on the way to and from business mornings and evenings, and shortly the first smaller-sized theatre programme, now in use in all theatres, appeared. The venture was successful from the start, returning a comfortable profit each week. Such advertisements as they could not secure for cash they accepted in trade; and this latter arrangement assisted materially in maintaining the households of the two publishers.

Edward's partner now introduced him into a debating

society called The Philomathean Society, made up of young men connected with Plymouth Church, of which Henry Ward Beecher was pastor. The debates took the form of a miniature congress, each member representing a State, and it is a curious coincidence that Edward drew, by lot, the representation of the Commonwealth of Pennsylvania. The members took these debates very seriously; no subject was too large for them to discuss. Edward became intensely interested in the society's doings, and it was not long before he was elected president.

The society derived its revenue from the dues of its members and from an annual concert given under its auspices in Plymouth Church. When the time for the concert under Edward's presidency came around, he decided that the occasion should be unique so as to insure a crowded house. He induced Mr. Beecher to preside; he got General Grant's promise to come and speak; he secured the gratuitous services of Emma C. Thursby, Annie Louise Cary, Clara Louise Kellogg, and Evelyn Lyon Hegeman, all of the first rank of concert-singers of that day, with the result that the church could not accommodate the crowd which naturally was attracted by such a programme.

It now entered into the minds of the two young theatre-programme publishers to extend their publishing interests by issuing an "organ" for their society, and the first issue of *The Philomathean Review* duly appeared with Mr. Colver as its publisher and Edward Bok as editor. Edward had now an opportunity to try his wings in an editorial capacity. The periodical was, of course, essentially an organ of the society; but gradually it took on a more general character, so that its circulation might extend over a larger portion of Brooklyn. With this extension came a further broadening of its contents, which now began to take on a literary character, and it was not long before its two projectors realized that the periodical had outgrown its name. It was decided—late in 1884—to change the name to *The Brooklyn Magazine*.

There was a periodical called *The Plymouth Pulpit*, which presented verbatim reports of the sermons of Mr. Beecher, and Edward got the idea of absorbing the *Pulpit* in the *Magazine*. But that required more capital than he and his partner could command. They consulted Mr. Beecher, who, attracted by the enterprise of the two boys, sent them with letters of introduction to a few of his most influential parishioners, with the result that the pair soon had a sufficient financial backing by some of the leading men of Brooklyn, like A. A. Low, H. B. Claflin, Rufus T. Bush, Henry W. Slocum, Seth Low, Rossiter W. Raymond, Horatio C. King, and others.

The young publishers could now go on. Understanding that Mr. Beecher's sermons might give a partial and denominational tone to the magazine, Edward arranged to publish also in its pages verbatim reports of the sermons of the Reverend T. De Witt Talmage, whose reputation was then at its zenith. The young editor now realized that he had a rather heavy cargo of sermons to carry each month; accordingly, in order that his magazine might not appear to be exclusively religious, he determined that its literary contents should be of a high order and equal in interest to the sermons. But this called for additional capital, and the capital furnished was not for that purpose.

It is here that Edward's autographic acquaintances stood him in good stead. He went in turn to each noted person he had met, explained his plight and stated his ambitions, with the result that very soon the magazine and the public were surprised at the distinction of the contributors to *The Brooklyn Magazine*. Each number contained a noteworthy list of them, and when an article by the President of the United States, then Rutherford B. Hayes, opened one of the numbers, the public was astonished, since up to that time the unwritten rule that a President's writings were confined to official pronouncements had scarcely been broken. William Dean Howells, General Grant, General Sherman, Phillips Brooks, General Sheridan, Canon Farrar, Cardinal Gibbons, Marion Harland, Margaret Sangster—the most prominent men and women of the day, some of whom had never written for magazines—began to appear in the young editor's contents. Editors wondered how the publishers could afford it, whereas, in fact, not a single name represented an honorarium. Each contributor had come gratuitously to the aid of the editor.

At first, the circulation of the magazine permitted the boys to wrap the copies themselves; and then they, with two other boys, would carry as huge bundles as they could lift, put them late at night on the front platform of the street-cars, and take them to the post-office. Thus the boys absolutely knew the growth of their circulation by the weight of their bundles and the number of their front-platform trips each month. Soon a baker's hand-cart was leased for an evening, and that was added to the capacity of the front platforms. Then one eventful month it was seen that a horse-truck would have to be employed. Within three weeks, a double horse-truck was necessary, and three trips had to be made.

By this time Edward Bok had become so intensely interested in the editorial problem, and his partner in the periodical publishing part, that they decided to sell out their theatre-programme interests and devote themselves to the magazine and its rapidly increasing circulation. All of Edward's editorial work had naturally to be done outside of his business hours, in other words, in the evenings and on Sundays; and the young editor found himself fully occupied. He now revived the old idea of selecting a subject and having ten or twenty writers express their views on it. It was the old symposium idea, but it had not been presented in American journalism for a number of years. He conceived the topic "Should America Have a Westminster Abbey?" and induced some twenty of the foremost men and women of the day to discuss it. When the discussion was presented in the magazine, the form being new and the theme novel, Edward was careful to send advance sheets to the newspapers, which treated it at length in reviews and editorials, with marked effect upon the circulation of the magazine.

All this time, while Edward Bok was an editor in his evenings he was, during the day, a stenographer and

clerk of the Western Union Telegraph Company. The
two occupations were hardly compatible, but each meant
a source of revenue to the boy, and he felt he must hold
on to both.

After his father passed away, the position of the boy's
desk—next to the empty desk of his father—was a
cause of constant depression to him. This was understood by the attorney for the company, Mr. Clarence
Cary, who sought the head of Edward's department,
with the result that Edward was transferred to Mr.
Cary's department as the attorney's private stenographer.

Edward had been much attracted to Mr. Cary, and
the attorney believed in the boy, and decided to show
his interest by pushing him along. He had heard of
the dual rôle which Edward was playing; he bought a
copy of the magazine, and was interested. Edward now
worked with new zest for his employer and friend; while
in every free moment he read law, feeling that, as almost
all his forbears had been lawyers, he might perhaps be
destined for the bar. This acquaintance with the fundamental basis of law, cursory as it was, became like a
gospel to Edward Bok. In later years, he was taught
its value by repeated experience in his contact with cor-
porate laws, contracts, property leases, and other matters; and he determined that, whatever the direction of
activity taken by his sons, each should spend at least
a year in the study of law.

The control of the Western Union Telegraph Company had now passed into the hands of Jay Gould and
his companions, and in the many legal matters arising

therefrom, Edward saw much, in his office, of "the little wizard of Wall Street." One day, the financier had to dictate a contract, and, coming into Mr. Cary's office, decided to dictate it then and there. An hour afterward Edward delivered the copy of the contract to Mr. Gould, and the financier was so struck by its accuracy and by the legibility of the handwriting that afterward he almost daily "happened in" to dictate to Mr. Cary's stenographer. Mr. Gould's private stenographer was in his own office in lower Broadway; but on his way down-town in the morning Mr. Gould invariably stopped at the Western Union Building, at 195 Broadway, and the habit resulted in the installation of a private office there. He borrowed Edward to do his stenography. The boy found himself taking not only letters from Mr. Gould's dictation, but, what interested him particularly, the financier's orders to buy and sell stock.

Edward watched the effects on the stock-market of these little notes which he wrote out and then shot through a pneumatic tube to Mr. Gould's brokers. Naturally, the results enthralled the boy, and he told Mr. Cary about his discoveries. This, in turn, interested Mr. Cary; Mr. Gould's dictations were frequently given in Mr. Cary's own office, where, as his desk was not ten feet from that of his stenographer, the attorney heard them, and began to buy and sell according to the magnate's decisions.

Edward had now become tremendously interested in the stock game which he saw constantly played by the great financier; and having a little money saved up, he concluded that he would follow in the wake of Mr. Gould's orders. One day, he naïvely mentioned his desire to Mr. Gould, when the financier seemed in a particularly favorable frame of mind; but Edward did not succeed in drawing out the advice he hoped for. "At least," reasoned Edward, "he knew of my intention; and if he considered it a violation of confidence he would have said as much."

Construing the financier's silence to mean at least not a prohibition, Edward went to his Sunday-school teacher, who was a member of a Wall Street brokerage firm, laid the facts before him, and asked him if he would buy for him some Western Union stock. Edward explained, however, that somehow he did not like the gambling idea of buying "on margin," and preferred to purchase the stock outright. He was shown that this would mean smaller profits; but the boy had in mind the loss of his father's fortune, brought about largely by "stock margins," and he did not intend to follow that example. So, prudently, under the brokerage of his Sunday-school teacher, and guided by the tips of no less a man than the controlling factor of stock-market finance, Edward Bok took his first plunge in Wall Street!

Of course the boy's buying and selling tallied precisely with the rise and fall of Western Union stock. It could scarcely have been otherwise. Jay Gould had the cards all in his hands; and as he bought and sold, so Edward bought and sold. The trouble was, the combination did not end there, as Edward might have foreseen had he been older and thus wiser. For as Edward bought and sold, so did his Sunday-school teacher, and all his customers who had seen the wonderful acumen of their broker in choosing exactly the right time to buy and sell Western Union. But Edward did not know this.

One day a rumor became current on the Street that an agreement had been reached by the Western Union Company and its bitter rival, the American Union Telegraph Company, whereby the former was to absorb the latter. Naturally, the report affected Western Union stock. But Mr. Gould denied it in toto; said the report was not true, no such consolidation was in view or had even been considered. Down tumbled the stock, of course.

But it so happened that Edward knew the rumor *was* true, because Mr. Gould, some time before, had personally given him the contract of consolidation to copy. The next day a rumor to the effect that the American Union was to absorb the Western Union appeared on the first page of every New York newspaper. Edward knew exactly whence this rumor emanated. He had heard it talked over. Again, Western Union stock dropped several points. Then he noticed that Mr. Gould became a heavy buyer. So became Edward—as heavy as he could. Jay Gould pooh-poohed the latest rumor. The boy awaited developments.

On Sunday afternoon, Edward's Sunday-school teacher asked the boy to walk home with him, and on reaching the house took him into the study and asked him whether he felt justified in putting all his savings in Western Union just at that time when the price was tumbling so fast and the market was so unsteady. Edward assured his teacher that he was right, although he explained that he could not disclose the basis of his assurance.

Edward thought his teacher looked worried, and after a little there came the revelation that he, seeing that Edward was buying to his limit, had likewise done so. But the broker had bought on margin, and had his margin wiped out by the decline in the stock caused by the rumors. He explained to Edward that he could recoup his losses, heavy though they were—in fact, he explained that nearly everything he possessed was involved—if Edward's basis was sure and the stock would recover.

Edward keenly felt the responsibility placed upon him. He could never clearly diagnose his feelings when he saw his teacher in this new light. The broker's "customers" had been hinted at, and the boy of eighteen wondered how far his responsibility went, and how many persons were involved. But the deal came out all right, for when, three days afterward, the contract was made public, Western Union, of course, skyrocketed, Jay Gould sold out, Edward sold out, the teacher-broker sold out, and all the customers sold out!

How long a string it was Edward never discovered, but he determined there and then to end his Wall Street experience; his original amount had multiplied; he was content to let well enough alone, and from that day to this Edward Bok has kept out of Wall Street. He had seen enough of its manipulations; and, although on "the inside," he decided that the combination of his teacher and his customers was a responsibility too great for him to carry.

Furthermore, Edward decided to leave the Western Union. The longer he remained, the less he liked its atmosphere. And the closer his contact with Jay Gould the more doubtful he became of the wisdom of such an association and perhaps its unconscious influence upon his own life in its formative period.

In fact, it was an experience with Mr. Gould that definitely fixed Edward's determination. The financier decided one Saturday to leave on a railroad inspection tour on the following Monday. It was necessary that a special meeting of one of his railroad interests should be held before his departure, and he fixed the meeting for Sunday at eleven-thirty at his residence on Fifth Avenue. He asked Edward to be there to take the notes of the meeting.

The meeting was protracted, and at one o'clock Mr. Gould suggested an adjournment for luncheon, the meeting to reconvene at two. Turning to Edward, the financier said: "You may go out to luncheon and return in an hour." So, on Sunday afternoon, with the Windsor Hotel on the opposite corner as the only visible place to get something to eat, but where he could not afford to go, Edward, with just fifteen cents in his pocket, was turned out to find a luncheon place.

He bought three apples for five cents—all that he could afford to spend, and even this meant that he must walk home from the ferry to his house in Brooklyn— and these he ate as he walked up and down Fifth Avenue until his hour was over. When the meeting ended at three o'clock, Mr. Gould said that, as he was leaving for the West early next morning, he would like Edward to write out his notes, and have them at his house by eight o'clock. There were over forty note-book pages of minutes. The remainder of Edward's Sunday after·· noon and evening was spent in transcribing the notes. By rising at half past five the next morning he reached Mr. Gould's house at a quarter to eight, handed him the minutes, and was dismissed without so much as a word of thanks or a nod of approval from the financier.

Edward felt that this exceeded the limit of fair treatment by employer of employee. He spoke of it to Mr. Cary, and asked whether he would object if he tried to get away from such influence and secure another position. His employer asked the boy in which direction he would like to go, and Edward unhesitatingly suggested the publishing business. He talked it over from every angle with his employer, and Mr. Cary not only agreed with him that his decision was wise, but promised to find him a position such as he had in mind.

It was not long before Mr. Cary made good his word, and told Edward that his friend Henry Holt, the publisher, would like to give him a trial.

The day before he was to leave the Western Union Telegraph Company the fact of his resignation became known to Mr. Gould. The financier told the boy there was no reason for his leaving, and that he would personally see to it that a substantial increase was made in his salary. Edward explained that the salary, while of importance to him, did not influence him so much as securing a position in a business in which he felt he would be happier.

"And what business is that?" asked the financier.

"The publishing of books," replied the boy.

"You are making a great mistake," answered the little man, fixing his keen gray eyes on the boy. "Books are a luxury. The public spends its largest money on necessities: on what it can't do without. It must telegraph; it need not read. It can read in libraries. A promising boy such as you are, with his life before him, should choose the right sort of business, not the wrong one."

But, as facts proved, the "little wizard of Wall Street" was wrong in his prediction; Edward Bok was not choosing the wrong business.

Years afterward when Edward was cruising up the Hudson with a yachting party one Saturday afternoon, the sight of Jay Gould's mansion, upon approaching Irvington, awakened the desire of the women on board to see his wonderful orchid collection. Edward explained his previous association with the financier and offered to recall himself to him, if the party wished to take the chance of recognition. A note was written to Mr. Gould, and sent ashore, and the answer came back that they were welcome to visit the orchid houses. Jay Gould, in person, received the party, and, placing it under the personal conduct of his gardener, turned to Edward and, indicating a bench, said: "Come and sit down here with me."

"Well," said the financier, who was in his domestic mood, quite different from his Wall Street aspect, "I see in the papers that you seem to be making your way in the publishing business."

Edward expressed surprise that the Wall Street magnate had followed his work.

"I have because I always felt you had it in you to make a successful man. But not in that business," he added quickly. "You were born for the Street. You would have made a great success there, and that is what I had in mind for you. In the publishing business you will go just so far; in the Street you could have gone as far as you liked. There is room there; there is none in the publishing business. It's not too late now, for that matter," continued the "little wizard," fastening his steel eyes on the lad beside him!

And Edward Bok has often speculated whither Jay Gould might have led him. To many a young man, a suggestion from such a source would have seemed the one to heed and follow. But Edward Bok's instinct never failed him. He felt that his path lay far apart from that of Jay Gould—and the farther the better!

In 1882 Edward, with a feeling of distinct relief, left the employ of the Western Union Telegraph Company and associated himself with the publishing business in which he had correctly divined that his future lay.

His chief regret on leaving his position was in severing the close relations, almost as of father and son, between Mr. Cary and himself. When Edward was left alone, with the passing away of his father, Clarence Cary had put his sheltering arm around the lonely boy, and with the tremendous encouragement of the phrase that the boy never forgot, "I think you have it in you, Edward, to make a successful man," he took him under his wing. It was a turning-point in Edward Bok's life, as he felt at the time and as he saw more clearly afterward.

He remained in touch with his friend, however, keeping him advised of his progress in everything he did, not only at that time, but all through his later years. And it was given to Edward to feel the deep satisfaction of having Mr. Cary say, before he passed away, that the boy had more than justified the confidence reposed in him. Mr. Cary lived to see him well on his way, until, indeed, Edward had had the proud happiness of introducing to his benefactor the son who bore his name, Cary William Bok.

CHAPTER VIII

STARTING A NEWSPAPER SYNDICATE

EDWARD felt that his daytime hours, spent in a publishing atmosphere as stenographer with Henry Holt and Company, were more in line with his editorial duties during the evenings. *The Brooklyn Magazine* was now earning a comfortable income for its two young proprietors, and their backers were entirely satisfied with the way it was being conducted. In fact, one of these backers, Mr. Rufus T. Bush, associated with the Standard Oil Company, who became especially interested, thought he saw in the success of the two boys a possible opening for one of his sons, who was shortly to be graduated from college. He talked to the publisher and editor about the idea, but the boys showed by their books that while there was a reasonable income for them, not wholly dependent on the magazine, there was no room for a third.

Mr. Bush now suggested that he buy the magazine for his son, alter its name, enlarge its scope, and make of it a national periodical. Arrangements were concluded, those who had financially backed the venture were fully paid, and the two boys received a satisfactory amount for their work in building up the magazine. Mr. Bush asked Edward to suggest a name for the new periodical, and in the following month of May, 1887, *The Brooklyn Magazine* became *The American Maga-*

zine, with its publication office in New York. But, though a great deal of money was spent on the new magazine, it did not succeed. Mr. Bush sold his interest in the periodical, which, once more changing its name, became *The Cosmopolitan Magazine*. Since then it has passed through the hands of several owners, but the name has remained the same. Before Mr. Bush sold *The American Magazine* he had urged Edward to come back to it as its editor, with promise of financial support; but the young man felt instinctively that his return would not be wise. The magazine had been *The Cosmopolitan* only a short time when the new owners, Mr. Paul J. Slicht and Mr. E. D. Walker, also solicited the previous editor to accept reappointment. But Edward, feeling that his baby had been rechristened too often for him to father it again, declined the proposition. He had not heard the last of it, however, for, by a curious coincidence, its subsequent owner, entirely ignorant of Edward's previous association with the magazine, invited him to connect himself with it. Thus three times could Edward Bok have returned to the magazine for whose creation he was responsible.

Edward was now without editorial cares; but he had already, even before disposing of the magazine, embarked on another line of endeavor. In sending to a number of newspapers the advance sheets of a particularly striking "feature" in one of his numbers of *The Brooklyn Magazine*, it occurred to him that he was furnishing a good deal of valuable material to these papers without cost. It is true his magazine was receiving the advertising value of editorial comment; but the boy wondered whether the newspapers would not be willing to pay for the privilege of simultaneous publication. An inquiry or two proved that they would. Thus Edward stumbled upon the "syndicate" plan of furnishing the same article to a group of newspapers, one in each city, for simultaneous publication. He looked over the ground, and found that while his idea was not a new one, since two "syndicate" agencies already existed, the field was by no means fully covered, and that the success of a third agency would depend entirely upon its ability to furnish the newspapers with material equally good or better than they received from the others. After following the material furnished by these agencies for two or three weeks, Edward decided that there was plenty of room for his new ideas.

He discussed the matter with his former magazine partner, Colver, and suggested that if they could induce Mr. Beecher to write a weekly comment on current events for the newspapers it would make an auspicious beginning. They decided to talk it over with the famous preacher. For to be a "Plymouth boy"—that is, to go to the Plymouth Church Sunday-school and to attend church there—was to know personally and become devoted to Henry Ward Beecher. And the two were synonymous. There was no distance between Mr. Beecher and his "Plymouth boys." Each understood the other. The tie was that of absolute comradeship.

"I don't believe in it, boys," said Mr. Beecher when Edward and his friend broached the syndicate letter to him. "No one yet ever made a cent out of my supposed literary work."

All the more reason, was the argument, why some one should.

Mr. Beecher smiled! How well he knew the youthful enthusiasm that rushes in, etc.

"Well, all right, boys! I like your pluck," he finally said. "I'll help you if I can."

The boys agreed to pay Mr. Beecher a weekly sum of two hundred and fifty dollars—which he knew was considerable for them.

When the first article had been written they took him their first check. He looked at it quizzically, and then at the boys. Then he said simply: "Thank you." He took a pin and pinned the check to his desk. There it remained, much to the curiosity of the two boys.

The following week he had written the second article and the boys gave him another check. He pinned that up over the other. "I like to look at them," was his only explanation, as he saw Edward's inquiring glance one morning.

The third check was treated the same way. When the boys handed him the fourth, one morning, as he was pinning it up over the others, he asked: "When do you get your money from the newspapers?"

He was told that the bills were going out that morning for the four letters constituting a month's service.

"I see," he remarked.

A fortnight passed, then one day Mr. Beecher asked: "Well, how are the checks coming in?"

"Very well," he was assured.

"Suppose you let me see how much you've got in," he suggested, and the boys brought the accounts to him.

After looking at them he said: "That's very interesting. How much have you in the bank?"

He was told the balance, less the checks given to him. "But I haven't turned them in yet," he explained. "Anyhow, you have enough in bank to meet the checks you have given me, and a profit besides, haven't you?"

He was assured they had.

Then, taking his bank-book from a drawer, he unpinned the six checks on his desk, indorsed each thus:

For deposit Mechn ics Bank H. W. Beecher

wrote a deposit-slip, and, handing the book to Edward, said:

"Just hand that in at the bank as you go by, will you?"

Edward was very young then, and Mr. Beecher's methods of financiering seemed to him quite in line with current notions of the Plymouth pastor's lack of business knowledge. But as the years rolled on the incident appeared in a new light—a striking example of the great preacher's wonderful considerateness.

Edward had offered to help Mr. Beecher with his correspondence; at the close of one afternoon, while he was with the Plymouth pastor at work, an organ-grinder and a little girl came under the study window. A cold, driving rain was pelting down. In a moment Mr.

Beecher noticed the girl's bare toes sticking out of her worn shoes.

He got up, went into the hall, and called for one of his granddaughters.

"Got any good, strong rain boots?" he asked when she appeared.

"Why, yes, grandfather. Why?" was the answer.

"More than one pair?" Mr. Beecher asked.

"Yes, two or three, I think."

"Bring me your strongest pair, will you, dear?" he asked. And as the girl looked at him with surprise he said: "Just one of my notions."

"Now, just bring that child into the house and put them on her feet for me, will you?" he said when the shoes came. "I'll be able to work so much better."

One rainy day, as Edward was coming up from Fulton Ferry with Mr. Beecher, they met an old woman soaked with the rain. "Here, you take this, my good woman," said the clergyman, putting his umbrella over her head and thrusting the handle into the astonished woman's hand. "Let's get into this," he said to Edward simply, as he hailed a passing car.

"There is a good deal of fraud about beggars," he remarked as he waved a sot away from him one day; "but that doesn't apply to women and children," he added; and he never passed such mendicants without stopping. All the stories about their being tools in the hands of accomplices failed to convince him. "They're women and children," he would say, and that settled it for him.

"What's the matter, son? Stuck?" he said once to

a newsboy who was crying with a heavy bundle of papers under his arm.

"Come along with me, then," said Mr. Beecher, taking the boy's hand and leading him into the newspaper office a few doors up the street.

"This boy is stuck," he simply said to the man behind the counter. "Guess *The Eagle* can stand it better than this boy; don't you think so?"

To the grown man Mr. Beecher rarely gave charity. He believed in a return for his alms.

"Why don't you go to work?" he asked of a man who approached him one day in the street.

"Can't find any," said the man.

"Looked hard for it?" was the next question.

"I have," and the man looked Mr. Beecher in the eye.

"Want some?" asked Mr. Beecher.

"I do," said the man.

"Come with me," said the preacher. And then to Edward, as they walked along with the man following behind, he added: "That man is honest."

"Let this man sweep out the church," he said to the sexton when they had reached Plymouth Church.

"But, Mr. Beecher," replied the sexton with wounded pride, "it doesn't need it."

"Don't tell him so, though," said Mr. Beecher with a merry twinkle of the eye; and the sexton understood.

Mr. Beecher was constantly thoughtful of a struggling young man's welfare, even at the expense of his own material comfort. Anxious to save him from the labor of writing out the newspaper articles, Edward, himself employed during the daylight hours which Mr. Beecher preferred for his original work, suggested a stenographer. The idea appealed to Mr. Beecher, for he was very busy just then. He hesitated, but as Edward persisted, he said: "All right; let him come to-morrow."

The next day he said: "I asked that stenographer friend of yours not to come again. No use of my trying to dictate. I am too old to learn new tricks. Much easier for me to write myself."

Shortly after that, however, Mr. Beecher dictated to Edward some material for a book he was writing. Edward naturally wondered at this, and asked the stenographer what had happened.

"Nothing," he said. "Only Mr. Beecher asked me how much it would cost you to have me come to him each week. I told him, and then he sent me away."

That was Henry Ward Beecher!

Edward Bok was in the formative period between boyhood and young manhood when impressions meant lessons, and associations meant ideals. Mr. Beecher never disappointed. The closer one got to him, the greater he became—in striking contrast to most public men, as Edward had already learned.

Then, his interests and sympathies were enormously wide. He took in so much! One day Edward was walking past Fulton Market. in New York City, with Mr. Beecher.

"Never skirt a market," the latter said; "always go through it. It's the next best thing, in the winter, to going South."

Of course all the marketmen knew him, and they knew, too, his love for green things.

"What do you think of these apples, Mr. Beecher?" one marketman would stop to ask.

Mr. Beecher would answer heartily: "Fine! Don't see how you grow them. All that my trees bear is a crop of scale. Still, the blossoms are beautiful in the spring, and I like an apple-leaf. Ever examine one?" The marketman never had. "Well, now, do, the next time you come across an apple-tree in the spring."

And thus he would spread abroad an interest in the beauties of nature which were commonly passed over.

"Wonderful man, Beecher is," said a market dealer in green goods once. "I had handled thousands of bunches of celery in my life and never noticed how beautiful its top leaves were until he picked up a bunch once and told me all about it. Now I haven't the heart to cut the leaves off when a customer asks me."

His idea of his own vegetable-gardening at Boscobel, his Peekskill home, was very amusing. One day Edward was having a hurried dinner, preparatory to catching the New York train. Mr. Beecher sat beside the boy, telling him of some things he wished done in Brooklyn.

"No, I thank you," said Edward, as the maid offered him some potatoes.

"Look here, young man," said Mr. Beecher, "don't pass those potatoes so lightly. They're of my own raising—and I reckon they cost me about a dollar a piece," he added with a twinkle in his eye.

He was an education in so many ways! One instance taught Edward the great danger of passionate speech that might unconsciously wound, and the manliness of instant recognition of the error. Swayed by an occasion, or by the responsiveness of an audience, Mr. Beecher would sometimes say something which was not meant as it sounded. One evening, at a great political meeting at Cooper Union, Mr. Beecher was at his brightest and wittiest. In the course of his remarks he had occasion to refer to ex-President Hayes; some one in the audience called out: "He was a softy!"

"No," was Mr. Beecher's quick response. "The country needed a poultice at that time, and got it."

"He's dead now, anyhow," responded the voice.

"Not dead, my friend: he only sleepeth."

It convulsed the audience, of course, and the reporters took it down in their books.

After the meeting Edward drove home with Mr. Beecher. After a while he asked: "Well, how do you think it went?"

Edward replied he thought it went very well, except that he did not like the reference to ex-President Hayes.

"What reference? What did I say?"

Edward repeated it.

"Did I say that?" he asked. Edward looked at him. Mr. Beecher's face was tense. After a few moments he said: "That's generally the way with extemporaneous remarks: they are always dangerous. The best impromptu speeches and remarks are the carefully prepared kind," he added.

Edward told him he regretted the reference because he knew that General Hayes would read it in the New York papers, and he would be nonplussed to understand it, considering the cordial relations which existed between the two men. Mr. Beecher knew of Edward's relations with the ex-President, and they had often talked of him together.

Nothing more was said of the incident. When the Beecher home was reached Mr. Beecher said: "Just come in a minute." He went straight to his desk, and wrote and wrote. It seemed as if he would never stop. At last he handed Edward an eight-page letter, closely written, addressed to General Hayes.

"Read that, and mail it, please, on your way home. Then it'll get there just as quickly as the New York papers will."

It was a superbly fine letter,—one of those letters which only Henry Ward Beecher could write in his tenderest moods. And the reply which came from Fremont, Ohio, was no less fine!

CHAPTER IX

ASSOCIATION WITH HENRY WARD BEECHER

As a letter-writer, Henry Ward Beecher was a constant wonder. He never wrote a commonplace letter. There was always himself in it—in whatever mood it found him.

It was not customary for him to see all his mail. As a rule Mrs. Beecher opened it, and attended to most of it. One evening Edward was helping Mrs. Beecher handle an unusually large number of letters. He was reading one when Mr. Beecher happened to come in and read what otherwise he would not have seen:

REVEREND HENRY WARD BEECHER.
Dear Sir:
I journeyed over from my New York hotel yesterday morning to hear you preach, expecting, of course, to hear an exposition of the gospel of Jesus Christ. Instead, I heard a political harangue, with no reason or cohesion in it. You made an ass of yourself.
Very truly yours,

—— ——.

"That's to the point," commented Mr. Beecher with a smile; and then seating himself at his desk, he turned the sheet over and wrote:

MY DEAR SIR:—
I am sorry you should have taken so long a journey to hear Christ preached, and then heard what you are polite enough

to call a "political harangue." I am sorry, too, that you think I made an ass of myself. In this connection I have but one consolation: that you didn't make an ass of *yourself*. The Lord did that.

Henry Ward Beecher.

When the Reverend T. De Witt Talmage began to come into public notice in Brooklyn, some of Mr. Beecher's overzealous followers unwisely gave the impression that the Plymouth preacher resented sharing with another the pulpit fame which he alone had so long unquestioningly held. Nothing, of course, was further from Mr. Beecher's mind. As a matter of fact, the two men were exceedingly good friends. Mr. Beecher once met Doctor Talmage in a crowded business thoroughfare, where they got so deeply interested in each other's talk that they sat down in some chairs standing in front of a furniture store. A gathering throng of intensely amused people soon brought the two men to the realization that they had better move. Then Mr. Beecher happened to see that back of their heads had been, respectively, two signs: one reading, "This style $3.45," the other, "This style $4.25."

"Well," said Mr. Beecher, as he and Doctor Talmage walked away laughing, "I was ticketed higher than you, Talmage, anyhow."

"You're worth more," rejoined Doctor Talmage.

On another occasion, as the two men met they began to bandy each other.

"Now, Talmage," said Mr. Beecher, his eyes twinkling, "let's have it out. My people say that Plymouth holds more people than the Tabernacle, and your folks stand up for the Tabernacle. Now which is it? What is your estimate?"

"Well, I should say that the Tabernacle holds about fifteen thousand people," said Doctor Talmage with a smile.

"Good," said Mr. Beecher, at once catching the spirit. "And I say that Plymouth accommodates, comfortably, twenty thousand people. Now, let's tell our respective trustees that it's settled, once for all."

Mr. Beecher could never be induced to take note of what others said of him. His friends, with more heart than head, often tried to persuade him to answer some attack, but he invariably waved them off. He always saw the ridiculous side of those attacks; never their serious import.

At one time a fellow Brooklyn minister, a staunch Prohibitionist, publicly reproved Mr. Beecher for being inconsistent in his temperance views, to the extent that he preached temperance but drank beer at his own dinner-table. This attack angered the friends of Mr. Beecher, who tried to persuade him to answer the charge. But the Plymouth pastor refused. "Friend —— is a good fellow," was the only comment they could elicit.

"But he ought to be broadened," persisted the friends.

"Well now," said Mr. Beecher, "that isn't always possible. For instance," he continued, as that inimitable merry twinkle came into his eyes, "sometime ago Friend —— criticised me for something I had said. I thought he ought not to have done so, and the next time we met I told him so. He persisted, and I felt the only way to treat him was as I would an unruly child. So I just took hold of him, laid him face down over my knee, and proceeded to impress him as our fathers used to do of old. And, do you know, I found that the Lord had not made a place on him for me to lay my hand upon."

And in the laughter which met this sally Mr. Beecher ended with "You see, it isn't always possible to broaden a man."

Mr. Beecher was rarely angry. Once, however, he came near it; yet he was more displeased than angry. Some of his family and Edward had gone to a notable public affair at the Brooklyn Academy of Music, where a box had been placed at Mr. Beecher's disposal. One member of the family was a very beautiful girl who had brought a girl-friend. Both were attired in full evening décolleté costume. Mr. Beecher came in late from another engagement. A chair had been kept vacant for him in the immediate front of the box, since his presence had been widely advertised, and the audience was expecting to see him. When he came in, he doffed his coat and was about to go to the chair reserved for him, when he stopped, stepped back, and sat down in a chair in the rear of the box. It was evident from his face that something had displeased him. Mrs. Beecher leaned over and asked him, but he offered no explanation. Nothing was said.

Edward went back to the house with Mr. Beecher; after talking awhile in the study, the preacher, wishing to show him something, was going up-stairs with his guest and had nearly reached the second landing when there was the sound of a rush, the gas was quickly turned low, and two white figures sped into one of the rooms.

"My dears," called Mr. Beecher.

"Yes, Mr. Beecher," came a voice from behind the door of the room in question.

"Come here one minute," said Mr. Beecher.

"But we cannot," said the voice. "We are ready for bed. Wait until——"

"No; come as you are," returned Mr. Beecher.

"Let me go down-stairs," Edward interrupted.

"No; you stay right here," said Mr. Beecher.

"Why, Mr. Beecher! How can we? Isn't Edward with you?"

"You are keeping me waiting for you," was the quiet and firm answer.

There was a moment's hesitation. Then the door opened and the figures of the two girls appeared.

"Now, turn up the gas, please, as it was," said Mr. Beecher.

"But, Mr. Beecher——"

"You heard me?"

Up went the light, and the two beautiful girls of the box stood in their night-dresses.

"Now, why did you run away?" asked Mr. Beecher.

"Why, Mr. Beecher! How can you ask such a question?" pouted one of the girls, looking at her dress and then at Edward.

"Exactly," said Mr. Beecher. "Your modesty leads you to run away from this young man because he might possibly see you under a single light in dresses that cover your entire bodies, while that same modesty did not prevent you all this evening from sitting beside him, under a myriad of lights, in dresses that exposed nearly half of your bodies. That's what I call a distinction with a difference—with the difference to the credit neither of your intelligence nor of your modesty. There is some modesty in the dresses you have on: there was precious little in what you girls wore this evening. Good night."

"You do not believe, Mr. Beecher," Edward asked later, "in décolleté dressing for girls?"

"No, and even less for women. A girl has some excuse of youth on her side; a woman none at all."

A few moments later he added:

"A proper dress for any girl or woman is one that reveals the lady, but not her person."

Edward asked Mrs. Beecher one day whether Mr. Beecher had ever expressed an opinion of his sister's famous book, *Uncle Tom's Cabin*, and she told this interesting story of how the famous preacher read the story:

"When the story was first published in *The National Era*, in chapters, all our family, excepting Mr. Beecher, looked impatiently for its appearance each week. But, try as we might, we could not persuade Mr. Beecher to read it, or let us tell him anything about it.

" 'It's folly for you to be kept in constant excitement week after week,' he would say. 'I shall wait till the work is completed, and take it all at one dose.'

"After the serial ended, the book came to Mr. Beecher

on the morning of a day when he had a meeting on hand
for the afternoon and a speech to make in the evening.
The book was quietly laid one side, for he always scru-
pulously avoided everything that could interfere with
work he was expected to do.   But the next day was a
free day.   Mr. Beecher rose even earlier than usual, and
as soon as he was dressed he began to read *Uncle Tom's
Cabin*.   When breakfast was ready he took his book
with him to the table, where reading and eating went
on together; but he spoke never a word.   After morning
prayers, he threw himself on the sofa, forgot everything
but his book, and read uninterruptedly till dinner-time.
Though evidently intensely interested, for a long time
he controlled any marked indication of it.   Before
noon I knew the storm was gathering that would con-
quer his self-control, as it had done with us all.   He
frequently 'gave way to his pocket-handkerchief,' to
use one of his old humorous remarks, in a most vigorous
manner.   In return for his teasing me for reading the
work weekly, I could not refrain from saying demurely,
as I passed him once: 'You seem to have a severe cold,
Henry.   How could you have taken it?'   But what did
I gain?   Not even a half-annoyed shake of the head, or
the semblance of a smile.   I might as well have spoken
to the Sphinx.

"When reminded that the dinner-bell had rung, he
rose and went to the table, still with his book in his
hand.   He asked the blessing with a tremor in his voice,
which showed the intense excitement under which he
was laboring.   We were alone at the table, and there
was nothing to distract his thoughts.   He drank his

coffee, ate but little, and returned to his reading, with no thought of indulging in his usual nap. His almost uncontrollable excitement revealed itself in frequent half-suppressed sobs.

"Mr. Beecher was a very slow reader. I was getting uneasy over the marks of strong feeling and excitement, and longed to have him finish the book. I could see that he entered into the whole story, every scene, as if it were being acted right before him, and he himself were the sufferer. He had always been a pronounced Abolitionist, and the story he was reading roused intensely all he had felt on that subject.

"The night came on. It was growing late, and I felt impelled to urge him to retire. Without raising his eyes from the book, he replied:

" 'Soon; soon; you go; I'll come soon.'

"Closing the house, I went to our room; but not to sleep. The clock struck twelve, one, two, three; and then, to my great relief, I heard Mr. Beecher coming up-stairs. As he entered, he threw *Uncle Tom's Cabin* on the table, exclaiming: 'There; I've done it! But if Hattie Stowe ever writes anything more like that I'll—well! She has nearly killed me.'

"And he never picked up the book from that day."

Any one who knew Henry Ward Beecher at all knew of his love of books. He was, however, most prodigal in lending his books and he always forgot the borrowers. Then when he wanted a certain volume from his library he could not find it. He would, of course, have forgotten the borrower, but he had a unique method of tracing the book.

One evening the great preacher suddenly appeared at a friend's house and, quietly entering the drawing-room without removing his overcoat, he walked up to his friend and said:

"Rossiter, why don't you bring back that Ruskin of mine that I lent you?"

The man colored to the roots of his hair. "Why, Mr. Beecher," he said, "I'll go up-stairs and get it for you right away. I would not have kept it so long, only you told me I might."

At this Beecher burst into a fit of merry laughter. "Found! Found!" he shouted, as he took off his overcoat and threw himself into a chair.

When he could stop laughing, he said: "You know, Rossiter, that I am always ready to lend my books to any one who will make good use of them and bring them back, but I always forget to whom I lend them. It happened, in this case, that I wanted that volume of Ruskin about a week ago; but when I went to the shelf for it, it was gone. I knew I must have lent it, but to whom I could not remember. During the past week, I began to demand the book of every friend I met to whom I might have lent it. Of course, every one of them protested innocence; but at last I've struck the guilty man. I shall know, in future, how to find my missing books. The plan works beautifully."

One evening, after supper, Mr. Beecher said to his wife: "Mother, what material have we among our papers about our early Indiana days?"

Mr. Beecher had long been importuned to write his

autobiography, and he had decided to do it after he had finished his *Life of Christ*.

Mrs. Beecher had two boxes brought into the room.

"Suppose you look into that box, if you will," said Mr. Beecher to Edward, "and I'll take this one, and we'll see what we can find about that time. Mother, you supervise and see how we look on the floor."

And Mr. Beecher sat down on the floor in front of one box, shoemaker-fashion, while Edward, likewise on the floor, started on the other box.

It was a dusty job, and the little room began to be filled with particles of dust which set Mrs. Beecher coughing. At last she said: "I'll leave you two to finish. I have some things to do up-stairs, and then I'll retire. Don't be too late, Henry," she said.

It was one of those rare evenings for Mr. Beecher— absolutely free from interruption; and, with his memory constantly taken back to his early days, he continued in a reminiscent mood that was charmingly intimate to the boy.

"Found something?" he asked at one intermission when quiet had reigned longer than usual, and he saw Edward studying a huge pile of papers.

"No, sir," said the boy. "Only a lot of papers about a suit."

"What suit?" asked Mr. Beecher mechanically, with his head buried in his box.

"I don't know, sir," Edward replied naïvely, little knowing what he was reopening to the preacher. "'Til-ton versus Beecher' they are marked."

Mr. Beecher said nothing, and after the boy had

fingered the papers he chanced to look in the preacher's direction and found him watching him intently with a curiously serious look in his face.

"Must have been a big suit," commented the boy. "Here's another pile of papers about it."

Edward could not make out Mr. Beecher's steady look at him as he sat there on the floor mechanically playing with a paper in his hand.

"Yes," he finally said, "it was a big suit. What does it mean to you?" he asked suddenly.

"To me?" Edward asked. "Nothing, sir. Why?"

Mr. Beecher said nothing for a few moments, and turned to his box to examine some more papers.

Then the boy asked: "Was the Beecher in this suit you, Mr. Beecher?"

Again was turned on him that serious, questioning look.

"Yes," he said after a bit. Then he thought again for a few moments and said: "How old were you in 1875?"

"Twelve," the boy replied.

"Twelve," he repeated. "Twelve."

He turned again to his box and Edward to his.

"There doesn't seem to be anything more in this box," the boy said, "but more papers in that suit," and he began to put the papers back.

"What do you know about that 'suit,' as you call it?" asked Mr. Beecher, stopping in his work.

"Nothing," was the reply. "I never heard of it."

"Never heard of it?" he repeated, and he fastened that curious look upon Edward again. It was so compelling that it held the boy. For several moments they looked at each other. Neither spoke.

"That seems strange," he said, at last, as he renewed the search of his box. "Never heard of it," he repeated almost to himself.

Then for fully five minutes not a word was spoken.

"But you will some day," said Mr. Beecher suddenly.

"I will what, Mr. Beecher?" asked the boy. He had forgotten the previous remark.

Mr. Beecher looked at Edward and sighed. "Hear about it," he said.

"I don't think I understand you," was the reply.

"No, I don't think you do," he said. "I mean, you will some day hear about that suit. And I don't know," then he hesitated, "but—but you might as well get it straight. You say you were twelve then," he mused. "What were you doing when you were twelve?"

"Going to school," was the reply.

"Yes, of course," said Mr. Beecher. "Well," he continued, turning on his haunches so that his back rested against the box, "I am going to tell you the story of that suit, and then you'll know it."

Edward said nothing, and then began the recital of a story that he was destined to remember. It was interesting then, as Mr. Beecher progressed; but how thrice interesting that wonderful recital was to prove as the years rolled by and the boy realized the wonderful telling of that of all stories by Mr. Beecher himself!

Slowly, and in that wonderfully low, mellow voice that so many knew and loved, step by step, came the unfolding of that remarkable story. Once or twice only did the voice halt, as when, after he had explained the basis of the famous suit, he said:

"Those were the charges. That is what it was all about."

Then he looked at Edward and asked: "Do you know just what such charges mean?"

"I think I do," Edward replied, and the question was asked with such feeling, and the answer was said so mechanically, that Mr. Beecher replied simply: "Perhaps."

"Well," he continued, "the suit *was* a 'long one,' as you said. For days and weeks, yes, for months, it went on, from January to July, and those were very full days: full of so many things that you would hardly understand."

And then he told the boy as much of the days in court as he thought he would understand, and how the lawyers worked and worked, in court all day, and up half the night, preparing for the next day. "Mostly around that little table there," he said, pointing to a white, marble-topped table against which the boy was leaning, and which now stands in Edward Bok's study.

"Finally the end came," he said, "after—well, months. To some it seemed years," said Mr. Beecher, and his eyes looked tired.

"Well," he continued, "the case went to the jury: the men, you know, who had to decide. There were twelve of them."

"Was it necessary that all twelve should think alike?" asked the boy.

"That was what was hoped, my boy," said Mr. Beecher—"that was what was hoped," he repeated.

"Well, they did, didn't they?" Edward asked, as Mr. Beecher stopped.

"Nine did," he replied. "Yes; nine did. But three didn't. Three thought—" Mr. Beecher stopped and did not finish the sentence. "But nine did," he repeated. "Nine to three it stood. That was the decision, and then the judge discharged the jury," he said.

There was naturally one question in the boyish mind to ask the man before him—one question! Yet, instinctively, something within him made him hesitate to ask that question. But at last his curiosity got the better of the still, small voice of judgment.

"And, Mr. Beecher—" the boy began.

But Mr. Beecher knew! He knew what was at the end of the tongue, looked clear into the boy's mind; and Edward can still see him lift that fine head and look into his eyes, as he said, slowly and clearly:

"And the decision of the nine was in exact accord with the facts."

He had divined the question!

As the two rose from the floor that night Edward looked at the clock. It was past midnight; Mr. Beecher had talked for two hours; the boy had spoken hardly at all.

As the boy was going out, he turned to Mr. Beecher sitting thoughtfully in his chair.

"Good night, Mr. Beecher," he said.

The Plymouth pastor pulled himself together, and with that wit that never forsook him he looked at the

clock, smiled, and answered: "Good morning, I should
say. God bless you, my boy." Then rising, he put his
arm around the boy's shoulders and walked with him to
the door.

CHAPTER X

THE FIRST "WOMAN'S PAGE," "LITERARY LEAVES,"
AND ENTERING SCRIBNER'S

MR. BEECHER's weekly newspaper "syndicate" letter
was not only successful in itself, it made liberal money
for the writer and for its two young publishers, but it
served to introduce Edward Bok's proposed agency to
the newspapers under the most favorable conditions.
With one stroke, the attention of newspaper editors had
been attracted, and Edward concluded to take quick
advantage of it. He organized the Bok Syndicate Press,
with offices in New York, and his brother, William J.
Bok, as partner and active manager. Edward's days
were occupied, of course, with his duties in the Holt
publishing house, where he was acquiring a first-hand
knowledge of the business.

Edward's attention was now turned, for the first
time, to women and their reading habits. He became
interested in the fact that the American woman was not
a newspaper reader. He tried to find out the psychology
of this, and finally reached the conclusion, on looking
over the newspapers, that the absence of any distinctive material for women was a factor. He talked the
matter over with several prominent New York editors,
who frankly acknowledged that they would like nothing better than to interest women, and make them
readers of their papers. But they were equally frank in

confessing that they were ignorant both of what women wanted, and, even if they knew, of where such material was to be had. Edward at once saw that here was an open field. It was a productive field, since, as woman was the purchasing power, it would benefit the newspaper enormously in its advertising if it could offer a feminine clientele.

There was a bright letter of New York gossip published in the *New York Star*, called "Bab's Babble." Edward had read it, and saw the possibility of syndicating this item as a woman's letter from New York. He instinctively realized that women all over the country would read it. He sought out the author, made arrangements with her and with former Governor Dorscheimer, owner of the paper, and the letter was sent out to a group of papers. It was an instantaneous success, and a syndicate of ninety newspapers was quickly organized.

Edward followed this up by engaging Ella Wheeler Wilcox, then at the height of her career, to write a weekly letter on women's topics. This he syndicated in conjunction with the other letter, and the editors invariably grouped the two letters. This, in turn, naturally led to the idea of supplying an entire page of matter of interest to women. The plan was proposed to a number of editors, who at once saw the possibilities in it and promised support. The young syndicator now laid under contribution all the famous women writers of the day; he chose the best of the men writers to write on women's topics; and it was not long before the syndicate was supplying a page of women's material. The newspapers played up the innovation, and thus was introduced into the newspaper press of the United States the "Woman's Page."

The material supplied by the Bok Syndicate Press was of the best; the standard was kept high; the writers were selected from among the most popular authors of the day; and readability was the cardinal note. The women bought the newspapers containing the new page, the advertiser began to feel the presence of the new reader, and every newspaper that could not get the rights for the "Bok Page," as it came to be known, started a "Woman's Page" of its own. Naturally, the material so obtained was of an inferior character. No single newspaper could afford what the syndicate, with the expense divided among a hundred newspapers, could pay. Nor had the editors of these woman's pages either a standard or a policy. In desperation they engaged any person they could to "get a lot of woman's stuff." It *was* stuff, and of the trashiest kind. So that almost coincident with the birth of the idea began its abuse and disintegration; the result we see in the meaningless presentations which pass for "woman's pages" in the newspaper of to-day.

This is true even of the woman's material in the leading newspapers, and the reason is not difficult to find. The average editor has, as a rule, no time to study the changing conditions of women's interests; his time is and must be engrossed by the news and editorial pages. He usually delegates the Sunday "specials" to some editor who, again, has little time to study the ever-changing women's problems, particularly in these days, and he relies upon unintelligent advice, or he places his "woman's page" in the hands of some woman with the comfortable assurance that, being a woman, she ought to know what interests her sex.

But having given the subject little thought, he attaches minor importance to the woman's "stuff," regarding it rather in the light of something that he "must carry to catch the women"; and forthwith he either forgets it or refuses to give the editor of his woman's page even a reasonable allowance to spend on her material. The result is, of course, inevitable: pages of worthless material. There is, in fact, no part of the Sunday newspaper of to-day upon which so much good and now expensive white paper is wasted as upon the pages marked for the home, for women, and for children.

Edward Bok now became convinced, from his book-publishing association, that if the American women were not reading the newspapers, the American public, as a whole, was not reading the number of books that it should, considering the intelligence and wealth of the people, and the cheap prices at which books were sold. He concluded to see whether he could not induce the newspapers to give larger and more prominent space to the news of the book world.

Owing to his constant contact with authors, he was in a peculiarly fortunate position to know their plans in advance of execution, and he was beginning to learn the ins and outs of the book-publishing world. He canvassed the newspapers subscribing to his syndicate features, but found a disinclination to give space to literary news. To the average editor, purely literary features held less of an appeal than did the features for women. Fewer persons were interested in books, they declared; besides, the publishing houses were not so liberal advertisers as the department stores. The whole question rested on a commercial basis.

Edward believed he could convince editors of the public interest in a newsy, readable New York literary letter, and he prevailed upon the editor of the *New York Star* to allow him to supplement the book reviews of George Parsons Lathrop in that paper by a column of literary chat called "Literary Leaves." For a number of weeks he continued to write this department, and confine it to the New York paper, feeling that he needed the experience for the acquirement of a readable style, and he wanted to be sure that he had opened a sufficient number of productive news channels to ensure a continuous flow of readable literary information.

Occasionally he sent to an editor here and there what he thought was a particularly newsy letter just "for his information, not for sale." The editor of the *Philadelphia Times* was the first to discover that his paper wanted the letter, and the *Boston Journal* followed suit. Then the editor of the *Cincinnati Times-Star* discovered the letter in the *New York Star*, and asked that it be supplied weekly with the letter. These newspapers renamed the letter "Bok's Literary Leaves," and the feature started on its successful career.

Edward had been in the employ of Henry Holt and Company as clerk and stenographer for two years when Mr. Cary sent for him and told him that there was an opening in the publishing house of Charles Scribner's Sons, if he wanted to make a change. Edward saw at once the larger opportunities possible in a house of the importance of the Scribners, and he immediately placed himself in communication with Mr. Charles Scribner, with the result that in January, 1884, he entered the employ of these publishers as stenographer to the two members of the firm and to Mr. Edward L. Burlingame, literary adviser to the house. He was to receive a salary of eighteen dollars and thirty-three cents per week, which was then considered a fair wage for steno-graphic work. The typewriter had at that time not come into use, and all letters were written in long-hand. Once more his legible handwriting had secured for him a position.

Edward Bok was now twenty-one years of age. He had already done a prodigious amount of work for a boy of his years. He was always busy. Every spare mo-ment of his evenings was devoted either to writing his literary letter, to the arrangement or editing of articles for his newspaper syndicate, to the steady acquirement of autograph letters in which he still persisted, or to helping Mr. Beecher in his literary work. The Plym-outh pastor was particularly pleased with Edward's successful exploitation of his pen work; and he after-ward wrote: "Bok is the only man who ever seemed to make my literary work go and get money out of it."

Enterprise and energy the boy unquestionably pos-sessed, but one need only think back even thus far in his life to see the continuous good fortune which had followed him in the friendships he had made, and in the men with whom his life, at its most formative period, had come into close contact. If we are inclined to credit young Bok with an ever-willingness to work and a certain quality of initiative, the influences which played upon him must also be taken into account.

Take, for example, the peculiarly fortuitous circumstances under which he entered the Scribner publishing house. As stenographer to the two members of the firm, Bok was immediately brought into touch with the leading authors of the day, their works as they were discussed in the correspondence dictated to him, and the authors' terms upon which books were published. In fact, he was given as close an insight as it was possible for a young man to get into the inner workings of one of the large publishing houses in the United States, with a list peculiarly noted for the distinction of its authors and the broad scope of its books.

The Scribners had the foremost theological list of all the publishing houses; its educational list was exceptionally strong; its musical list excelled; its fiction represented the leading writers of the day; its general list was particularly noteworthy; and its foreign department, importing the leading books brought out in Great Britain and Europe, was an outstanding feature of the business. The correspondence dictated to Bok covered, naturally, all these fields, and a more remarkable opportunity for self-education was never offered a stenographer.

Mr. Burlingame was known in the publishing world for his singularly keen literary appreciation, and was accepted as one of the best judges of good fiction. Bok entered the Scribner employ as Mr. Burlingame was selecting the best short stories published within a decade for a set of books to be called "Short Stories by American Authors." The correspondence for this series was dictated to Bok, and he decided to read after Mr. Burlingame and thus get an idea of the best fiction of the day. So whenever his chief wrote to an author asking for permission to include his story in the proposed series, Bok immediately hunted up the story and read it.

Later, when the house decided to start *Scribner's Magazine*, and Mr. Burlingame was selected to be its editor, all the preliminary correspondence was dictated to Bok through his employers, and he received a first-hand education in the setting up of the machinery necessary for the publication of a magazine. All this he eagerly absorbed.

He was again fortunate in that his desk was placed in the advertising department of the house; and here he found, as manager, an old-time Brooklyn boy friend with whom he had gone to school: Frank N. Doubleday, to-day the senior partner of Doubleday, Page and Company. Bok had been attracted to advertising through his theatre programme and *Brooklyn Magazine* experience, and here was presented a chance to learn the art at first hand and according to the best traditions. So, whenever his stenographic work permitted, he assisted Mr. Doubleday in preparing and placing the advertisements of the books of the house.

Mr. Doubleday was just reviving the publication of a house-organ called *The Book Buyer*, and, given a chance to help in this, Bok felt he was getting back into the periodical field, especially since, under Mr.

Doubleday's guidance, the little monthly soon developed into a literary magazine of very respectable size and generally bookish contents.

The house also issued another periodical, *The Presbyterian Review*, a quarterly under the editorship of a board of professors connected with the Princeton and Union Theological Seminaries. This ponderous-looking magazine was not composed of what one might call "light reading," and as the price of a single copy was eighty cents, and the advertisements it could reasonably expect were necessarily limited in number, the periodical was rather difficult to move. Thus the whole situation at the Scribners' was adapted to give Edward an all-round training in the publishing business. It was an exceptional opportunity.

He worked early and late. An increase in his salary soon told him that he was satisfying his employers, and then, when the new *Scribner's Magazine* appeared, and a little later Mr. Doubleday was delegated to take charge of the business end of it, Bok himself was placed in charge of the advertising department, with the publishing details of the two periodicals on his hands.

He suddenly found himself directing a stenographer instead of being a stenographer himself. Evidently his apprentice days were over. He had, in addition, the charge of sending all the editorial copies of the new books to the press for review, and of keeping a record of those reviews. This naturally brought to his desk the authors of the house who wished to see how the press received their works.

The study of the writers who were interested in following the press notices of their books, and those who were indifferent to them became a fascinating game to young Bok. He soon discovered that the greater the author the less he seemed to care about his books once they were published. Bok noticed this, particularly, in the case of Robert Louis Stevenson, whose work had attracted him, but, although he used the most subtle means to inveigle the author into the office to read the press notices, he never succeeded. Stevenson never seemed to have the slightest interest in what the press said of his books.

One day Mr. Burlingame asked Bok to take some proofs to Stevenson at his home; thinking it might be a propitious moment to interest the author in the popular acclaim that followed the publication of *Doctor Jekyll and Mr. Hyde*, Bok put a bunch of press notices in his pocket. He found the author in bed, smoking his inevitable cigarette.

As the proofs were to be brought back, Bok waited, and thus had an opportunity for nearly two hours to see the author at work. No man ever went over his proofs more carefully than did Stevenson; his corrections were numerous; and sometimes for ten minutes at a time he would sit smoking and thinking over a single sentence, which, when he had satisfactorily shaped it in his mind, he would recast on the proof.

Stevenson was not a prepossessing figure at these times. With his sallow skin and his black dishevelled hair, with finger-nails which had been allowed to grow very long, with fingers discolored by tobacco—in short, with a general untidiness that was all his own, Stevenson, so

Bok felt, was an author whom it was better to read than to see. And yet his kindliness and gentleness more than offset the unattractiveness of his physical appearance.

After one or two visits from Bok, having grown accustomed to him, Stevenson would discuss some sentence in an article, or read some amended paragraph out loud and ask whether Bok thought it sounded better. To pass upon Stevenson as a stylist was, of course, hardly within Bok's mental reach, so he kept discreetly silent when Stevenson asked his opinion.

In fact, Bok reasoned it out that the novelist did not really expect an answer or an opinion, but was at such times thinking aloud. The mental process, however, was immensely interesting, particularly when Stevenson would ask Bok to hand him a book on words lying on an adjacent table. "So hard to find just the right word," Stevenson would say, and Bok got his first realization of the truth of the maxim: "Easy writing, hard reading; hard writing, easy reading."

On this particular occasion when Stevenson finished, Bok pulled out his clippings, told the author how his book was being received, and was selling, what the house was doing to advertise it, explained the forthcoming play by Richard Mansfield, and then offered the press notices.

Stevenson took the bundle and held it in his hand.

"That's very nice to tell me all you have," he said, "and I have been greatly interested. But you have really told me all about it, haven't you, so why should I read these notices? Hadn't I better get busy on another paper for Mr. Burlingame for the next magazine, else he'll be after me? You know how impatient these editors are." And he handed back the notices.

Bok saw it was of no use: Stevenson was interested in his work, but, beyond a certain point, not in the world's reception of it. Bok's estimate of the author rose immeasurably. His attitude was in such sharp contrast to that of others who came almost daily into the office to see what the papers said, often causing discomfiture to the young advertising director by insisting upon taking the notices with them. But Bok always countered this desire by reminding the author that, of course, in that case he could not quote from these desirable notices in his advertisements of the book. And, invariably, the notices were left behind!

It now fell to the lot of the young advertiser to arouse the interest of the public in what were to be some of the most widely read and best-known books of the day: Robert Louis Stevenson's *Dr. Jekyll and Mr. Hyde;* Frances Hodgson Burnett's *Little Lord Fauntleroy;* Andrew Carnegie's *Triumphant Democracy;* Frank R. Stockton's *The Lady, or the Tiger?* and his *Rudder Grange,* and a succession of other books.

The advertising of these books keenly sharpened the publicity sense of the developing advertising director. One book could best be advertised by the conventional means of the display advertisement; another, like *Triumphant Democracy,* was best served by sending out to the newspapers a "broadside" of pungent extracts; public curiosity in a novel like *The Lady, or the Tiger?* was, of course, whetted by the publication of literary notes as to the real dénouement the author had in mind in writing the story. Whenever Mr. Stockton came into the office Bok pumped him dry as to his experiences with the story, such as when, at a dinner party, his hostess served an ice-cream lady and a tiger to the author, and the whole company watched which he chose.

"And which did you choose?" asked the advertising director.

"*Et tu, Brute?*" Stockton smilingly replied. "Well, I'll tell you. I asked the butler to bring me another spoon, and then, with a spoon in each hand, I attacked both the lady and the tiger at the same time."

Once, when Stockton was going to Boston by the night boat, every room was taken. The ticket agent recognized the author, and promised to get him a desirable room if the author would tell which he had had in mind, the lady or the tiger.

"Produce the room," answered Stockton.

The man did. Stockton paid for it, and then said: "To tell you the truth, my friend, I don't know."

And that *was* the truth, as Mr. Stockton confessed to his friends. The idea of the story had fascinated him; when he began it he purposed to give it a definite ending. But when he reached the end he didn't know himself which to produce out of the open door, the lady or the tiger, "and so," he used to explain, "I made up my mind to leave it hanging in the air."

To the present generation of readers, all this reference to Stockton's story may sound strange, but for months it was the most talked-of story of the time, and sold into large numbers.

One day while Mr. Stockton was in Bok's office, A.

B. Frost, the illustrator, came in. Frost had become a full-fledged farmer with one hundred and twenty acres of Jersey land, and Stockton had a large farm in the South which was a financial burden to him.

"Well, Stockton," said Frost, "I have found a way at last to make a farm stop eating up money. Perhaps it will help you."

Stockton was busy writing, but at this bit of hopeful news he looked up, his eyes kindled, he dropped his pen, and eagerly said:

"Tell me."

And looking behind him to see that the way was clear, Frost answered:

"Pave it solid, old man."

When the stories of *Dr. Jekyll and Mr. Hyde* and *Little Lord Fauntleroy* were made into plays, Bok was given an opportunity for an entirely different kind of publicity. Both plays were highly successful; they ran for weeks in succession, and each evening Bok had circulars of the books in every seat of the theatre; he had a table filled with the books in the foyer of each theatre; and he bombarded the newspapers with stories of Mr. Mansfield's method of making the quick change from one character to the other in the dual rôle of the Stevenson play, and with anecdotes about the boy Tommy Russell in Mrs. Burnett's play. The sale of the books went merrily on, and kept pace with the success of the plays. And it all sharpened the initiative of the young advertiser and developed his sense for publicity.

One day while waiting in the anteroom of a publishing house to see a member of the firm, he picked up a book and began to read it. Since he had to wait for nearly an hour, he had read a large part of the volume when he was at last admitted to the private office. When his business was finished, Bok asked the publisher why this book was not selling.

"I don't know," replied the publisher. "We had great hopes for it, but somehow or other the public has not responded to it."

"Are you sure you are telling the public about it in the right way?" ventured Bok.

The Scribner advertising had by this time attracted the attention of the publishing world, and this publisher was entirely ready to listen to a suggestion from his youthful caller.

"I wish we published it," said Bok. "I think I could make it a go. It's all in the book."

"How would you advertise it?" asked the publisher.

Bok promised the publisher he would let him know. He carried with him a copy of the book, wrote some advertisements for it, prepared an attractive "broadside" of extracts, to which the book easily lent itself, wrote some literary notes about it, and sent the whole collection to the publisher. Every particle of "copy" which Bok had prepared was used, the book began to sell, and within three months it was the most discussed book of the day.

The book was Edward Bellamy's *Looking Backward*.

CHAPTER XI

THE CHANCES FOR SUCCESS

EDWARD BOK does not now remember whether the
mental picture had been given him, or whether he had
conjured it up for himself; but he certainly was pos-
sessed of the idea, as are so many young men entering
business, that the path which led to success was very
difficult: that it was overfilled with a jostling, bustling,
panting crowd, each eager to reach the goal; and all
ready to dispute every step that a young man should
take; and that favoritism only could bring one to the
top.

After Bok had been in the world of affairs, he wondered
where were these choked avenues, these struggling
masses, these competitors for every inch of vantage.
Then he gradually discovered that they did not exist.

In the first place, he found every avenue leading to
success wide open and certainly not overpeopled. He
was surprised how few there were who really stood in a
young man's way. He found that favoritism was not
the factor that he had been led to suppose. He realized
it existed in a few isolated cases, but to these every one
had pointed and about these every one had talked until,
in the public mind, they had multiplied in number and
assumed a proportion that the facts did not bear out.

Here and there a relative "played a favorite," but
even with the push and influence behind him "the lucky

one," as he was termed, did not seem to make progress, unless he had merit. It was not long before Bok discovered that the possession of sheer merit was the only real factor that actually counted in any of the places where he had been employed or in others which he had watched; that business was so constructed and conducted that nothing else, in the face of competition, could act as current coin. And the amazing part of it all to Bok was how little merit there was. Nothing astonished him more than the low average ability of those with whom he worked or came into contact.

He looked at the top, and instead of finding it overcrowded, he was surprised at the few who had reached there; the top fairly begged for more to climb its heights.

For every young man, earnest, eager to serve, willing to do more than he was paid for, he found ten trying to solve the problem of how little they could actually do for the pay received.

It interested Bok to listen to the talk of his fellow-workers during luncheon hours and at all other times outside of office hours. When the talk did turn on the business with which they were concerned, it consisted almost entirely of wages, and he soon found that, with scarcely an exception, every young man was terribly underpaid, and that his employer absolutely failed to appreciate his work. It was interesting, later, when Bok happened to get the angle of the employer, to discover that, invariably, these same lamenting young men were those who, from the employer's point of view, were either greatly overpaid or so entirely worthless as to be marked for early decapitation.

Bok felt that this constant thought of the wages earned or deserved was putting the cart before the horse; he had schooled himself into the belief that if he did his work well, and accomplished more than was expected of him, the question of wages would take care of itself. But, according to the talk on every side, it was he who had the cart before the horse. Bok had not only tried always to fill the particular job set for him, but had made it a rule at the same time to study the position just ahead, to see what it was like, what it demanded, and then, as the opportunity presented itself, do a part of that job in addition to his own. As a stenographer, he tried always to clear off the day's work before he closed his desk. This was not always possible, but he kept it before him as a rule to be followed rather than violated.

One morning Bok's employer happened to come to the office earlier than usual, to find the letters he had dictated late in the afternoon before lying on his desk ready to be signed.

"These are the letters I gave you late yesterday afternoon, are they not?" asked the employer.

"Yes, sir."

"Must have started early this morning, didn't you?"

"No, sir," answered Bok. "I wrote them out last evening before I left."

"Like to get your notes written out before they get stale?"

"Yes, sir."

"Good idea," said the employer.

"Yes, sir," answered Bok, "and I think it is even a

better idea to get a day's work off before I take my apron off."

"Well said," answered the employer, and the following payday Bok found an increase in his weekly envelope.

It is only fair, however, to add here, parenthetically, that it is neither just nor considerate to a conscientious stenographer for an employer to delay his dictation until the end of the day's work, when, merely by judicious management of his affairs and time, he can give his dictation directly after opening his morning mail. There are two sides to every question; but sometimes the side of the stenographer is not kept in mind by the employer.

Bok found it a uniform rule among his fellow-workers to do exactly the opposite to his own idea; there was an astonishing unanimity in working by the clock; where the hour of closing was five o'clock the preparations began five minutes before, with the hat and overcoat over the back of the chair ready for the stroke of the hour. This concert of action was curiously universal, no "overtime" was ever to be thought of, and, as occasionally happened when the work did go over the hour, it was not, to use the mildest term, done with care, neatness, or accuracy; it was, to use a current phrase, "slammed off." Every moment beyond five o'clock in which the worker was asked to do anything was by just so much an imposition on the part of the employer, and so far as it could be safely shown, this impression was gotten over to him.

There was an entire unwillingness to let business

interfere with any anticipated pleasure or personal engagement. The office was all right between nine and five; one had to be there to earn a living; but after five, it was not to be thought of for one moment. The elevators which ran on the stroke of five were never large enough to hold the throng which besieged them. « The talk during lunch hour rarely, if ever, turned toward business, except as said before, when it dealt with underpaid services. In the spring and summer it was invariably of baseball, and scores of young men knew the batting averages of the different players and the standing of the clubs with far greater accuracy than they knew the standing or the discounts of the customers of their employers. In the winter the talk was all of dancing, boxing, or plays.

It soon became evident to Bok why scarcely five out of every hundred of the young men whom he knew made any business progress. They were not interested; it was a case of a day's work and a day's pay; it was not a question of how much one could do but how little one could get away with. The thought of how well one might do a given thing never seemed to occur to the average mind.

"Oh, what do you care?" was the favorite expression. "The boss won't notice it if you break your back over his work; you won't get any more pay."

And there the subject was dismissed, and thoroughly dismissed, too.

Eventually, then, Bok learned that the path that led to success was wide open: the competition was negligible. There was no jostling. In fact, travel on it was just a trifle lonely. One's fellow-travellers were excellent company, but they were few! It was one of Edward Bok's greatest surprises, but it was also one of his greatest stimulants. To go where others could not go, or were loath to go, where at least they were not, had a tang that savored of the freshest kind of adventure. And the way was so simple, so much simpler, in fact, than its avoidance, which called for so much argument, explanation, and discussion. One had merely to do all that one could do, a little more than one was asked or expected to do, and immediately one's head rose above the crowd and one was in an employer's eye—where it is always so satisfying for an employee to be! And as so few heads lifted themselves above the many, there was never any danger that they would not be seen.

Of course, Edward Bok had to prove to himself that his conception of conditions was right. He felt instinctively that it was, however, and with this stimulus he bucked the line hard. When others played, he worked, fully convinced that his play-time would come later. Where others shirked, he assumed. Where others lagged, he accelerated his pace. Where others were indifferent to things around them, he observed and put away the results for possible use later. He did not make of himself a pack-horse; what he undertook he did from interest in it, and that made it a pleasure to him when to others it was a burden. He instinctively reasoned it out that an unpleasant task is never accomplished by stepping aside from it, but that, unerringly, it will return later to be met and done.

Obstacles, to Edward Bok, soon became merely difficulties to be overcome, and he trusted to his instinct to show him the best way to overcome them. He soon learned that the hardest kind of work was back of every success; that nothing in the world of business just happened, but that everything was brought about, and only in one way—by a willingness of spirit and a determination to carry through. He soon exploded for himself the misleading and comfortable theory of luck: the only lucky people, he found, were those who worked hard. To them, luck came in the shape of what they had earned. There were exceptions here and there, as there are to every rule; but the majority of these, he soon found, were more in the seeming than in the reality. Generally speaking—and of course to this rule there are likewise exceptions, or as the Frenchman said, "All generalizations are false, including this one"—a man got in this world about what he worked for.

And that became, for himself, the rule of Edward Bok's life.

CHAPTER XII

BAPTISM UNDER FIRE

THE personnel of the Scribner house was very youthful from the members of the firm clear down the line. It was veritably a house of young men.

The story is told of a Boston publisher, sedate and fairly elderly, who came to the Scribner house to transact business with several of its departments. One of his errands concerning itself with advertising, he was introduced to Bok, who was then twenty-four. Looking the youth over, he transacted his business as well as he felt it could be transacted with a manager of such tender years, and then sought the head of the educational department: this brought him to another young man of twenty-four.

With his yearnings for some one more advanced in years full upon him, the visitor now inquired for the business manager of the new magazine, only to find a man of twenty-six. His next introduction was to the head of the out-of-town business department, who was twenty-seven.

At this point the Boston man asked to see Mr. Scribner. This disclosed to him Mr. Arthur H. Scribner, the junior partner, who owned to twenty-eight summers. Mustering courage to ask faintly for Mr. Charles Scribner himself, he finally brought up in that gentleman's office only to meet a man just turning thirty-three!

"This *is* a young-looking crowd," said Mr. Scribner one day, looking over his young men. And his eye rested on Bok. "Particularly you, Bok. Doubleday looks his years better than you do, for at least he has a moustache." Then, contemplatively: "You raise a moustache, Bok, and I'll raise your salary."

This appealed to Bok very strongly, and within a month he pointed out the result to his employer. "Stand in the light here," said Mr. Scribner. "Well, yes," he concluded dubiously, "it's there—something at least. All right; I'll keep my part of the bargain."

He did. But the next day he was nonplussed to see that the moustache had disappeared from the lip of his youthful advertising manager. "Couldn't quite stand it, Mr. Scribner," was the explanation. "Besides, you didn't say I should keep it: you merely said to raise it."

But the increase did not follow the moustache. To Bok's great relief, it stuck!

This youthful personnel, while it made for *esprit de corps*, had also its disadvantages. One day as Bok was going out to lunch, he found a small-statured man, rather plainly dressed, wandering around the retail department, hoping for a salesman to wait on him. The young salesman on duty, full of inexperience, had a ready smile and quick service ever ready for "carriage trade," as he called it; but this particular customer had come afoot, and this, together with his plainness of dress, did not impress the young salesman. His attention was called to the wandering customer, and it was suggested that he find out what was wanted. When Bok returned from lunch, the young salesman, who, with a beaming smile, had just most ceremoniously bowed the plainly dressed little customer out of the street-door, said: "You certainly struck it rich that time when you suggested my waiting on that little man! Such an order! Been here ever since. Did you know who it was?"

"No," returned Bok. "Who was it?"

"Andrew Carnegie," beamed the salesman.

Another youthful clerk in the Scribner retail book-store, unconscious of the customer's identity, waited one day on the wife of Mark Twain.

Mrs. Clemens asked the young salesman for a copy of Taine's *Ancient Régime*.

"Beg pardon," said the clerk, "what book did you say?"

Mrs. Clemens repeated the author and title of the book.

Going to the rear of the store, the clerk soon returned, only to inquire: "May I ask you to repeat the name of the author?"

"Taine, T-a-i-n-e," replied Mrs. Clemens.

Then did the youthfulness of the salesman assert itself. Assuming an air of superior knowledge, and looking at the customer with an air of sympathy, he corrected Mrs. Clemens:

"Pardon me, madam, but you have the name a trifle wrong. You mean Twain—not Taine."

With so many young men of the same age, there was a natural sense of team-work and a spirit of comrade-ship that made for successful co-operation. This spirit extended outside of business hours. At luncheon there was a Scribner table in a neighboring restaurant, and evenings saw the Scribner department heads mingling as friends. It was a group of young men who understood and liked each other, with the natural result that business went easier and better because of it.

But Bok did not have much time for evening enjoyment, since his outside interests had grown and prospered and they kept him busy. His syndicate was regularly supplying over a hundred newspapers: his literary letter had become an established feature in thirty different newspapers.

Of course, his opportunities for making this letter interesting were unusual. Owing to his Scribner connection, however, he had taken his name from the letter and signed that of his brother. He had, also, constantly to discriminate between the information that he could publish without violation of confidence and that which he felt he was not at liberty to print. This gave him excellent experience; for the most vital of all essentials in the journalist is the ability unerringly to decide what to print and what to regard as confidential.

Of course, the best things that came to him he could not print. Whenever there was a question, he gave the benefit of the doubt to the confidential relation in which his position placed him with authors; and his Dutch caution, although it deprived him of many a toothsome morsel for his letter, soon became known to his confrères, and was a large asset when, as an editor, he had to follow the golden rule of editorship that teaches one to keep the ears open but the mouth shut.

This Alpha and Omega of all the commandments in

the editorial creed some editors learn by sorrowful experience. Bok was, again, fortunate in learning it under the most friendly auspices. He continued to work without sparing himself, but his star remained in the ascendency. Just how far a man's own efforts and standards keep a friendly star centred over his head is a question. But Edward Bok has always felt that he was materially helped by fortuitous conditions not of his own creation or choice.

He was now to receive his first public baptism of fire. He had published a symposium, through his newspaper syndicate, discussing the question, "Should Clergymen Smoke?" He had induced all the prominent clergymen in the country to contribute their views, and so distinguished was the list that the article created widespread attention.

One of the contributors was the Reverend Richard S. Storrs, D.D., one of the most distinguished of Brooklyn's coterie of clergy of that day. A few days after the publication of the article, Bok was astounded to read in the *Brooklyn Eagle* a sensational article, with large headlines, in which Doctor Storrs repudiated his contribution to the symposium, declared that he had never written or signed such a statement, and accused Edward Bok of forgery.

Coming from a man of Doctor Storrs's prominence, the accusation was, of course, a serious one. Bok realized this at once. He foresaw the damage it might work to the reputation of a young man trying to climb the ladder of success, and wondered why Doctor Storrs had seen fit to accuse him in this public manner instead of calling upon him for a personal explanation. He thought perhaps he might find such a letter from Doctor Storrs when he reached home, but instead he met a small corps of reporters from the Brooklyn and New York newspapers. He told them frankly that no one was more surprised at the accusation than he, but that the original contributions were in the New York office of the syndicate, and he could not corroborate his word until he had looked into the papers and found Doctor Storrs's contribution.

That evening Bok got at the papers in the case, and found out that, technically, Doctor Storrs was right: he had not written or signed such a statement. The compiler of the symposium, the editor of one of New York's leading evening papers whom Bok had employed, had found Doctor Storrs's declaration in favor of a clergyman's use of tobacco in an address made some time before, had extracted it and incorporated it into the symposium. It was, therefore, Doctor Storrs's opinion on the subject, but not written for the occasion for which it was used. Bok felt that his editor had led him into an indiscretion. Yet the sentiments were those of the writer whose name was attached to them, so that the act was not one of forgery. The editor explained that he had sent the extract to Doctor Storrs, who had not returned it, and he had taken silence to mean consent to the use of the material.

Bok decided to say nothing until he heard from Doctor Storrs personally, and so told the newspapers. But the clergyman did not stop his attack. Of course, the newspapers egged him on and extracted from him the further accusation that Bok's silence proved his guilt. Bok now took the case to Mr. Beecher, and asked his advice.

"Well, Edward, you are right and you are wrong," said Mr. Beecher. "And so is Storrs, of course. It is beneath him to do what he has done. Storrs and I are not good friends, as you know, and so I cannot go to him and ask him the reason of his disclaimer. Otherwise I would. Of course, he may have forgotten his remarks: that is always possible in a busy man's life. He may not have received the letter enclosing them. That is likewise possible. But I have a feeling that Storrs has some reason for wishing to repudiate his views on this subject just at this time. What it is I do not, of course, know, but his vehemence makes me think so. I think I should let him have his rein. Keep you quiet. It may damage you a little here and there, but in the end it won't harm you. In the main point, you are right. You are not a forger. The sentiments are his and he uttered them, and he should stand by them. He threatens to bring you into court, I see from to-day's paper. Wait until he does so."

Bok, chancing to meet Doctor Talmage, told him Mr. Beecher's advice, and he endorsed it. "Remember, boy," said Doctor Talmage, "silence is never so golden as when you are under fire. I know, for I have been there, as you know, more than once. Keep quiet; and always believe this: that there is a great deal of common sense abroad in the world, and a man is always safe in trusting it to do him justice."

They were not pleasant and easy days for Bok, for

Doctor Storrs kept up the din for several days. Bok waited for the word to appear in court. But this never came, and the matter soon died down and out. And, although Bok met the clergyman several times afterward in the years that followed, no reference was ever made by him to the incident.

But Edward Bok had learned a valuable lesson of silence under fire—an experience that was to stand him in good stead when he was again publicly attacked not long afterward.

This occurred in connection with a notable anniversary celebration in honor of Henry Ward Beecher, in which the entire city of Brooklyn was to participate. It was to mark a mile-stone in Mr. Beecher's ministry and in his pastorate of Plymouth Church. Bok planned a world-wide tribute to the famed clergyman: he would get the most distinguished men and women of this and other countries to express their esteem for the Plymouth pastor in written congratulations, and he would bind these into a volume for presentation to Mr. Beecher on the occasion. He consulted members of the Beecher family, and, with their acquiescence, began to assemble the material. He was in the midst of the work when Henry Ward Beecher passed away. Bok felt that the tributes already received were too wonderful to be lost to the world, and, after again consulting Mrs. Beecher and her children, he determined to finish the collection and publish it as a memorial for private distribution. After a prodigious correspondence, the work was at last completed; and in June, 1887, the volume was published, in a limited edition of five hundred copies.

Bok distributed copies of the volume to the members of Mr. Beecher's family, he had orders from Mr. Beecher's friends, one hundred copies were offered to the American public and one hundred copies were issued in an English edition.

With such a figure to whom to do honor, the contributors, of course, included the foremost men and women of the time. Grover Cleveland was then President of the United States, and his tribute was a notable one. Mr. Gladstone, the Duke of Argyll, Pasteur, Canon Farrar, Bartholdi, Salvini, and a score of others represented English and European opinion. Oliver Wendell Holmes, John Greenleaf Whittier, T. De Witt Talmage, Robert G. Ingersoll, Charles Dudley Warner, General Sherman, Julia Ward Howe, Andrew Carnegie, Edwin Booth, Rutherford B. Hayes—there was scarcely a leader of thought and of action of that day unrepresented. The edition was, of course, quickly exhausted; and when to-day a copy occasionally appears at an auction sale, it is sold at a high price.

The newspapers gave very large space to the distinguished memorial, and this fact angered a journalist, Joseph Howard, Junior, a man at one time close to Mr. Beecher, who had befriended him. Howard had planned to be the first in the field with a hastily prepared biography of the great preacher, and he felt that Bok had forestalled him. Forthwith, he launched a vicious attack on the compiler of the memorial, accusing him of "making money out of Henry Ward Beecher's dead body" and of "seriously offending the family of Mr. Beecher, who had had no say in the memorial, which was therefore without authority, and hence extremely distasteful to all."

Howard had convinced a number of editors of the justice of his position, and so he secured a wide publication for his attack. For the second time, Edward Bok was under fire, and remembering his action on the previous occasion, he again remained silent, and again the argument was put forth that his silence implied guilt. But Mrs. Beecher and members of the Beecher family did not observe silence, and quickly proved that not only had Bok compiled the memorial as a labor of love and had lost money on it, but that he had the full consent of the family in its preparation.

When, shortly afterward, Howard's hastily compiled "biography" of Mr. Beecher appeared, a reporter asked Mrs. Beecher whether she and her family had found it accurate.

"Accurate, my child," said Mrs. Beecher. "Why, it is so accurate in its absolute falsity that neither I nor the boys can find one fact or date given correctly, although we have studied it for two days. Even the year of Mr. Beecher's birth is wrong, and that is the smallest error!"

Edward Bok little dreamed that these two experiences with public criticism were to serve him as a foretaste of future attacks when he would get the benefit of hundreds of pencils especially sharpened for him.

CHAPTER XIII

PUBLISHING INCIDENTS AND ANECDOTES

ONE evening some literary men were dining togethei previous to going to a private house where a number of authors were to give readings from their books. At the table the talk turned on the carelessness with which the public reads books. Richard Harding Davis, one of the party, contended that the public read more carefully than the others believed. It was just at the time when Du Maurier's *Trilby* was in every one's hands.

"Don't you believe it," said one of the diners. "I'll warrant you could take a portion of some well-known story to-night and palm it off on most of your listeners as new stuff."

"Done," said Davis. "Come along, and I'll prove you wrong."

The reading was to be at the house of John Kendrick Bangs at Yonkers. When Davis's "turn" in the programme came, he announced that he would read a portion from an unpublished story written by himself. Immediately there was a flutter in the audience, particularly among the younger element.

Pulling a roll of manuscript out of his pocket, Davis began:

"It was a fine, sunny, showery day in April. The big studio window——"

He got no farther. Almost the entire audience broke into a shout of laughter and applause. Davis had read thirteen of the opening words of *Trilby*.

All publishing houses employ "readers" outside of those in their own offices for the reading of manuscripts on special subjects. One of these "outside readers" was given a manuscript for criticism. He took it home and began its reading. He had finished only a hundred pages or so when, by a curious coincidence, the card of the author of the manuscript was brought to the "reader." The men were close friends.

Hastily gathering up the manuscript, the critic shoved the work into a drawer of his desk, and asked that his friend be shown in.

The evening was passed in conversation; as the visitor rose to leave, his host, rising also and seating himself on his desk, asked:

"What have you been doing lately? Haven't seen much of you."

"No," said the friend. "It may interest you to know that I have been turning to literary work, and have just completed what I consider to be an important book."

"Really?" commented the "reader."

"Yes," went on his friend. "I submitted it a few days ago to one of the big publishing houses. But, great Scott, you can never tell what these publishers will do with a thing of that sort. They give their manuscripts to all kinds of fools to read. I suppose, by this time, some idiot, who doesn't know a thing of the subject about which I have written, is sitting on my manuscript."

Mechanically, the "reader" looked at the desk upon which he was sitting, thought of the manuscript lying in the drawer directly under him, and said:

"Yes, that may be. Quite likely, in fact."

Of no novel was the secret of the authorship ever so well kept as was that of *The Breadwinners*, which, published anonymously in 1883, was the talk of literary circles for a long time, and speculation as to its authorship was renewed in the newspapers for years afterward. Bok wanted very much to find out the author's name so that he could announce it in his literary letter. He had his suspicions, but they were not well founded until an amusing little incident occurred which curiously revealed the secret to him.

Bok was waiting to see one of the members of a publishing firm when a well-known English publisher, visiting in America, was being escorted out of the office, the conversation continuing as the two gentlemen walked through the outer rooms. "My chief reason," said the English publisher, as he stopped at the end of the outer office where Bok was sitting, "for hesitating at all about taking an English set of plates of the novel you speak of is because it is of anonymous authorship, a custom of writing which has grown out of all decent proportions in your country since the issue of that stupid book, *The Breadwinners*."

As these last words were spoken, a man seated at a desk directly behind the speaker looked up, smiled, and resumed reading a document which he had dropped in to sign. A smile also spread over the countenance of the American publisher as he furtively glanced over the shoulder of the English visitor and caught the eye of the smiling man at the desk.

Bok saw the little comedy, realized at once that he had discovered the author of *The Breadwinners*, and stated to the publisher that he intended to use the incident in his literary letter. But it proved to be one of those heart-rending instances of a delicious morsel of news that must be withheld from the journalist's use. The publisher acknowledged that Bok had happened upon the true authorship, but placed him upon his honor to make no use of the incident. And Bok learned again the vital journalistic lesson that there are a great many things in the world that the journalist knows and yet cannot write about. He would have been years in advance of the announcement finally made that John Hay wrote the novel.

At another time, while waiting, Bok had an experience which, while interesting, was saddening instead of amusing. He was sitting in Mark Twain's sitting-room in his home in Hartford waiting for the humorist to return from a walk. Suddenly sounds of devotional singing came in through the open window from the direction of the outer conservatory. The singing was low, yet the sad tremor in the voice seemed to give it special carrying power.

"You have quite a devotional servant," Bok said to a maid who was dusting the room.

"Oh, that is not a servant who is singing, sir," was the answer. "You can step to this window and see for yourself."

Bok did so, and there, sitting alone on one of the

rustic benches in the flower-house, was a small, elderly woman. Keeping time with the first finger of her right hand, as if with a baton, she was slightly swaying her frail body as she sang, softly yet sweetly, Charles Wesley's hymn, "Jesus, Lover of My Soul," and Sarah Flower Adams's "Nearer, My God, to Thee."

But the singer was not a servant. It was Harriet Beecher Stowe!

On another visit to Hartford, shortly afterward, Bok was just turning into Forrest Street when a little old woman came shambling along toward him, unconscious, apparently, of people or surroundings. In her hand she carried a small tree-switch. Bok did not notice her until just as he had passed her he heard her calling to him: "Young man, young man." Bok retraced his steps, and then the old lady said: "Young man, you have been leaning against something white," and taking her tree-switch she whipped some wall dust from the sleeve of Bok's coat. It was not until that moment that Bok recognized in his self-appointed "brush" no less a personage than Harriet Beecher Stowe.

"This is Mrs. Stowe, is it not?" he asked, after tendering his thanks to her.

Those blue eyes looked strangely into his as she answered:

"That is my name, young man. I live on this street. Are you going to have me arrested for stopping you?" with which she gathered up her skirts and quickly ran away, looking furtively over her shoulder at the amazed young man, sorrowfully watching the running figure!

Speaking of Mrs. Stowe brings to mind an unscrupulous and yet ingenious trick just about this time played by a young man attached to one of the New York publishing houses. One evening at dinner this chap happened to be in a bookish company when the talk turned to the enthusiasm of the Southern negro for an illustrated Bible. The young publishing clerk listened intently, and next day he went to a Bible publishing house in New York which issued a Bible gorgeous with pictures and entered into an arrangement with the proprietors whereby he should have the Southern territory. He resigned his position, and within a week he was in the South. He made arrangements with an artist friend to make a change in each copy of the Bible which he contracted for. The angels pictured therein were white in color. He had these made black, so he could show that there were black angels as well as white ones. The Bibles cost him just eighty cents apiece. He went about the South and offered the Bibles to the astonished and open-mouthed negroes for eight dollars each, two dollars and a half down and the rest in monthly payments. His sales were enormous. Then he went his rounds all over again and offered to close out the remaining five dollars and a half due him by a final payment of two dollars and a half each. In nearly every case the bait was swallowed, and on each Bible he thus cleared four dollars and twenty cents net!

Running the elevator in the building where a prominent publishing firm had its office was a negro of more than ordinary intelligence. The firm had just published a subscription book on mechanical engineering, a chapter of which was devoted to the construction and operation of passenger elevators. One of the agents selling the book thought he might find a customer in Washington.

"Wash," said the book-agent, "you ought to buy a copy of this book, do you know it?"

"No, boss, don't want no books. Don't git no time fo' readin' books," drawled Wash. "It teks all mah time to run dis elevator."

"But this book will help you to run your elevator. See here: there's a whole chapter here on elevators," persisted the canvasser.

"Don't want no help to run dis elevator," said the darky. "Dis elevator runs all right now."

"But," said the canvasser, "this will help you to run it better. You will know twice as much when you get through."

"No, boss, no, dat's just it," returned Wash. "Don't want to learn nothing, boss," he said. "Why, boss, I know more now than I git paid for."

There was one New York newspaper that prided itself on its huge circulation, and its advertising canvassers were particularly insistent in securing the advertisements of publishers. Of course, the real purpose of the paper was to secure a certain standing for itself, which it lacked, rather than to be of any service to the publishers.

By dint of perseverance, its agents finally secured from one of the ten-cent magazines, then so numerous, a large advertisement of a special number, and in order to test the drawing power of the newspaper as a medium, there was inserted a line in large black type:

"SEND TEN CENTS FOR A NUMBER."

But the compositor felt that magazine literature should be even cheaper than it was, and to that thought in his mind his fingers responded, so that when the advertisement appeared, this particular bold-type line read:

"SEND TEN CENTS FOR A YEAR."

This wonderful offer appealed with singular force to the class of readers of this particular paper, and they decided to take advantage of it. The advertisement appeared on Sunday, and Monday's first mail brought the magazine over eight hundred letters with ten cents enclosed "for a year's subscription as per your advertisement in yesterday's ——." The magazine management consulted its lawyer, who advised the publisher to make the newspaper pay the extra ninety cents on each subscription, and, although this demand was at first refused, the proprietors of the daily finally yielded. At the end of the first week eight thousand and fifty-five letters with ten cents enclosed had reached the magazine, and finally the total was a few over twelve thousand!

CHAPTER XIV

LAST YEARS IN NEW YORK

EDWARD BOK'S lines were now to follow those of advertising for several years. He was responsible for securing the advertisements for *The Book Buyer* and *The Presbyterian Review*. While the former was, frankly, a house-organ, its editorial contents had so broadened as to make the periodical of general interest to book-lovers, and with the subscribers constituting the valuable list of Scribner book-buyers, other publishers were eager to fish in the Scribner pond.

With *The Presbyterian Review*, the condition was different. A magazine issued quarterly naturally lacks the continuity desired by the advertiser; the scope of the magazine was limited, and so was the circulation. It was a difficult magazine to "sell" to the advertiser, and Bok's salesmanship was taxed to the utmost. Although all that the publishers asked was that the expense of getting out the periodical be met, with its two hundred and odd pages even this was difficult. It was not an attractive proposition.

The most interesting feature of the magazine to Bok appeared to be the method of editing. It was ostensibly edited by a board, but, practically, by Professor Francis L. Patton, D.D., of Princeton Theological Seminary (afterward president of Princeton University), and Doctor Charles A. Briggs, of Union Theological Seminary. The views of these two theologians differed rather widely, and when, upon several occasions, they met in Bok's office, on bringing in their different articles to go into the magazine, lively discussions ensued. Bok did not often get the drift of these discussions, but he was intensely interested in listening to the diverse views of the two theologians.

One day the question of heresy came up between the two men, and during a pause in the discussion, Bok, looking for light, turned to Doctor Briggs and asked: "Doctor, what really is heresy?"

Doctor Briggs, taken off his guard for a moment, looked blankly at his young questioner, and repeated: "What is heresy?"

"Yes," repeated Bok, "just what is heresy, Doctor?"

"That's right," interjected Doctor Patton, with a twinkle in his eyes, "what *is* heresy, Briggs?"

"Would you be willing to write it down for me?" asked Bok, fearful that he should not remember Doctor Briggs's definition even if he were told.

And Doctor Briggs wrote:

Heresy is anything in doctrine or practice that departs from the mind of the Church as officially defined.

CHARLES A. BRIGGS.

"Let me see," asked Doctor Patton, and when he read it, he muttered: "Humph, pretty broad, pretty broad."

"Well," answered the nettled Doctor Briggs, "perhaps you can give a less broad definition, Patton."

"No, no," answered the Princeton theologian, as the

slightest wink came from the eye nearest Bok, "I wouldn't attempt it for a moment. Too much for me."

On another occasion, as the two were busy in their discussion of some article to be inserted in the magazine, Bok listening with all his might, Doctor Patton, suddenly turning to the young listener, asked, in the midst of the argument: "Whom are the Giants going to play this afternoon, Bok?"

Doctor Briggs's face was a study. For a moment the drift of the question was an enigma to him: then realizing that an important theological discussion had been interrupted by a trivial baseball question, he gathered up his papers and stamped violently out of the office. Doctor Patton made no comment, but, with a smile, he asked Bok: "Johnnie Ward going to play to-day, do you know? Thought I might ask Mr. Scribner if you could go up to the game this afternoon."

It is unnecessary to say to which of the two men Bok was the more attracted, and when it came, each quarter, to figuring how many articles could go into the *Review* without exceeding the cost limit fixed by the house, it was always a puzzle to Doctor Briggs why the majority of the articles left out were invariably those that he had brought in, while many of those which Doctor Patton handed in somehow found their place, upon the final assembling, among the contents.

"Your articles are so long," Bok would explain.

"Long?" Doctor Briggs would echo. "You don't measure theological discussions by the yardstick, young man."

"Perhaps not," the young assembler would maintain.

"But we have to do some measuring here by the composition-stick, just the same."

And the Union Seminary theologian was never able, successfully, to vault that hurdle!

From his boyhood days (up to the present writing) Bok was a pronounced baseball "fan," and so Doctor Patton appealed to a warm place in the young man's heart when he asked him the questions about the New York baseball team. There was, too, a baseball team among the Scribner young men of which Bok was a part. This team played, each Saturday afternoon, a team from another publishing house, and for two seasons it was unbeatable. Not only was this baseball aggregation close to the hearts of the Scribner employees, but, in an important game, the junior member of the firm played on it and the senior member was a spectator. Frank N. Doubleday played on first base; William D. Moffat, later of Moffat, Yard & Company, and now editor of *The Mentor*, was behind the bat; Bok pitched; Ernest Dressel North, the present authority on rare editions of books, was in the field, as were also Ray Safford, now a director in the Scribner corporation, and Owen W. Brewer, at present a prominent figure in Chicago's book world. It was a happy group, all closely banded together in their business interests and in their human relations as well.

With *Scribner's Magazine* now in the periodical field, Bok would be asked on his trips to the publishing houses to have an eye open for advertisements for that periodical as well. Hence his education in the solicitation of advertisements became general, and gave him a sympa-

thetic understanding of the problems of the advertising
solicitor which was to stand him in good stead when, in
his later experience, he was called upon to view the business problems of a magazine from the editor's position.
His knowledge of the manufacture of the two magazines
in his charge was likewise educative, as was the fascinating study of typography which always had, and has to-
day, a wonderful attraction for him.

It was, however, in connection with the advertising
of the general books of the house, and in his relations
with their authors, that Bok found his greatest interest.
It was for him to find the best manner in which to introduce to the public the books issued by the house,
and the general study of the psychology of publicity
which this called for attracted Bok greatly.

Bok was now asked to advertise a novel published by
the Scribners which, when it was issued, and for years
afterward, was pointed to as a proof of the notion that
a famous name was all that was necessary to ensure the
acceptance of a manuscript by even a leading publishing
house. The facts in the case were that this manuscript
was handed in one morning by a friend of the house with
the remark that he submitted it at the suggestion of the
author, who did not desire that his identity should be
known until after the manuscript had been read and
passed upon by the house. It was explained that the
writer was not a famous author; in fact, he had never
written anything before; this was his first book of any
sort; he merely wanted to "try his wings." The manuscript was read in due time by the Scribner readers, and
the mutual friend was advised that the house would be

glad to publish the novel, and was ready to execute and send a contract to the author if the firm knew in whose name the agreement should be made. Then came the first intimation of the identity of the author: the friend wrote that if the publishers would look in the right-hand corner of the first page of the manuscript they would find there the author's name. Search finally revealed an asterisk. The author of the novel (*Valentino*) was William Waldorf Astor.

Although the Scribners did not publish Mark Twain's books, the humorist was a frequent visitor to the retail store, and occasionally he would wander back to the publishing department located at the rear of the store, which was then at 743 Broadway.

Smoking was not permitted in the Scribner offices, and, of course, Mark Twain was always smoking. He generally smoked a granulated tobacco which he kept in a long check bag made of silk and rubber. When he sauntered to the back of the Scribner store, he would generally knock the residue from the bowl of the pipe, take out the stem, place it in his vest pocket, like a pencil, and drop the bowl into the bag containing the granulated tobacco. When he wanted to smoke again (which was usually five minutes later) he would fish out the bowl, now automatically filled with tobacco, insert the stem, and strike a light. One afternoon as he wandered into Bok's office, he was just putting his pipe away. The pipe, of the corncob variety, was very aged and black. Bok asked him whether it was the only pipe he had.

"Oh, no," Mark answered, "I have several. But

they're all like this. I never smoke a new corncob pipe. A new pipe irritates the throat. No corncob pipe is fit for anything until it has been used at least a fortnight."

"How do you break in a pipe, then?" asked Bok.

"That's the trick," answered Mark Twain. "I get a cheap man—a man who doesn't amount to much, anyhow: who would be as well, or better, dead—and pay him a dollar to break in the pipe for me. I get him to smoke the pipe for a couple of weeks, then put in a new stem, and continue operations as long as the pipe holds together."

Bok's newspaper syndicate work had brought him into contact with Fanny Davenport, then at the zenith of her career as an actress. Miss Davenport, or Mrs. Melbourne McDowell as she was in private life, had never written for print; but Bok, seeing that she had something to say about her art and the ability to say it, induced her to write for the newspapers through his syndicate. The actress was overjoyed to have revealed to her a hitherto unsuspected gift; Bok published her articles successfully, and gave her a publicity that her press agent had never dreamed of. Miss Davenport became interested in the young publisher, and after watching the methods which he employed in successfully publishing her writings, decided to try to obtain his services as her assistant manager. She broached the subject, offered him a five years' contract for forty weeks' service, with a minimum of fifteen weeks each year to spend in or near New York, at a salary, for the first year, of three thousand dollars, increasing annually until the fifth year, when he was to receive sixty-four hundred dollars.

Bok was attracted to the work: he had never seen the United States, was anxious to do so, and looked upon the chance as a good opportunity. Miss Davenport had the contract made out, executed it, and then, in high glee, Bok took it home to show it to his mother. He had reckoned without question upon her approval, only to meet with an immediate and decided negative to the proposition as a whole, general and specific. She argued that the theatrical business was not for him; and she saw ahead and pointed out so strongly the mistake he was making that he sought Miss Davenport the next day and told her of his mother's stand. The actress suggested that she see the mother; she did, that day, and she came away from the interview a wiser if a sadder woman. Miss Davenport frankly told Bok that with such an instinctive objection as his mother seemed to have, he was right to follow her advice and the contract was not to be thought of.

It is difficult to say whether this was or was not for Bok the turning-point which comes in the life of every young man. Where the venture into theatrical life would have led him no one can, of course, say. One thing is certain: Bok's instinct and reason both failed him in this instance. He believes now that had his venture into the theatrical field been temporary or permanent, the experiment, either way, would have been disastrous.

Looking back and viewing the theatrical profession even as it was in that day (of a much higher order than now), he is convinced he would never have been happy in it. He might have found this out in a year or more, after the novelty of travelling had worn off, and asked release from his contract; in that case he would have broken his line of progress in the publishing business. From whatever viewpoint he has looked back upon this, which he now believes to have been the crisis in his life, he is convinced that his mother's instinct saved him from a grievous mistake.

The Scribner house, in its foreign-book department, had imported some copies of Bourrienne's *Life of Napoleon*, and a set had found its way to Bok's desk for advertising purposes. He took the books home to glance them over, found himself interested, and sat up half the night to read them. Then he took the set to the editor of the *New York Star*, and suggested that such a book warranted a special review, and offered to leave the work for the literary editor.

"You have read the books?" asked the editor.

"Every word," returned Bok.

"Then, why don't you write the review?" suggested the editor.

This was a new thought to Bok. "Never wrote a review," he said.

"Try it," answered the editor. "Write a column."

"A column wouldn't scratch the surface of this book," suggested the embryo reviewer.

"Well, give it what it is worth," returned the editor.

Bok did. He wrote a page of the paper.

"Too much, too much," said the editor. "Heavens, man, we've got to get some news into this paper."

"Very well," returned the reviewer.   "Read it, and cut it where you like.   That's the way I see the book."

And next Sunday the review appeared, word for word, as Bok had written it.   His first review had successfully passed!

But Bok was really happiest in that part of his work which concerned itself with the writing of advertisements.   The science of advertisement writing, which meant to him the capacity to say much in little space, appealed strongly.   He found himself more honestly attracted to this than to the writing of his literary letter, his editorials, or his book reviewing, of which he was now doing a good deal.   He determined to follow where his bent led; he studied the mechanics of unusual advertisements wherever he saw them; he eagerly sought a knowledge of typography and its best handling in an advertisement, and of the value and relation of illustrations to text.   He perceived that his work along these lines seemed to give satisfaction to his employers, since they placed more of it in his hands to do; and he sought in every way to become proficient in the art.

To publishers whose advertisements he secured for the periodicals in his charge, he made suggestions for the improvement of their announcements, and found his suggestions accepted.   He early saw the value of white space as one of the most effective factors in advertising; but this was a difficult argument, he soon found, to convey successfully to others.   A white space in an advertisement was to the average publisher something to fill up; Bok saw in it something to cherish for its effectiveness.   But he never got very far with his idea: he could not convince (perhaps because he failed to express his ideas convincingly) his advertisers of what he felt and believed so strongly.

An occasion came in which he was permitted to prove his contention. The Scribners had published Andrew Carnegie's volume, *Triumphant Democracy*, and the author desired that some special advertising should be done in addition to that allowed by the appropriation made by the house. To Bok's grateful ears came the injunction from the steel magnate: "Use plenty of white space." In conjunction with Mr. Doubleday, Bok prepared and issued this extra advertising, and for once, at least, the wisdom of using white space was demonstrated. But it was only a flash in the pan. Publishers were unwilling to pay for "unused space," as they termed it. Each book was a separate unit, others argued: it was not like advertising one article continuously in which money could be invested; and only a limited amount could be spent on a book which ran its course, even at its best, in a very short time.

And, rightly or wrongly, book advertising has continued much along the same lines until the present day. In fact, in no department of manufacturing or selling activity has there been so little progress during the past fifty years as in bringing books to the notice of the public. In all other lines, the producer has brought his wares to the public, making it easier and still easier for it to obtain his goods, while the public, if it wants a book, must still seek the book instead of being sought by it.

That there is a tremendous unsupplied book demand in this country there is no doubt: the wider distribution and easier access given to periodicals prove this point. Now and then there has been tried an unsupported or not well-thought-out plan for bringing books to a public not now reading them, but there seems little or no understanding of the fact that there lies an uncultivated field of tremendous promise to the publisher who will strike out on a new line and market his books, so that the public will not have to ferret out a book-store or wind through the maze of a department store. The American reading public is not the book-reading public that it should be or could be made to be; but the habit must be made easy for it to acquire. Books must be placed where the public can readily get at them. It will not, of its own volition, seek them. It did not do so with magazines; it will not do so with books.

In the meanwhile, Bok's literary letter had prospered until it was now published in some forty-five newspapers. One of these was the *Philadelphia Times*. In that paper, each week, the letter had been read by Mr. Cyrus H. K. Curtis, the owner and publisher of *The Ladies' Home Journal*. Mr. Curtis had decided that he needed an editor for his magazine, in order to relieve his wife, who was then editing it, and he fixed upon the writer of *Literary Leaves* as his man. He came to New York, consulted Will Carleton, the poet, and found that while the letter was signed by William J. Bok, it was actually written by his brother who was with the Scribners. So he sought Bok out there.

The publishing house had been advertising in the Philadelphia magazine, so that the visit of Mr. Curtis was not an occasion for surprise. Mr. Curtis told Bok he had read his literary letter in the *Philadelphia Times*, and suggested that perhaps he might write a similar department for *The Ladies' Home Journal*. Bok saw no reason why he should not, and told Mr. Curtis so, and promised to send over a trial instalment. The Philadelphia publisher then deftly went on, explained editorial conditions in his magazine, and, recognizing the ethics of the occasion by not offering Bok another position while he was already occupying one, asked him if he knew the man for the place.

"Are you talking at me or through me?" asked Bok.

"Both," replied Mr. Curtis.

This was in April of 1889.

Bok promised Mr. Curtis he would look over the field, and meanwhile he sent over to Philadelphia the promised trial "literary gossip" instalment. It pleased Mr. Curtis, who suggested a monthly department, to which Bok consented. He also turned over in his mind the wisdom of interrupting his line of progress with the Scribners, and in New York, and began to contemplate the possibilities in Philadelphia and the work there.

He gathered a collection of domestic magazines then published, and looked them over to see what was already in the field. Then he began to study himself, his capacity for the work, and the possibility of finding it congenial. He realized that it was absolutely foreign to his Scribner work: that it meant a radical departure. But his work with his newspaper syndicate naturally occurred to him, and he studied it with a view of its adaptation to the field of the Philadelphia magazine.

His next step was to take into his confidence two or three friends whose judgment he trusted and discuss the possible change. Without an exception, they advised against it. The periodical had no standing, they argued; Bok would be out of sympathy with its general atmosphere after his Scribner environment; he was now in the direct line of progress in New York publishing houses; and, to cap the climax, they each argued in turn, he would be buried in Philadelphia: New York was the centre, etc., etc.

More than any other single argument, this last point destroyed Bok's faith in the judgment of his friends. He had had experience enough to realize that a man could not be buried in any city, provided he had the ability to stand out from his fellow-men. He knew from his biographical reading that cream will rise to the surface anywhere, in Philadelphia as well as in New York: it all depended on whether the cream was there: it was up to the man. Had he within him that peculiar, subtle something that, for the want of a better phrase, we call the editorial instinct? That was all there was to it, and that decision had to be his and his alone!

A business trip for the Scribners now calling him West, Bok decided to stop at Philadelphia, have a talk with Mr. Curtis, and look over his business plant. He did this, and found Mr. Curtis even more desirous than before to have him consider the position. Bok's instinct was strongly in favor of an acceptance. A natural impulse moved him, without reasoning, to action. Reasoning led only to a cautious mental state, and caution is a strong factor in the Dutch character. The longer he pursued a conscious process of reasoning, the farther he got from the position. But the instinct remained strong.

On his way back from the West, he stopped in Philadelphia again to consult his friend, George W. Childs; and here he found the only person who was ready to encourage him to make the change.

Bok now laid the matter before his mother, in whose feminine instinct he had supreme confidence. With her, he met with instant discouragement. But in subsequent talks he found that her opposition was based not upon the possibilities inherent in the position, but on a mother's natural disinclination to be separated from one of her sons. In the case of Fanny Davenport's offer the mother's instinct was strong against the proposition itself. But in the present instance it was the mother's love that was speaking; not her instinct or judgment.

Bok now consulted his business associates, and, to a man, they discouraged the step, but almost invariably upon the argument that it was suicidal to leave New York. He had now a glimpse of the truth that there is no man so provincially narrow as the untravelled New Yorker who believes in his heart that the sun rises in the East River and sets in the North River.

He realized more keenly than ever before that the decision rested with him alone. On September 1, 1889, Bok wrote to Mr. Curtis, accepting the position in Philadelphia; and on October 13 following he left the Scribners, where he had been so fortunate and so happy, and, after a week's vacation, followed where his instinct so strongly led, but where his reason wavered.

On October 20, 1889, Edward Bok became the editor of *The Ladies' Home Journal*.

CHAPTER XV

SUCCESSFUL EDITORSHIP

THERE is a popular notion that the editor of a woman's magazine should be a woman. At first thought, perhaps, this sounds logical. But it is a curious fact that by far the larger number of periodicals for women, the world over, are edited by men; and where, as in some cases, a woman is the proclaimed editor, the direction of the editorial policy is generally in the hands of a man, or group of men, in the background. Why this is so has never been explained, any more than why the majority of women's dressmakers are men; why music, with its larger appeal to women, has been and is still being composed, largely, by men, and why its greatest instrumental performers are likewise men; and why the church, with its larger membership of women, still has, as it always has had, men for its greatest preachers.

In fact, we may well ponder whether the full editorial authority and direction of a modern magazine, either essentially feminine in its appeal or not, can safely be entrusted to a woman when one considers how largely executive is the nature of such a position, and how thoroughly sensitive the modern editor must be to the hundred and one practical business matters which to-day enter into and form so large a part of the editorial duties. We may question whether women have as yet had sufficient experience in the world of business to cope successfully with the material questions of a pivotal editorial position. Then, again, it is absolutely essential in the conduct of a magazine with a feminine or home appeal to have on the editorial staff women who are experts in their line; and the truth is that women will work infinitely better under the direction of a man than of a woman.

It would seem from the present outlook that, for some time, at least, the so-called woman's magazine of large purpose and wide vision is very likely to be edited by a man. It is a question, however, whether the day of the woman's magazine, as we have known it, is not passing. Already the day has gone for the woman's magazine built on the old lines which now seem so grotesque and feeble in the light of modern growth. The interests of women and of men are being brought closer with the years, and it will not be long before they will entirely merge. This means a constantly diminishing necessity for the distinctly feminine magazine.

Naturally, there will always be a field in the essentially feminine pursuits which have no place in the life of a man, but these are rapidly being cared for by books, gratuitously distributed, issued by the manufacturers of distinctly feminine and domestic wares; for such publications the best talent is being employed, and the results are placed within easy access of women, by means of newspaper advertisement, the store-counter, or the mails. These will sooner or later—and much sooner than later—supplant the practical portions of the woman's magazine, leaving only the general contents, which are equally interesting to men and to women. Hence the field for the magazine with the essentially feminine appeal is contracting rather than broadening, and it is likely to contract much more rapidly in the future.

The field was altogether different when Edward Bok entered it in 1889. It was not only wide open, but fairly crying out to be filled. The day of *Godey's Lady's Book* had passed; *Peterson's Magazine* was breathing its last; and the home or women's magazines that had attempted to take their place were sorry affairs. It was this consciousness of a void ready to be filled that made the Philadelphia experiment so attractive to the embryo editor. He looked over the field and reasoned that if such magazines as did exist could be fairly successful, if women were ready to buy such, how much greater response would there be to a magazine of higher standards, of larger initiative—a magazine that would be an authoritative clearing-house for all the problems confronting women in the home, that brought itself closely into contact with those problems and tried to solve them in an entertaining and efficient way; and yet a magazine of uplift and inspiration: a magazine, in other words, that would give light and leading in the woman's world.

The method of editorial expression in the magazines of 1889 was also distinctly vague and prohibitively impersonal. The public knew the name of scarcely a single editor of a magazine: there was no personality that stood out in the mind: the accepted editorial expression was the indefinite "we"; no one ventured to use the first person singular and talk intimately to the reader. Edward Bok's biographical reading had taught him that the American public loved a personality: that it was always ready to recognize and follow a leader, provided, of course, that the qualities of leadership were demonstrated. He felt the time had come—the reference here and elsewhere is always to the realm of popular magazine literature appealing to a very wide audience—for the editor of some magazine to project his personality through the printed page and to convince the public that he was not an oracle removed from the people, but a real human being who could talk and not merely write on paper.

He saw, too, that the average popular magazine of 1889 failed of large success because it wrote down to the public—a grievous mistake that so many editors have made and still make. No one wants to be told, either directly or indirectly, that he knows less than he does, or even that he knows as little as he does: every one is benefited by the opposite implication, and the public will always follow the leader who comprehends this bit of psychology. There is always a happy medium between shooting over the public's head and shooting too far under it. And it is because of the latter aim that we find the modern popular magazine the worthless thing that, in so many instances, it is to-day.

It is the rare editor who rightly gauges his public psychology. Perhaps that is why, in the enormous growth of the modern magazine, there have been produced so few successful editors. The average editor is obsessed with the idea of "giving the public what it wants," whereas, in fact, the public, while it knows what it wants when it sees it, cannot clearly express its wants, and never wants the thing that it does ask for, although it thinks it does at the time. But woe to the editor and his periodical if he heeds that siren voice!

The editor has, therefore, no means of finding it out aforehand by putting his ear to the ground. Only by the simplest rules of psychology can he edit rightly so that he may lead, and to the average editor of to-day, it is to be feared, psychology is a closed book. His mind is all too often focussed on the circulation and advertising, and all too little on the intangibles that will bring to his periodical the results essential in these respects.

The editor is the pivot of a magazine. On him everything turns. If his gauge of the public is correct, readers will come: they cannot help coming to the man who has something to say himself, or who presents writers who have. And if the reader comes, the advertiser must come. He must go where his largest market is: where the buyers are. The advertiser, instead of being the most difficult factor in a magazine proposition, as is so often mistakenly thought, is, in reality, the simplest. He has no choice but to advertise in the successful periodical. He must come along. The editor need never worry about him. If the advertiser shuns the periodical's pages, the fault is rarely that of the advertiser: the editor can generally look for the reason nearer home.

One of Edward Bok's first acts as editor was to offer a series of prizes for the best answers to three questions he put to his readers: what in the magazine did they like least and why; what did they like best and why; and what omitted feature or department would they like to see installed? Thousands of answers came, and these the editor personally read carefully and classified. Then he gave his readers' suggestions back to them in articles and departments, but never on the level suggested by them. He gave them the subjects they asked for, but invariably on a slightly higher plane; and each year he raised the standard a notch. He always kept "a huckleberry or two" ahead of his readers. His psychology was simple: come down to the level which the public sets and it will leave you at the moment you do it. It always expects of its leaders that they shall keep a notch above or a step ahead. The American public always wants something a little better than it asks for, and the successful man, in catering to it, is he who follows this golden rule.

CHAPTER XVI

FIRST YEARS AS A WOMAN'S EDITOR

EDWARD BOK has often been referred to as the one
"who made *The Ladies' Home Journal* out of nothing,"
who "built it from the ground up," or, in similar terms,
implying that when he became its editor in 1889 the
magazine was practically non-existent.   This is far from
the fact.   The magazine was begun in 1883, and had
been edited by Mrs. Cyrus H. K. Curtis, for six years,
under her maiden name of Louisa Knapp, before Bok
undertook its editorship.   Mrs. Curtis had laid a solid
foundation of principle and policy for the magazine:
it had achieved a circulation of 440,000 copies a month
when she transferred the editorship, and it had already
acquired such a standing in the periodical world as to
attract the advertisements of Charles Scribner's Sons,
which Mr. Doubleday, and later Bok himself, gave to
the Philadelphia magazine—advertising which was never
given lightly, or without the most careful investigation
of the worth of the circulation of a periodical.

What every magazine publisher knows as the most
troublous years in the establishment of a periodical,
the first half-dozen years of its existence, had already
been weathered by the editor and publisher.   The wife
as editor and the husband as publisher had combined to
lay a solid basis upon which Bok had only to build: his
task was simply to rear a structure upon the foundation
already laid.   It is to the vision and to the genius of the

first editor of *The Ladies' Home Journal* that the unprecedented success of the magazine is primarily due. It was the purpose and the policy of making a magazine of authoritative service for the womanhood of America, a service which would visualize for womanhood its highest domestic estate, that had won success for the periodical from its inception. It is difficult to believe, in the multiplicity of similar magazines to-day, that such a purpose was new; that *The Ladies' Home Journal* was a path-finder; but the convincing proof is found in the fact that all the later magazines of this class have followed in the wake of the periodical conceived by Mrs. Curtis, and have ever since been its imitators.

When Edward Bok succeeded Mrs. Curtis, he immediately encountered another popular misconception of a woman's magazine—the conviction that if a man is the editor of a periodical with a distinctly feminine appeal, he must, as the term goes, "understand women." If Bok had believed this to be true, he would never have assumed the position. How deeply rooted is this belief was brought home to him on every hand when his decision to accept the Philadelphia position was announced. His mother, knowing her son better than did any one else, looked at him with amazement. She could not believe that he was serious in his decision to cater to women's needs when he knew so little about them. His friends, too, were intensely amused, and took no pains to hide their amusement from him. They knew him to be the very opposite of "a lady's man," and when they were not convulsed with hilarity they were incredulous and marvelled.

No man, perhaps, could have been chosen for the position who had a less intimate knowledge of women. Bok had no sister, no women confidantes: he had lived with and for his mother. She was the only woman he really knew or who really knew him. His boyhood days had been too full of poverty and struggle to permit him to mingle with the opposite sex. And it is a curious fact that Edward Bok's instinctive attitude toward women was that of avoidance. He did not dislike women, but it could not be said that he liked them. They had never interested him. Of women, therefore, he knew little; of their needs less. Nor had he the slightest desire, even as an editor, to know them better, or to seek to understand them. Even at that age, he knew that, as a man, he could not, no matter what effort he might make, and he let it go at that.

What he saw in the position was not the need to know women; he could employ women for that purpose. He perceived clearly that the editor of a magazine was largely an executive: his was principally the work of direction; of studying currents and movements, watching their formation, their tendency, their efficacy if advocated or translated into actuality; and then selecting from the horizon those that were for the best interests of the home. For a home was something Edward Bok did understand. He had always lived in one; had struggled to keep it together, and he knew every inch of the hard road that makes for domestic permanence amid adverse financial conditions. And at the home he aimed rather than at the woman in it.

It was upon his instinct that he intended to rely rather

than upon any knowledge of woman. His first act in
the editorial chair of *The Ladies' Home Journal* showed
him to be right in this diagnosis of himself, for the incident proved not only how correct was his instinct, but
how woefully lacking he was in any knowledge of the
feminine nature.

He had divined the fact that in thousands of cases
the American mother was not the confidante of her
daughter, and reasoned if an inviting human personality
could be created on the printed page that would supply
this lamentable lack of American family life, girls would
flock to such a figure. But all depended on the confidence
which the written word could inspire. He tried several
writers, but in each case the particular touch that he
sought for was lacking. It seemed so simple to him,
and yet he could not translate it to others. Then,
in desperation, he wrote an instalment of such a department as he had in mind himself, intending to show
it to a writer he had in view, thus giving her a visual
demonstration. He took it to the office the next morning, intending to have it copied, but the manuscript
accidentally attached itself to another intended for the
composing-room, and it was not until the superintendent
of the composing-room during the day said to him, "I
didn't know Miss Ashmead wrote," that Bok knew
where his manuscript had gone.

"Miss Ashmead?" asked the puzzled editor.

"Yes, Miss Ashmead in your department," was the
answer.

The whereabouts of the manuscript was then disclosed, and the editor called for its return. He had

called the department "Side Talks with Girls" by Ruth Ashmead.

"My girls all hope this is going into the magazine," said the superintendent when he returned the manuscript.

"Why?" asked the editor.

"Well, they say it's the best stuff for girls they have ever read. They'd love to know Miss Ashmead better."

Here was exactly what the editor wanted, but he was the author! He changed the name to Ruth Ashmore, and decided to let the manuscript go into the magazine. He reasoned that he would then have a month in which to see the writer he had in mind, and he would show her the proof. But a month filled itself with other duties, and before the editor was aware of it, the composition-room wanted "copy" for the second instalment of "Side Talks with Girls." Once more the editor furnished the copy!

Within two weeks after the second article had been written, the magazine containing the first instalment of the new department appeared, and the next day two hundred letters were received for "Ruth Ashmore," with the mail-clerk asking where they should be sent. "Leave them with me, please," replied the editor. On the following day the mail-clerk handed him five hundred more.

The editor now took two letters from the top and opened them. He never opened the third! That evening he took the bundle home, and told his mother of his predicament. She read the letters and looked at her son. "You have no right to read these," she said. The son readily agreed.

His instinct had correctly interpreted the need, but he never dreamed how far the feminine nature would reveal itself on paper.

The next morning the editor, with his letters, took the train for New York and sought his friend, Mrs. Isabel A. Mallon, the "Bab" of his popular syndicate letter.

"Have you read this department?" he asked, pointing to the page in the magazine.

"I have," answered Mrs. Mallon. "Very well done, too, it is. Who is 'Ruth Ashmore'?"

"You are," answered Edward Bok. And while it took considerable persuasion, from that time on Mrs. Mallon became Ruth Ashmore, the most ridiculed writer in the magazine world, and yet the most helpful editor that ever conducted a department in periodical literature. For sixteen years she conducted the department, until she passed away, her last act being to dictate a letter to a correspondent. In those sixteen years she had received one hundred and fifty-eight thousand letters: she kept three stenographers busy, and the number of girls who to-day bless the name of Ruth Ashmore is legion.

But the newspaper humorists who insisted that Ruth Ashmore was none other than Edward Bok never knew the partial truth of their joke!

The editor soon supplemented this department with one dealing with the spiritual needs of the mature woman. "The King's Daughters" was then an organization at the summit of its usefulness, with Margaret Bottome its president. Edward Bok had heard Mrs. Bottome speak, had met her personally, and decided that she was the editor for the department he had in mind.

"I want it written in an intimate way as if there were only two persons in the world, you and the person reading. I want heart to speak to heart. We will make that the title," said the editor, and unconsciously he thus created the title that has since become familiar wherever English is spoken: "Heart to Heart Talks." The title gave the department an instantaneous hearing; the material in it carried out its spirit, and soon Mrs. Bottome's department rivalled, in popularity, the page by Ruth Ashmore.

These two departments more than anything else, and the irresistible picture of a man editing a woman's magazine, brought forth an era of newspaper paragraphing and a flood of so-called "humorous" references to the magazine and editor. It became the vogue to poke fun at both. The humorous papers took it up, the cartoonists helped it along, and actors introduced the name of the magazine on the stage in plays and skits. Never did a periodical receive such an amount of gratuitous advertising. Much of the wit was absolutely without malice: some of it was written by Edward Bok's best friends, who volunteered to "let up" would he but raise a finger.

But he did not raise the finger. No one enjoyed the "paragraphs" more heartily when the wit was good, and in that case, if the writer was unknown to him, he sought him out and induced him to write for him. In this way, George Fitch was found on the Peoria, Illinois, *Transcript* and introduced to his larger public in the magazine and book world through *The Ladies' Home Journal*, whose editor he believed he had "most unmercifully roasted"; —but he had done it so cleverly that the editor at once saw his possibilities.

When all his friends begged Bok to begin proceedings against the *New York Evening Sun* because of the libellous (?) articles written about him by "The Woman About Town," the editor admired the style rather than the contents, made her acquaintance, and secured her as a regular writer: she contributed to the magazine some of the best things published in its pages. But she did not abate her opinions of Bok and his magazine in her articles in the newspaper, and Bok did not ask it of her: he felt that she had a right to her opinions—those he was not buying; but he was eager to buy her direct style in treating subjects he knew no other woman could so effectively handle.

And with his own limited knowledge of the sex, he needed, and none knew it better than did he, the ablest women he could obtain to help him realize his ideals. Their personal opinions of him did not matter so long as he could command their best work. Sooner or later, when his purposes were better understood, they might alter those opinions. For that he could afford to wait. But he could not wait to get their work.

By this time the editor had come to see that the power of a magazine might lie more securely behind the printed page than in it. He had begun to accustom his readers to writing to his editors upon all conceivable problems.

This he decided to encourage. He employed an expert in each line of feminine endeavor, upon the distinct understanding that the most scrupulous attention should be given to her correspondence: that every letter, no matter how inconsequential, should be answered quickly, fully, and courteously, with the questioner always encouraged to come again if any problem of whatever nature came to her. He told his editors that ignorance on any question was a misfortune, not a crime; and he wished their correspondence treated in the most courteous and helpful spirit.

Step by step, the editor built up this service behind the magazine until he had a staff of thirty-five editors on the monthly pay-roll; in each issue, he proclaimed the willingness of these editors to answer immediately any questions by mail, he encouraged and cajoled his readers to form the habit of looking upon his magazine as a great clearing-house of information. Before long, the letters streamed in by the tens of thousands during a year. The editor still encouraged, and the total ran into the hundreds of thousands, until during the last year, before the service was finally stopped by the Great War of 1917-18, the yearly correspondence totalled nearly a million letters.

The work of some of these editors never reached the printed page, and yet was vastly more important than any published matter could possibly be. Out of the work of Ruth Ashmore, for instance, there grew a class of cases of the most confidential nature. These cases,

distributed all over the country, called for special investigation and personal contact. Bok selected Mrs.
Lyman Abbott for this piece of delicate work, and,
through the wide acquaintance of her husband, she was
enabled to reach, personally, every case in every locality,
and bring personal help to bear on it. These cases
mounted into the hundreds, and the good accomplished
through this quiet channel cannot be overestimated.

The lack of opportunity for an education in Bok's
own life led him to cast about for some plan whereby
an education might be obtained without expense by any
one who desired. He finally hit upon the simple plan
of substituting free scholarships for the premiums then
so frequently offered by periodicals for subscriptions
secured. Free musical education at the leading con-
servatories was first offered to any girl who would secure
a certain number of subscriptions to *The Ladies' Home
Journal*, the complete offer being a year's free tuition,
with free room, free board, free piano in her own room,
and all travelling expenses paid. The plan was an immediate success: the solicitation of a subscription by a
girl desirous of educating herself made an irresistible
appeal.

This plan was soon extended, so as to include all the
girls' colleges, and finally all the men's colleges, so that
a free education might be possible at any educational
institution. So comprehensive it became that to the
close of 1919, one thousand four hundred and fifty-
five free scholarships had been awarded. The plan has
now been in operation long enough to have produced
some of the leading singers and instrumental artists of

the day, whose names are familiar to all, as well as instructors in colleges and scores of teachers; and to have sent several score of men into conspicuous positions in the business and professional world.

Edward Bok has always felt that but for his own inability to secure an education, and his consequent desire for self-improvement, the realization of the need in others might not have been so strongly felt by him, and that his plan whereby thousands of others were benefited might never have been realized.

The editor's correspondence was revealing, among other deficiencies, the wide-spread unpreparedness of the average American girl for motherhood, and her desperate ignorance when a new life was given her. On the theory that with the realization of a vital need there is always the person to meet it, Bok consulted the authorities of the Babies' Hospital of New York, and found Doctor Emmet Holt's house physician, Doctor Emelyn L. Coolidge. To the authorities in the world of babies, Bok's discovery was, of course, a known and serious fact.

Doctor Coolidge proposed that the magazine create a department of questions and answers devoted to the problems of young mothers. This was done, and from the publication of the first issue the questions began to come in. Within five years the department had grown to such proportions that Doctor Coolidge proposed a plan whereby mothers might be instructed, by mail, in the rearing of babies—in their general care, their feeding, and the complete hygiene of the nursery.

Bok had already learned, in his editorial experience, carefully to weigh a woman's instinct against a man's judgment, but the idea of raising babies by mail floored him. He reasoned, however, that a woman, and more particularly one who had been in a babies' hospital for years, knew more about babies than he could possibly know. He consulted baby-specialists in New York and Philadelphia, and, with one accord, they declared the plan not only absolutely impracticable but positively dangerous. Bok's confidence in woman's instinct, however, persisted, and he asked Doctor Coolidge to map out a plan.

This called for the services of two physicians: Miss Marianna Wheeler, for many years superintendent of the Babies' Hospital, was to look after the prospective mother before the baby's birth; and Doctor Coolidge, when the baby was born, would immediately send to the young mother a printed list of comprehensive questions, which, when answered, would be immediately followed by a full set of directions as to the care of the child, including carefully prepared food formulæ. At the end of the first month, another set of questions was to be forwarded for answer by the mother, and this monthly service was to be continued until the child reached the age of two years. The contact with the mother would then become intermittent, dependent upon the condition of mother and child. All the directions and formulæ were to be used only under the direction of the mother's attendant physician, so that the fullest cooperation might be established between the physician on the case and the advisory department of the magazine.

Despite advice to the contrary, Bok decided, after

consulting a number of mothers, to establish the system. It was understood that the greatest care was to be exercised: the most expert advice, if needed, was to be sought and given, and the thousands of cases at the Babies' Hospital were to be laid under contribution.

There was then begun a magazine department which was to be classed among the most clear-cut pieces of successful work achieved by *The Ladies' Home Journal.*

Step by step, the new departure won its way, and was welcomed eagerly by thousands of young mothers. It was not long before the warmest commendation from physicians all over the country was received. Promptness of response and thoroughness of diagnosis were, of course, the keynotes of the service: where the cases were urgent, the special delivery post and, later, the night-letter telegraph service were used.

The plan is now in its eleventh year of successful operation. Some idea of the enormous extent of its service can be gathered from the amazing figures that, at the close of the tenth year, show over forty thousand prospective mothers have been advised, while the number of babies actually "raised" by Doctor Coolidge approaches eighty thousand. Fully ninety-five of every hundred of these babies registered have remained under the monthly letter-care of Doctor Coolidge until their first year, when the mothers receive a diet list which has proved so effective for future guidance that many mothers cease to report regularly. Eighty-five out of every hundred babies have remained in the registry until their graduation at the age of two. Over eight large sets of library drawers are required for the records of the babies always under the supervision of the registry.

Scores of physicians who vigorously opposed the work at the start have amended their opinions and now not only give their enthusiastic endorsement, but have adopted Doctor Coolidge's food formulæ for their private and hospital cases.

It was this comprehensive personal service, built up back of the magazine from the start, that gave the periodical so firm and unique a hold on its clientele.   It was not the printed word that was its chief power: scores of editors who have tried to study and diagnose the appeal of the magazine from the printed page, have remained baffled at the remarkable confidence elicited from its readers.   They never looked back of the magazine, and therefore failed to discover its secret.   Bok went through three financial panics with the magazine, and while other periodicals severely suffered from diminished circulation at such times, *The Ladies' Home Journal* always held its own.   Thousands of women had been directly helped by the magazine; it had not remained an inanimate printed thing, but had become a vital need in the personal lives of its readers.

So intimate had become this relation, so efficient was the service rendered, that its readers could not be pried loose from it;   where women were willing and ready, when the domestic pinch came, to let go of other reading matter, they explained to their husbands or fathers that *The Ladies' Home Journal* was a necessity—they did not feel that they could do without it.   The very quality for which the magazine had been held up to ridicule by the unknowing and unthinking had become, with hundreds of thousands of women, its source of power and the bulwark of its success.

Bok was beginning to realize the vision which had lured him from New York: that of putting into the field of American magazines a periodical that should become such a clearing-house as virtually to make it an institution.

He felt that, for the present at least, he had sufficiently established the personal contact with his readers through the more intimate departments, and decided to devote his efforts to the literary features of the magazine.

CHAPTER XVII

EUGENE FIELD'S PRACTICAL JOKES

EUGENE FIELD was one of Edward Bok's close friends and also his despair, as was likely to be the case with those who were intimate with the Western poet. One day Field said to Bok: "I am going to make you the most widely paragraphed man in America." The editor passed the remark over, but he was to recall it often as his friend set out to make his boast good.

The fact that Bok was unmarried and the editor of a woman's magazine appealed strongly to Field's sense of humor. He knew the editor's opposition to patent medicines, and so he decided to join the two facts in a paragraph, put on the wire at Chicago, to the effect that the editor was engaged to be married to Miss Lavinia Pinkham, the granddaughter of Mrs. Lydia Pinkham, of patent-medicine fame. The paragraph carefully described Miss Pinkham, the school where she had been educated, her talents, her wealth, etc. Field was wise enough to put the paragraph not in his own column in the *Chicago News*, lest it be considered in the light of one of his practical jokes, but on the news page of the paper, and he had it put on the Associated Press wire.

He followed this up a few days later with a paragraph announcing Bok's arrival at a Boston hotel. Then came a paragraph saying that Miss Pinkham was sailing for

Paris to buy her trousseau. The paragraphs were worded in the most matter-of-fact manner, and completely fooled the newspapers, even those of Boston. Field was delighted at the success of his joke, and the fact that Bok was in despair over the letters that poured in upon him added to Field's delight.

He now asked Bok to come to Chicago. "I want you to know some of my cronies," he wrote. "Julia [his wife] is away, so we will shift for ourselves." Bok arrived in Chicago one Sunday afternoon, and was to dine at Field's house that evening. He found a jolly company: James Whitcomb Riley, Sol Smith Russell the actor, Opie Read, and a number of Chicago's literary men.

When seven o'clock came, some one suggested to Field that something to eat might not be amiss.

"Shortly," answered the poet. "Wife is out; cook is new, and dinner will be a little late. Be patient." But at eight o'clock there was still no dinner. Riley began to grow suspicious and slipped down-stairs. He found no one in the kitchen and the range cold. He came back and reported. "Nonsense," said Field. "It can't be." All went down-stairs to find out the truth. "Let's get supper ourselves," suggested Russell. Then it was discovered that not a morsel of food was to be found in the refrigerator, closet, or cellar. "That's a joke on us," said Field. "Julia has left us without a crumb to eat."

It was then nine o'clock. Riley and Bok held a council of war and decided to slip out and buy some food, only to find that the front, basement, and back doors were locked and the keys missing! Field was very sober. "Thorough woman, that wife of mine," he commented. But his friends knew better.

Finally, the Hoosier poet and the Philadelphia editor crawled through one of the basement windows and started on a foraging expedition. Of course, Field lived in a residential section where there were few stores, and on Sunday these were closed. There was nothing to do but to board a down-town car. Finally they found a delicatessen shop open, and the two hungry men amazed the proprietor by nearly buying out his stock.

It was after ten o'clock when Riley and Bok got back to the house with their load of provisions to find every door locked, every curtain drawn, and the bolt sprung on every window. Only the cellar grating remained, and through this the two dropped their bundles and themselves, and appeared in the dining-room, dirty and dishevelled, to find the party at table enjoying a supper which Field had carefully hidden and brought out when they had left the house.

Riley, cold and hungry, and before this time the victim of Field's practical jokes, was not in a merry humor and began to recite paraphrases of Field's poems. Field retorted by paraphrasing Riley's poems, and mimicking the marked characteristics of Riley's speech. This started Sol Smith Russell, who mimicked both. The fun grew fast and furious, the entire company now took part, Mrs. Field's dresses were laid under contribution, and Field, Russell, and Riley gave an impromptu play. And it was upon this scene that Mrs. Field, after a continuous ringing of the door-bell and nearly battering down the door, appeared at seven o'clock the next morning!

It was fortunate that Eugene Field had a patient wife; she needed every ounce of patience that she could command. And no one realized this more keenly than did her husband. He once told of a dream he had which illustrated the endurance of his wife.

"I thought," said Field, "that I had died and gone to heaven. I had some difficulty in getting past St. Peter, who regarded me with doubt and suspicion, and examined my records closely, but finally permitted me to enter the pearly gates. As I walked up the street of the heavenly city, I saw a venerable old man with long gray hair and flowing beard. His benignant face encouraged me to address him. 'I have just arrived and I am entirely unacquainted,' I said. 'May I ask your name?'

"'My name,' he replied, 'is Job.'

"'Indeed,' I exclaimed, 'are you that Job whom we were taught to revere as the most patient being in the world?'

"'The same,' he said, with a shadow of hesitation; 'I did have quite a reputation for patience once, but I hear that there is a woman now on earth, in Chicago, who has suffered more than I ever did, and she has endured it with great resignation.'

"'Why,' said I, 'that is curious. I am just from earth, and from Chicago, and I do not remember to have heard of her case. What is her name?'

"'Mrs. Eugene Field,' was the reply.

"Just then I awoke," ended Field.

The success of Field's paragraph engaging Bok to Miss Pinkham stimulated the poet to greater effort. Bok had gone to Europe; Field, having found out the date of his probable return, just about when the steamer was due, printed an interview with the editor "at quarantine" which sounded so plausible that even the men in Bok's office in Philadelphia were fooled and prepared for his arrival. The interview recounted, in detail, the changes in women's fashions in Paris, and so plausible had Field made it, based upon information obtained at Marshall Field's, that even the fashion papers copied it.

All this delighted Field beyond measure. Bok begged him to desist; but Field answered by printing an item to the effect that there was the highest authority for denying "the reports industriously circulated some time ago to the effect that Mr. Bok was engaged to be married to a New England young lady, whereas, as a matter of fact, it is no violation of friendly confidence that makes it possible to announce that the Philadelphia editor is engaged to Mrs. Frank Leslie, of New York."

It so happened that Field put this new paragraph on the wire just about the time that Bok's actual engagement was announced. Field was now deeply contrite, and sincerely promised Bok and his fiancée to reform. "I'm through, you mooning, spooning calf, you," he wrote Bok, and his friend believed him, only to receive a telegram the next day from Mrs. Field warning him that "Gene is planning a series of telephonic conversations with you and Miss Curtis at college that I think should not be printed." Bok knew it was of no use trying to curb Field's industry, and so he wired the editor of the *Chicago News* for his cooperation. Field, now checked, asked Bok and his fiancée and the parents of both to come to Chicago, be his guests for the World's Fair, and "let me make amends."

It was a happy visit. Field was all kindness, and, of course, the entire party was charmed by his personality. But the boy in him could not be repressed. He had kept it down all through the visit. "No, not a joke—cross my heart," he would say, and then he invited the party to lunch with him on their way to the train when they were leaving for home. "But we shall be in our travelling clothes, not dressed for a luncheon," protested the women. It was an unfortunate protest, for it gave Field an idea! "Oh," he assured them, "just a goodbye luncheon at the club; just you folks and Julia and me." They believed him, only to find upon their arrival at the club an assembly of over sixty guests at one of the most elaborate luncheons ever served in Chicago, with each woman guest carefully enjoined by Field, in his invitation, to "put on her prettiest and most elaborate costume in order to dress up the table!"

One day Field came to Philadelphia to give a reading in Camden in conjunction with George W. Cable. It chanced that his friend, Francis Wilson, was opening that same evening in Philadelphia in a new comic opera which Field had not seen. He immediately refused to give his reading, and insisted upon going to the theatre. The combined efforts of his manager, Wilson, Mr. Cable, and his friends finally persuaded him to keep his engagement and join in a double-box party later at the theatre. To make sure that he would keep his lecture appointment, Bok decided to go to Camden with him. Field and Cable were to appear alternately.

Field went on for his first number; and when he came off, he turned to Bok and said: "No use, Bok, I'm a sick man. I must go home. Cable can see this through," and despite every protestation Field bundled himself into his overcoat and made for his carriage. "Sick, Bok, really sick," he muttered as they rode along. Then seeing a fruit-stand he said: "Buy me a bag of oranges, like a good fellow. They'll do me good."

When Philadelphia was reached, he suggested: "Do you know I think it would do me good to go and see Frank in the new play? Tell the driver to go to the theatre like a good boy." Of course, that had been his intent all along! When the theatre was reached he insisted upon taking the oranges with him. "They'll steal 'em if you leave 'em there," he said.

Field lost all traces of his supposed illness the moment he reached the box. Francis Wilson was on the stage with Marie Jansen. "Isn't it beautiful?" said Field, and directing the attention of the party to the players, he reached under his chair for the bag of oranges, took one out, and was about to throw it at Wilson when Bok caught his arm, took the orange away from him, and grabbed the bag. Field never forgave Bok for this act of watchfulness. "Treason," he hissed—"going back on a friend."

The one object of Field's ambition was to achieve the distinction of so "fussing" Francis Wilson that he would be compelled to ring down the curtain. He had tried every conceivable trick: had walked on the stage in one of Wilson's scenes; had started a quarrel with an usher in the audience—everything that ingenuity could conceive he had practised on his friend. Bok had known this penchant of Field's, and when he insisted on taking the bag of oranges into the theatre, Field's purpose was evident!

One day Bok received a wire from Field: "City of New Orleans purposing give me largest public reception on sixth ever given an author. Event of unusual quality. Mayor and city officials peculiarly desirous of having you introduce me to vast audience they propose to have. Hate to ask you to travel so far, but would be great favor to me. Wire answer." Bok wired back his willingness to travel to New Orleans and oblige his friend. It occurred to Bok, however, to write to a friend in New Orleans and ask the particulars. Of course, there was never any thought of Field going to New Orleans or of any reception. Bok waited for further advices, and a long letter followed from Field giving him a glowing picture of the reception planned. Bok sent a message to his New Orleans friend to be telegraphed from New Orleans on the sixth: "Find whole thing to be a fake. Nice job to put over on me. Bok." Field was overjoyed at the apparent success of his joke and gleefully told his Chicago friends all about it—until he found out that the joke had been on him. "Durned dirty, I call it," he wrote Bok.

It was a lively friendship that Eugene Field gave to Edward Bok, full of anxieties and of continuous forebodings, but it was worth all that it cost in mental perturbation. No rarer friend ever lived: in his serious moments he gave one a quality of unforgetable friendship that remains a precious memory. But his desire for practical jokes was uncontrollable: it meant being constantly on one's guard, and even then the pranks could not always be thwarted!

CHAPTER XVIII

BUILDING UP A MAGAZINE

THE newspaper paragraphers were now having a delightful time with Edward Bok and his woman's magazine, and he was having a delightful time with them. The editor's publicity sense made him realize how valuable for his purposes was all this free advertising. The paragraphers believed, in their hearts, that they were annoying the young editor; they tried to draw his fire through their articles. But he kept quiet, put his tongue in his cheek, and determined to give them some choice morsels for their wit.

He conceived the idea of making familiar to the public the women who were back of the successful men of the day. He felt sure that his readers wanted to know about these women. But to attract his newspaper friends he labelled the series, "Unknown Wives of Well-Known Men" and "Clever Daughters of Clever Men."

The alliterative titles at once attracted the paragraphers; they fell upon them like hungry trout, and a perfect fusillade of paragraphs began. This is exactly what the editor wanted; and he followed these two series immediately by inducing the daughter of Charles Dickens to write of "My Father as I Knew Him," and Mrs. Henry Ward Beecher, of "Mr. Beecher as I Knew Him." Bok now felt that he had given the newspapers enough ammunition to last for some time; and he turned his attention to building up a more permanent basis for his magazine.

The two authors of that day who commanded more attention than any others were William Dean Howells and Rudyard Kipling. Bok knew that these two would give to his magazine the literary quality that it needed, and so he laid them both under contribution. He bought Mr. Howells's new novel, "The Coast of Bohemia," and arranged that Kipling's new novelette upon which he was working should come to the magazine. Neither the public nor the magazine editors had expected Bok to break out along these more permanent lines, and magazine publishers began to realize that a new competitor had sprung up in Philadelphia. Bok knew they would feel this; so before he announced Mr. Howells's new novel, he contracted with the novelist to follow this with his autobiography. This surprised the editors of the older magazines, for they realized that the Philadelphia editor had completely tied up the leading novelist of the day for his next two years' output.

Meanwhile, in order that the newspapers might be well supplied with barbs for their shafts, he published an entire number of his magazine written by famous daughters of famous men. This unique issue presented contributions by the daughters of Charles Dickens, Nathaniel Hawthorne, President Harrison, Horace Greeley, William M. Thackeray, William Dean Howells, General Sherman, Julia Ward Howe, Jefferson Davis, Mr. Gladstone, and a score of others. This issue simply filled the paragraphers with glee. Then once more Bok turned to material calculated to cement the foundation for a more permanent structure.

He noted, early in its progress, the gathering strength of the drift toward woman suffrage, and realized that the American woman was not prepared, in her knowledge of her country, to exercise the privilege of the ballot. Bok determined to supply the deficiency to his readers, and concluded to put under contract the President of the United States, Benjamin Harrison, the moment he left office, to write a series of articles explaining the United States. No man knew this subject better than the President; none could write better; and none would attract such general attention to his magazine, reasoned Bok. He sought the President, talked it over with him, and found him favorable to the idea. But the President was in doubt at that time whether he would be a candidate for another term, and frankly told Bok that he would be taking too much risk to wait for him. He suggested that the editor try to prevail upon his then secretary of state, James G. Blaine, to undertake the series, and offered to see Mr. Blaine and induce him to a favorable consideration. Bok acquiesced, and a few days afterward received from Mr. Blaine a request to come to Washington.

Bok had had a previous experience with Mr. Blaine which had impressed him to an unusual degree. Many years before, he had called upon him at his hotel in New York, seeking his autograph, had been received, and as the statesman was writing his signature he said: "Your name is a familiar one to me. I have had correspondence with an Edward Bok who is secretary of state for the Transvaal Republic. Are you related to him?"

Bok explained that this was his uncle, and that he was named for him.

Years afterward Bok happened to be at a public meeting where Mr. Blaine was speaking, and the statesman, seeing him, immediately called him by name. Bok knew of the reputed marvels of Mr. Blaine's memory, but this proof of it amazed him.

"It is simply inconceivable, Mr. Blaine," said Bok, "that you should remember my name after all these years."

"Not at all, my boy," returned Mr. Blaine. "Memorizing is simply association. You associate a fact or an incident with a name and you remember the name. It never leaves you. The moment I saw you I remembered you told me that your uncle was secretary of state for the Transvaal. That at once brought your name to me. You see how simple a trick it is."

But Bok did not see, since remembering the incident was to him an even greater feat of memory than recalling the name. It was a case of having to remember two things instead of one.

At all events, Bok was no stranger to James G. Blaine when he called upon him at his Lafayette Place home in Washington.

"You've gone ahead in the world some since I last saw you," was the statesman's greeting. "It seems to go with the name."

This naturally broke the ice for the editor at once.

"Let's go to my library where we can talk quietly.

What train are you making back to Philadelphia, by the way?"

"The four, if I can," replied Bok.

"Excuse me a moment," returned Mr. Blaine, and when he came back to the room, he said: "Now let's talk over this interesting proposition that the President has told me about."

The two discussed the matter and completed arrangements whereby Mr. Blaine was to undertake the work. Toward the latter end of the talk, Bok had covertly—as he thought—looked at his watch to keep track of his train.

"It's all right about that train," came from Mr. Blaine, with his back toward Bok, writing some data of the talk at his desk. "You'll make it all right."

Bok wondered how he should, as it then lacked only seventeen minutes of four. But as Mr. Blaine reached the front door, he said to the editor: "My carriage is waiting at the curb to take you to the station, and the coachman has your seat in the parlor car."

And with this knightly courtesy, Mr. Blaine shook hands with Bok, who was never again to see him, nor was the contract ever to be fulfilled. For early in 1893 Mr. Blaine passed away without having begun the work.

Again Bok turned to the President, and explained to him that, for some reason or other, the way seemed to point to him to write the articles himself. By that time President Harrison had decided that he would not succeed himself. Accordingly he entered into an agreement with the editor to begin to write the articles immediately upon his retirement from office. And the day after Inauguration Day every newspaper contained an Associated Press despatch announcing the former President's contract with *The Ladies' Home Journal.*

Shortly afterward, Benjamin Harrison's articles on "This Country of Ours" successfully appeared in the magazine.

During Bok's negotiations with President Harrison in connection with his series of articles, he was called to the White House for a conference. It was midsummer. Mrs. Harrison was away at the seashore, and the President was taking advantage of her absence by working far into the night.

The President, his secretary, and Bok sat down to dinner.

The Marine Band was giving its weekly concert on the green, and after dinner the President suggested that Bok and he adjourn to the "back lot" and enjoy the music.

"You have a coat?" asked the President.

"No, thank you," Bok answered. "I don't need one."

"Not in other places, perhaps," he said, "but here you do. The dampness comes up from the Potomac at nightfall, and it's just as well to be careful. It's Mrs. Harrison's dictum," he added smiling. "Halford, send up for one of my light coats, will you, please?"

Bok remarked, as he put on the President's coat, that this was probably about as near as he should ever get to the presidency.

"Well, it's a question whether you want to get

nearer to it," answered the President. He looked very white and tired in the moonlight.

"Still," Bok said with a smile, "some folks seem to like it well enough to wish to get it a second time."

"True," he answered, "but that's what pride will do for a man. Try one of these cigars."

A cigar! Bok had been taking his tobacco in smaller doses with paper around them. He had never smoked a cigar. Still, one cannot very well refuse a presidential cigar!

"Thank you," Bok said as he took one from the President's case. He looked at the cigar and remembered all he had read of Benjamin Harrison's black cigars. This one was black—inky black—and big.

"Allow me," he heard the President suddenly say, as he handed him a blazing match. There was no escape. The aroma was delicious, but— Two or three whiffs of that cigar, and Bok decided the best thing to do was to let it go out. He did.

"I have allowed you to talk so much," said the President after a while, "that you haven't had a chance to smoke. Allow me," and another match crackled into flame.

"Thank you," the editor said, as once more he lighted the cigar, and the fumes went clear up into the farthest corner of his brain.

"Take a fresh cigar," said the President after a while. "That doesn't seem to burn well. You *will* get one like that once in a while, although I am careful about my cigars."

"No, thanks, Mr. President," Bok said hurriedly. "It's I, not the cigar."

"Well, prove it to me with another," was the quick rejoinder, as he held out his case, and in another minute a match again crackled. "There is only one thing worse than a bad smoke, and that is an office-seeker," chuckled the President.

Bok couldn't prove that the cigars were bad, naturally. So smoke that cigar he did, to the bitter end, and it was bitter! In fifteen minutes his head and stomach were each whirling around, and no more welcome words had Bok ever heard than when the President said: "Well, suppose we go in. Halford and I have a day's work ahead of us yet."

The President went to work.

Bok went to bed. He could not get there quick enough, and he didn't—that is, not before he had experienced that same sensation of which Oliver Wendell Holmes wrote: he never could understand, he said, why young authors found so much trouble in getting into the magazines, for his first trip to Europe was not a day old before, without even the slightest desire or wish on his part, he became a contributor to the Atlantic!

The next day, and for days after, Bok smelled, tasted, and felt that presidential cigar!

A few weeks afterward, Bok was talking after dinner with the President at a hotel in New York, when once more the cigar-case came out and was handed to Bok.

"No, thank you, Mr. President," was the instant reply, as visions of his night in the White House came back to him. "I am like the man from the West who was willing to try anything once."

And he told the President the story of the White House cigar.

The editor decided to follow General Harrison's discussion of American affairs by giving his readers a glimpse of foreign politics, and he fixed upon Mr. Gladstone as the one figure abroad to write for him. He sailed for England, visited Hawarden Castle, and proposed to Mr. Gladstone that he should write a series of twelve autobiographical articles which later could be expanded into a book.

Bok offered fifteen thousand dollars for the twelve articles—a goodly price in those days—and he saw that the idea and the terms attracted the English statesman. But he also saw that the statesman was not quite ready. He decided, therefore, to leave the matter with him, and keep the avenue of approach favorably open by inducing Mrs. Gladstone to write for him. Bok knew that Mrs. Gladstone had helped her husband in his literary work, that she was a woman who had lived a full-rounded life, and after a day's visit and persuasion, with Mr. Gladstone as an amused looker-on, the editor closed a contract with Mrs. Gladstone for a series of reminiscent articles "From a Mother's Life."

Some time after Bok had sent the check to Mrs. Gladstone, he received a letter from Mr. Gladstone expressing the opinion that his wife must have written with a golden pen, considering the size of the honorarium. "But," he added, "she is so impressed with this as the first money she has ever earned by her pen that she is reluctant to part with the check. The result is that she has not offered it for deposit, and has decided to frame it. Considering the condition of our exchequer, I have tried to explain to her, and so have my son and daughter, that if she were to present the check for payment and allow it to pass through the bank, the check would come back to you and that I am sure your company would return it to her as a souvenir of the momentous occasion. Our arguments are of no avail, however, and it occurred to me that an assurance from you might make the check more useful than it is at present!"

Bok saw with this disposition that, as he had hoped, the avenue of favorable approach to Mr. Gladstone had been kept open. The next summer Bok again visited Hawarden, where he found the statesman absorbed in writing a life of Bishop Butler, from which it was difficult for him to turn away. He explained that it would take at least a year or two to finish this work. Bok saw, of course, his advantage, and closed a contract with the English statesman whereby he was to write the twelve autobiographical articles immediately upon his completion of the work then under his hand.

Here again, however, as in the case of Mr. Blaine, the contract was never fulfilled, for Mr. Gladstone passed away before he could free his mind and begin on the work.

The vicissitudes of an editor's life were certainly beginning to demonstrate themselves to Edward Bok.

The material that the editor was publishing and the authors that he was laying under contribution began to have marked effect upon the circulation of the magazine, and it was not long before the original figures were doubled, an edition—enormous for that day—of seven hundred and fifty thousand copies was printed and sold each month, the magical figure of a million was in sight, and the periodical was rapidly taking its place as one of the largest successes of the day.

Mr. Curtis's single proprietorship of the magazine had been changed into a corporation called The Curtis Publishing Company, with a capital of five hundred thousand dollars, with Mr. Curtis as president, and Bok as vice-president.

The magazine had by no means an easy road to travel financially. The doubling of the subscription price to one dollar per year had materially checked the income for the time being; the huge advertising bills, sometimes exceeding three hundred thousand dollars a year, were difficult to pay; large credit had to be obtained, and the banks were carrying a considerable quantity of Mr. Curtis's notes. But Mr. Curtis never wavered in his faith in his proposition and his editor. In the first he invested all he had and could borrow, and to the latter he gave his undivided support. The two men worked together rather as father and son—as, curiously enough, they were to be later—than as employer and employee. To Bok, the daily experience of seeing Mr. Curtis finance his proposition in sums that made the publishing world of that day gasp with sceptical astonishment was a wonderful opportunity, of which the editor took full advantage so as to learn the intricacies of a world which up to that time he had known only in a limited way.

What attracted Bok immensely to Mr. Curtis's methods was their perfect simplicity and directness. He believed absolutely in the final outcome of his proposition: where others saw mist and failure ahead, he saw clear weather and the port of success. Never did he waver: never did he deflect from his course. He knew no path save the direct one that led straight to success, and, through his eyes, he made Bok see it with equal clarity until Bok wondered why others could not see it. But they could not. Cyrus Curtis would never be able, they said, to come out from under the load he had piled up. Where they differed from Mr. Curtis was in their lack of vision: they could not see what he saw!

It has been said that Mr. Curtis banished patent-medicine advertisements from his magazine only when he could afford to do so. That is not true, as a simple incident will show. In the early days, he and Bok were opening the mail one Friday full of anxiety because the pay-roll was due that evening, and there was not enough money in the bank to meet it. From one of the letters dropped a certified check for five figures for a contract equal to five pages in the magazine. It was a welcome sight, for it meant an easy meeting of the pay-roll for that week and two succeeding weeks. But the check was from a manufacturing patent-medicine company. Without a moment's hesitation, Mr. Curtis slipped it back into the envelope, saying: "Of course, *that* we can't take." He returned the check, never gave the matter a second thought, and went out and borrowed more money to meet his pay-roll!

With all respect to American publishers, there are very few who could have done this—or indeed, would do it to-day, under similar conditions—particularly in that day when it was the custom for all magazines to accept patent-medicine advertising; *The Ladies' Home Journal* was practically the only publication of standing in the United States refusing that class of business!

Bok now saw advertising done on a large scale by a man who believed in plenty of white space surrounding the announcement in the advertisement. He paid Mr. Howells $10,000 for his autobiography, and Mr. Curtis spent $50,000 in advertising it. "It is not expense," he would explain to Bok, "it is investment. We are investing in a trade-mark. It will all come back in time." And when the first $100,000 did not come back as Mr. Curtis figured, he would send another $100,000 after it, and then both came back.

Bok's experience in advertisement writing was now to stand him in excellent stead. He wrote all the advertisements and from that day to the day of his retirement, practically every advertisement of the magazine was written by him.

Mr. Curtis believed that the editor should write the advertisements of a magazine's articles. "You are the one who knows them, what is in them and your purpose," he said to Bok, who keenly enjoyed this advertisement writing. He put less and less in his advertisements. Mr. Curtis made them larger and larger in the space which they occupied in the media used. In this way *The Ladies' Home Journal* advertisements became distinctive for their use of white space, and as the advertising world began to say: "You can't miss them." Only one feature was advertised at one time, but the "feature" was always carefully selected for its wide popular appeal, and then Mr. Curtis spared no expense to advertise it abundantly. As much as $400,000 was spent in one year in advertising only a few features— a gigantic sum in those days, approached by no other periodical. But Mr. Curtis believed in showing the advertising world that he was willing to take his own medicine.

Naturally, such a campaign of publicity announcing the most popular attractions offered by any magazine of the day had but one effect: the circulation leaped forward by bounds, and the advertising columns of the magazine rapidly filled up.

The success of *The Ladies' Home Journal* began to look like an assured fact, even to the most sceptical.

As a matter of fact, it was only at its beginning, as both publisher and editor knew. But they desired to fill the particular field of the magazine so quickly and fully that there would be small room for competition. The woman's magazine field was to belong to them!

CHAPTER XIX

PERSONALITY LETTERS

EDWARD BOK was always interested in the manner in which personality was expressed in letters. For this reason he adopted, as a boy, the method of collecting not mere autographs, but letters characteristic of their writers which should give interesting insight into the most famous men and women of the day. He secured what were really personality letters.

One of these writers was Mark Twain. The humorist was not kindly disposed toward autograph collectors, and the fact that in this case the collector aimed to raise the standard of the hobby did not appease him. Still, it brought forth a characteristic letter:

I hope I shall not offend you; I shall certainly say nothing with the intention to offend you. I must explain myself, however, and I will do it as kindly as I can. What you ask me to do, I am asked to do as often as one-half dozen times a week. Three hundred letters a year! One's impulse is to freely consent, but one's time and necessary occupations will not permit it. There is no way but to decline in all cases, making no exceptions, and I wish to call your attention to a thing which has probably not occurred to you, and that is this: that no man takes pleasure in exercising his trade as a pastime. Writing is my trade, and I exercise it only when I am obliged to. You might make your request of a doctor, or a builder, or a sculptor, and there would be no impropriety in it, but if you asked either of those for a specimen of his rrade, his handiwork, he would be justified in rising to a point of order. It would never be fair to ask a doctor for one of his corpses to remember him by.

MARK TWAIN.

At another time, after an interesting talk with Mark Twain, Bok wrote an account of the interview, with the humorist's permission. Desirous that the published account should be in every respect accurate, the manuscript was forwarded to Mark Twain for his approval. This resulted in the following interesting letter:

MY DEAR MR. BOK:

No, no—it is like most interviews, pure twaddle, and valueless.

For several quite plain and simple reasons, an "interview" must, as a rule, be an absurdity. And chiefly for this reason: it is an attempt to use a boat on land, or a wagon on water, to speak figuratively. Spoken speech is one thing, written speech is quite another. Print is a proper vehicle for the latter, but it isn't for the former. The moment "talk" is put into print you recognize that it is not what it was when you heard it; you perceive that an immense something has disappeared from it. That is its soul. You have nothing but a dead carcass left on your hands. Color, play of feature, the varying modulations of voice, the laugh, the smile, the informing inflections, everything that gave that body warmth, grace, friendliness, and charm, and commended it to your affection, or at least to your tolerance, is gone, and nothing is left, but a pallid, stiff and repulsive cadaver.

Such is "talk," almost invariably, as you see it lying in state in an "interview." The interviewer seldom tries to tell one *how* a thing was said; he merely puts in the naked remark, and stops there. When one writes for print, his methods are very different. He follows forms which have but little resemblance to conversation, but they make the reader understand what the writer is trying to convey. And when the writer is making a story, and finds it necessary to report some of the talk of his characters, observe how cautiously and anxiously he goes at that risky and difficult thing:

"If he had dared to say that thing in my presence," said Alfred, taking a mock heroic attitude, and casting an arch glance upon the company, "blood would have flowed."

"If he had dared to say that thing in my presence," said Hawkwood, with that in his eye which caused more than one heart in that guilty assemblage to quake, "blood would have flowed."

"If he had dared to say that thing in my presence," said the paltry blusterer, with valor on his tongue and pallor on his lips, "blood would have flowed."

So painfully aware is the novelist that naked talk in print conveys no meaning, that he loads, and often overloads, almost every utterance of his characters with explanations and interpretations. It is a loud confession that print is a poor vehicle for "talk," it is a recognition that uninterpreted talk in print would result in confusion to the reader, not instruction.

Now, in your interview you have certainly been most accurate, you have set down the sentences I uttered as I said them. But you have not a word of explanation; what my manner was at several points is not indicated. Therefore, no reader can possibly know where I was in earnest and where I was joking; or whether I was joking altogether or in earnest altogether. Such a report of a conversation has no value. It can convey many meanings to the reader, but never the right one. To add interpretations which would convey the right meaning is a something which would require—what? An art so high and fine and difficult that no possessor of it would ever be allowed to waste it on interviews.

No; spare the reader and spare me; leave the whole interview out; it is rubbish. I wouldn't talk in my sleep if I couldn't talk better than that.

If you wish to print anything print this letter; it may have some value, for it may explain to a reader here and there why it is that in interviews as a rule men seem to talk like anybody but themselves.

Sincerely yours,

MARK TWAIN.

The Harpers had asked Bok to write a book descriptive of his autograph-letter collection, and he had consented. The propitious moment, however, never came in his busy life. One day he mentioned the fact to Doctor Oliver Wendell Holmes and the poet said: "Let me write the introduction for it." Bok, of course, eagerly accepted, and within a few days he received the following, which, with the book, never reached publication:

How many autograph writers have had occasion to say with the Scotch trespasser climbing his neighbor's wall, when asked where he was going

Bok again!

Edward Bok has persevered like the widow in scripture, and the most obdurate subjects of his quest have found it for their interest to give in, lest by his continual coming he should weary them. We forgive him; almost admire him for his pertinacity; only let him have no imitators. The tax he has levied must not be imposed a second time.

An autograph of a distinguished personage means more to an imaginative person than a prosaic looker-on dreams of. Along these lines ran the consciousness and the guiding will of Napoleon, or Washington, of Milton or Goethe. His breath warmed the sheet of paper which you have before you. The microscope will show you the trail of flattened particles left by the tesselated epidermis of his hand as it swept along the manuscript. Nay, if we had but the right developing fluid to flow over it, the surface of the sheet would offer you his photograph as the light pictured it at the instant of writing.

Look at Mr. Bok's collection with such thoughts, . . . and you will cease to wonder at his pertinacity and applaud the conquests of his enthusiasm.

OLIVER WENDELL HOLMES.

Whenever biographers of the New England school of writers have come to write of John Greenleaf Whittier, they have been puzzled as to the scanty number of letters and private papers left by the poet. This letter, written to Bok, in comment upon a report that the poet had burned all his letters, is illuminating:

DEAR FRIEND·

The report concerning the burning of my letters is only true so far as this: some years ago I destroyed a large collection of letters I had received not from any regard to my own reputation, but from the fear that to leave them liable to publicity might be injurious or unpleasant to the writers or their friends. They covered much of the anti-slavery period and the War of the Rebellion, and many of them I knew were strictly private and confidential. I was not able at the time to look over the MS. and thought it safest to make a bonfire of it all. I have always regarded a private and confidential letter as sacred and its publicity in any shape a shameful breach of trust, unless authorized by the writer. I only wish my own letters to thousands of correspondents may be as carefully disposed of.

You may use this letter as you think wise and best.

Very truly thy friend,
JOHN G. WHITTIER.

Once in a while a bit of untold history crept into a letter sent to Bok; as for example in the letter, referred to in a previous chapter from General Jubal A. Early, the Confederate general, in which he gave an explanation, never before fully given, of his reasons for the burning of Chambersburg, Pennsylvania:

The town of Chambersburg was burned on the same day on which the demand on it was made by McCausland and refused. It was ascertained that a force of the enemy's cavalry was approaching, and there was no time for delay. Moreover, the refusal was peremptory, and there was no reason for delay unless the demand was a mere idle threat.

I had no knowledge of what amount of money there might be in Chambersburg. I knew that it was a town of some twelve thousand inhabitants. The town of Frederick, in Maryland, which was a much smaller town than Chambersburg, had in June very promptly responded to my demand on it for $200,000, some of the inhabitants, who were friendly to me, expressing a regret that I had not made it $500,000. There were one or more National Banks at Chambersburg, and the town ought to have been able to raise the sum I demanded. I never heard that the refusal was based on the inability to pay such a sum, and there was no offer to pay any sum. The value of the houses destroyed by Hunter, with their contents, was fully $100,000 in gold, and at the time I made the demand the price of gold in greenbacks had very nearly reached $3.00 and was going up rapidly. Hence it was that I required the $500,000 in greenbacks, if the gold was not paid, to provide against any further depreciation of the paper money.

I would have been fully justified by the laws of retaliation in war in burning the town without giving the inhabitants the opportunity of redeeming it.

J. A. EARLY.

Bok wrote to Eugene Field, once, asking him why in all his verse he had never written any love-songs, and suggesting that the story of Jacob and Rachel would have made a theme for a beautiful love-poem. Field's reply is interesting and characteristic, and throws a light on an omission in his works at which many have wondered:

DEAR BOK:
I'll see what I can do with the suggestion as to Jacob and Rachel. Several have asked me why I have never written any love-songs. That is hard to answer. I presume it is because I married so young. I was married at twenty-three, and did not begin to write until I was twenty-nine. Most of my lullabies are, in a sense, love-songs; so is "To a Usurper," "A Valentine," "The Little Bit of a Woman," "Lovers' Lane," etc., but not the kind commonly called love-songs. I am sending you herewith my first love-song, and even into it has crept a cadence that makes it a love-song of maturity rather than of youth. I do not know that you will care to have it, but it will interest you as the first. . . .
Ever sincerely yours.
EUGENE FIELD.

During the last years of his life, Bok tried to interest Benjamin Harrison, former President of the United States, in golf, since his physician had ordered "moderate outdoor exercise." Bok offered to equip him with the necessary clubs and balls. When he received the balls, the ex-president wrote:

"Thanks. But does not a bottle of liniment go with each ball?"

When William Howard Taft became President of the United States, the impression was given out that journalists would not be so welcome at the White House as they had been during the administration of President

Roosevelt. Mr. Taft, writing to Bok about another matter, asked why he had not called and talked it over while in Washington. Bok explained the impression that was current; whereupon came the answer, swift and definite!

There are no *personæ non gratæ* at the White House. I long ago learned the waste of time in maintaining such a class.

There was in circulation during Henry Ward Beecher's lifetime a story, which is still revived every now and then, that on a hot Sunday morning in early summer, he began his sermon in Plymouth Church by declaring that "It is too damned hot to preach." Bok wrote to the great preacher, asked him the truth of this report, and received this definite denial:

My Dear Friend:
No, I never did begin a sermon with the remark that "it is d—d hot," etc. It is a story a hundred years old, revamped every few years to suit some new man. When I am dead and gone, it will be told to the rising generation respecting some other man, and then, as now, there will be fools who will swear that they heard it!
                                        Henry Ward Beecher.

When Bok's father passed away, he left, among his effects, a large number of Confederate bonds. Bok wrote to Jefferson Davis, asking if they had any value, and received this characteristic answer:

I regret my inability to give an opinion. The theory of the Confederate Government, like that of the United States, was to separate the sword from the purse. Therefore, the Confederate States Treasury was under the control not of the Chief Executive, but of the Congress and the Secretary of the Treasury. This may explain my want of special information in regard to the Confederate States Bonds. Generally, I may state that the Confederate Government cannot have preserved a fund for the redemption of its Bonds other than the cotton subscribed by our citizens for that purpose. At the termination of the War, the United States Government, claiming to be the successor of the Confederate Government, seized all its property which could be found, both at home and abroad. I have not heard of any purpose to apply these assets to the payment of the liabilities of the Confederacy, and, therefore, have been at a loss to account for the demand which has lately been made for the Confederate Bonds.

JEFFERSON DAVIS.

Always the soul of courtesy itself, and most obliging in granting the numerous requests which came to him for his autograph, William Dean Howells finally turned; and Bok always considered himself fortunate that the novelist announced his decision to him in the following characteristic letter:

The requests for my autograph have of late become so burdensome that I am obliged either to refuse all or to make some sort of limitation. Every author must have an uneasy fear that his signature is "collected" at times like postage-stamps, and at times "traded" among the collectors for other signatures. That would not matter so much if the applicants were always able to spell his name, or were apparently acquainted with his work or interested in it.

I propose, therefore, to give my name hereafter only to such askers as can furnish me proof by intelligent comment upon it that they have read some book of mine. If they can inclose a bookseller's certificate that they have bought the book, their case will be very much strengthened; but I do not insist upon this. In all instances a card and a stamped and directed envelope must be inclosed. I will never "add a sentiment" except in the case of applicants who can give me proof that they have read all my books, now some thirty or forty in number.

W. D. HOWELLS.

It need hardly be added that Mr. Howells's good nature prevented his adherence to his rule!

Rudyard Kipling is another whose letters fairly vibrate with personality; few men can write more interestingly, or, incidentally, considering his microscopic handwriting, say more on a letter page.

Bok was telling Kipling one day about the scrapple so dear to the heart of the Philadelphian as a breakfast dish. The author had never heard of it or tasted it, and wished for a sample. So, upon his return home, Bok had a Philadelphia market-man send some of the Philadelphia-made article, packed in ice, to Kipling in his English home. There were several pounds of it and Kipling wrote:

By the way, that scrapple—which by token is a dish for the Gods—arrived in perfect condition, and I ate it all, or as much as I could get hold of. I am extremely grateful for it. It's all nonsense about pig being unwholesome. There isn't a Mary-ache in a barrel of scrapple.

Then later came this afterthought:

A noble dish is that scrapple, *but* don't eat three slices and go to work straight on top of 'em. That's the way to dyspepsia!

P. S. I wish to goodness you'd give another look at England before long. It's quite a country; really it is. Old, too, I believe.

It was Kipling who suggested that Bok should name his Merion home "Swastika." Bok asked what the author knew about the mystic sign:

There is a huge book (I've forgotten the name, but the Smithsonian will know), he wrote back, about the Swastika (pronounced Swas-ti-ka to rhyme with "car's ticker"), in literature, art, religion, dogma, etc. I believe there are two sorts of Swastikas, one ఔ and one 卍; one is bad, the other is good, but which is which I know not for sure. The Hindu trader opens his yearly account-books with a Swastika as "an auspicious beginning," and all the races of the earth have used it. It's an inexhaustible subject, and some man in the Smithsonian ought to be full of it. Anyhow, the sign on the door or the hearth should protect you against fire and water and thieves.

By this time should have reached you a Swastika door-knocker, which I hope may fit in with the new house and the new name. It was made by a village-smith; and you will see that it has my initials, to which I hope you will add yours, that the story may be complete.

We are settled out here in Cape Town, eating strawberries in January and complaining of the heat, which for the last two days has been a little more than we pampered folk are used to; say 70° at night. But what a lovely land it is, and how superb are the hydrangeas! Figure to yourself four acres of 'em, all in bloom on the hillside near our home!

Bok had visited the Panama Canal before its completion and had talked with the men, high and low, working on it, asking them how they felt about President Roosevelt's action in "digging the Canal first and talking about it afterwards." He wrote the result of his talks to Colonel Roosevelt, and received this reply:

I shall always keep your letter, for I shall want my children and grandchildren to see it after I am gone. I feel just as you do about the Canal. It is the greatest contribution I was able to make to my country; and while I do not believe my countrymen appreciate this at the moment, I am extremely pleased to know that the men on the Canal do, for they are the men who have done and are doing the great job. I am awfully pleased that you feel the way you do.

THEODORE ROOSEVELT.

In 1887, General William Tecumseh Sherman was much talked about as a candidate for the presidency, until his famous declaration came out: "I will not run if nominated, and will not serve if elected." During the weeks of talk, however, much was said of General Sherman's religious views, some contending that he was a Roman Catholic; others that he was a Protestant.

Bok wrote to General Sherman and asked him. His answer was direct:

My family is strongly Roman Catholic, but I am not. Until I ask some favor the public has no claim to question me further.

When Mrs. Sherman passed away, Doctor T. DeWitt Talmage wrote General Sherman a note of condolence, and what is perhaps one of the fullest expositions of his religious faith to which he ever gave expression came from him in a most remarkable letter, which Doctor Talmage gave to Bok.

New York, December 12, 1886.

MY DEAR FRIEND:

Your most tender epistle from Mansfield, Ohio, of December 9 brought here last night by your son awakens in my brain a flood of memories. Mrs. Sherman was by nature and inheritance an Irish Catholic. Her grandfather, Hugh Boyle, was a highly educated classical scholar, whom I remember well,—married the half sister of the mother of James G. Blaine at Brownsville, Pa., settled in our native town Lancaster, Fairfield County, Ohio, and became the Clerk of the County Court. He had two daughters, Maria and Susan. Maria became the wife of Thomas Ewing, about 1819, and was the mother of my wife, Ellen Boyle Ewing. She was so staunch to what she believed the *true Faith* that I am sure that though she loved her children better than herself, she would have seen them die with less pang, than to depart from the "Faith." Mr. Ewing was a great big man, an intellectual giant, and looked down on religion as something domestic, something consoling which ought to be encouraged; and to him it made little difference whether the religion was Methodist, Presbyterian, Baptist, or Catholic, provided the acts were "half as good" as their professions.

In 1829 my father, a Judge of the Supreme Court of Ohio, died at Lebanon away from home, leaving his widow, Mary Hoyt of Norwalk, Conn. (sister to Charles and James Hoyt of Brooklyn) with a frame house in Lancaster, an income of $200 a year and eleven as hungry, rough, and uncouth children as ever existed on earth. But father had been kind, generous, manly, with a big heart; and when it ceased to beat friends turned up— Our Uncle Stoddard took Charles, the oldest; W. I. married the next, Elisabeth (still living); Amelia was soon married to a merchant in Mansfield, McCorab; I, the third son, was adopted by Thomas Ewing, a neighbor, and John fell to his namesake in Mt. Vernon, a merchant.

Surely "Man proposes and God disposes." I could fill a hundred pages, but will not bore you. A half century has passed and you, a Protestant minister, write me a kind, affectionate letter about my Catholic wife from Mansfield, one of my family homes, where my mother, Mary Hoyt, died, and where our Grandmother, Betsey Stoddard, lies buried. Oh, what a flood of memories come up at the name of Betsey Stoddard,—daughter of the Revd. Mr. Stoddard, who preached three times every Sunday, and as often in between as he could cajole a congregation at ancient Woodbury, Conn.,--who came down from Mansfield to Lancaster, three days' hard journey to regulate the family of her son Judge Sherman, whose gentle wife was as afraid of Grandma as any of us boys. She never spared the rod or broom, but she had more square solid sense to the yard than any woman I ever saw. From her Charles, John, and I inherit what little sense we possess.

Lancaster, Fairfield County, was our paternal home, Mansfield that of Grandmother Stoddard and her daughter, Betsey Parker. There Charles and John settled, and when in 1846 I went to California Mother also went there, and there died in 1851.

When a boy, once a year I had to drive my mother in an old "dandy wagon" on her annual visit. The distance was 75 miles, further than Omaha is from San Francisco. We always took three days and stopped at every house to gossip with the woman folks, and dispense medicines and syrups to the sick, for in those days all had the chills or ague. If I could I would not awaken Grandmother Betsey Stoddard because she would be horrified at the backsliding of the servants of Christ,—but oh ! how I would like to take my mother, Mary Hoyt, in a railroad car out to California, to Santa Barbara and Los Angeles, among the vineyards of grapes, the groves of oranges, lemons and pomegranates. How clearly recurs to me the memory of her exclamation when I told her I had been ordered around Cape Horn to California. Her idea was about as definite as mine or yours as to, Where is Stanley? but she saw me return with some nuggets to make her life more comfortable.

She was a strong Presbyterian to the end, but she loved my Ellen, and the love was mutual. All my children have inherited their mother's faith, and she would have given anything if I would have simply said Amen; but it is simply impossible.

But I am sure that you know that the God who created the minnow, and who has moulded the rose and carnation, given each its sweet fragrance, will provide for those mortal men who strive to do right in the world which he himself has stocked with birds, animals, and men;—at all events, I will trust Him with absolute confidence.

With great respect and affection,
Yours truly,
W. T. SHERMAN.

CHAPTER XX

MEETING A REVERSE OR TWO

WITH the hitherto unreached magazine circulation of a million copies a month in sight, Edward Bok decided to give a broader scope to the periodical. He was determined to lay under contribution not only the most famous writers of the day, but also to seek out those well-known persons who usually did not contribute to the magazines; always keeping in mind the popular appeal of his material, but likewise aiming constantly to widen its scope and gradually to lift its standard.

Sailing again for England, he sought and secured the acquaintance of Rudyard Kipling, whose alert mind was at once keenly interested in what Bok was trying to do. He was willing to co-operate, with the result that Bok secured the author's new story, *William the Conqueror*. When Bok read the manuscript, he was delighted; he had for some time been reading Kipling's work with enthusiasm, and he saw at once that here was one of the author's best tales.

At that time, Frances E. Willard had brought her agitation for temperance prominently before the public, and Bok had promised to aid her by eliminating from his magazine, so far as possible, all scenes which represented alcoholic drinking. It was not an iron-clad rule, but, both from the principle fixed for his own life and in the interest of the thousands of young people who read his magazine, he believed it would be better to minimize all incidents portraying alcoholic drinking or drunkenness. Kipling's story depicted several such scenes; so when Bok sent the proofs he suggested that if Kipling could moderate some of these scenes, it would be more in line with the policy of the magazine. Bok did not make a special point of the matter, leaving it to Kipling's judgment to decide how far he could make such changes and preserve the atmosphere of his story.

From this incident arose the widely published story that Bok cabled Kipling, asking permission to omit a certain drinking reference, and substitute something else, whereupon Kipling cabled back: "Substitute Mellin's Food." As a matter of fact (although it is a pity to kill such a clever story), no such cable was ever sent and no such reply ever received. As Kipling himself wrote to Bok: "No, I said nothing about Mellin's Food. I wish I had." An American author in London happened to hear of the correspondence between the editor and the author, it appealed to his sense of humor, and the published story was the result. If it mattered, it is possible that Brander Matthews could accurately reveal the originator of the much-published yarn.

From Kipling's house Bok went to Tunbridge Wells to visit Mary Anderson, the one-time popular American actress, who had married Antonio de Navarro and retired from the stage. A goodly number of editors had tried to induce the retired actress to write, just as a number of managers had tried to induce her to return to the stage. All had failed. But Bok never accepted the failure of others as a final decision for himself; and after two or three visits, he persuaded Madame de Navarro to write her reminiscences, which he published with marked success in the magazine.

The editor was very desirous of securing something for his magazine that would delight children, and he hit upon the idea of trying to induce Lewis Carroll to write another *Alice in Wonderland* series. He was told by English friends that this would be difficult, since the author led a secluded life at Oxford and hardly ever admitted any one into his confidence. But Bok wanted to beard the lion in his den, and an Oxford graduate volunteered to introduce him to an Oxford don through whom, if it were at all possible, he could reach the author. The journey to Oxford was made, and Bok was introduced to the don, who turned out to be no less a person than the original possessor of the highly colored vocabulary of the "White Rabbit" of the *Alice* stories.

"Impossible," immediately declared the don. "You couldn't persuade Dodgson to consider it." Bok, however, persisted, and it so happened that the don liked what he called "American perseverance."

"Well, come along," he said. "We'll beard the lion in his den, as you say, and see what happens. You know, of course, that it is the Reverend Charles L. Dodgson that we are going to see, and I must introduce you to that person, not to Lewis Carroll. He is a tutor in mathematics here, as you doubtless know; lives a rigidly secluded life; dislikes strangers; makes no friends; and yet withal is one of the most delightful men in the world if he wants to be."

But as it happened upon this special occasion when

Bok was introduced to him in his chambers in Tom Quad, Mr. Dodgson did not "want to be" delightful. There was no doubt that back of the studied reserve was a kindly, charming, gracious gentleman, but Bok's profession had been mentioned and the author was on rigid guard.

When Bok explained that one of the special reasons for his journey from America this summer was to see him, the Oxford mathematician sufficiently softened to ask the editor to sit down. Bok then broached his mission.

"You are quite in error, Mr. Bok," was the Dodgson comment. "You are not speaking to the person you think you are addressing."

For a moment Bok was taken aback. Then he decided to go right to the point.

"Do I understand, Mr. Dodgson, that you are not 'Lewis Carroll': that you did not write *Alice in Wonderland?*"

For an answer the tutor rose, went into another room, and returned with a book which he handed to Bok. "This is my book," he said simply. It was entitled *An Elementary Treatise on Determinants*, by C. L. Dodgson. When he looked up, Bok found the author's eyes riveted on him.

"Yes," said Bok. "I know, Mr. Dodgson. If I remember correctly, this is the same book of which you sent a copy to Her Majesty, Queen Victoria, when she wrote to you for a personal copy of your *Alice*."

Dodgson made no comment. The face was absolutely without expression save a kindly compassion intended to convey to the editor that he was making a terrible mistake.

"As I said to you in the beginning, Mr. Bok, you are in error. You are not speaking to 'Lewis Carroll.'" And then: "Is this the first time you have visited Oxford?"

Bok said it was; and there followed the most delightful two hours with the Oxford mathematician and the Oxford don, walking about and into the wonderful college buildings, and afterward the three had a bite of lunch together. But all efforts to return to "Lewis Carroll" were futile. While saying good-by to his host, Bok remarked:

"I can't help expressing my disappointment, Mr. Dodgson, in my quest in behalf of the thousands of American children who love you and who would so gladly welcome 'Lewis Carroll' back."

The mention of children and their love for him momentarily had its effect. For an instant a different light came into the eyes, and Bok instinctively realized Dodgson was about to say something. But he checked himself. Bok had almost caught him off his guard.

"I am sorry," he finally said at the parting at the door, "that you should be disappointed, for the sake of the children as well as for your own sake. I only regret that I cannot remove the disappointment."

And as the trio walked to the station, the don said: "That is his attitude toward all, even toward me. He is not 'Lewis Carroll' to any one; is extremely sensitive on the point, and will not acknowledge his identity. That is why he lives so much to himself. He is in daily dread that some one will mention *Alice* in his presence. Curious, but there it is."

Edward Bok's next quest was to be even more disappointing; he was never even to reach the presence of the person he sought. This was Florence Nightingale, the Crimean nurse. Bok was desirous of securing her own story of her experiences, but on every hand he found an unwillingness even to take him to her house. "No use," said everybody. "She won't see any one. Hates publicity and all that sort of thing, and shuns the public." Nevertheless, the editor journeyed to the famous nurse's home on South Street, in the West End of London, only to be told that "Miss Nightingale never receives strangers."

"But I am not a stranger," insisted the editor. "I am one of her friends from America. Please take my card to her."

This mollified the faithful secretary, but the word instantly came back that Miss Nightingale was not receiving any one that day. Bok wrote her a letter asking for an appointment, which was never answered. Then he wrote another, took it personally to the house, and awaited an answer, only to receive the message that "Miss Nightingale says there is no answer to the letter."

Bok had with such remarkable uniformity secured whatever he sought, that these experiences were new to him. Frankly, they puzzled him. He was not easily baffled, but baffled he now was, and that twice in succession. Turn as he might, he could find no way in which to reopen an approach to either the Oxford tutor or the Crimean nurse. They were plainly too much for him, and he had to acknowledge his defeat. The experience was good for him; he did not realize this at the time, nor did he enjoy the sensation of not getting what he wanted. Nevertheless, a reverse or two was due. Not that his success was having any undesirable effect upon him; his Dutch common sense saved him from any such calamity. But at thirty years' of age it is not good for any one, no matter how well balanced, to have things come his way too fast and too consistently. And here were breaks. He could not have everything he wanted, and it was just as well that he should find that out.

In his next quest he found himself again opposed by his London friends. Unable to secure a new *Alice in Wonderland* for his child readers, he determined to give them Kate Greenaway. But here he had selected another recluse. Everybody discouraged him. The artist never saw visitors, he was told, and she particularly shunned editors and publishers. Her own publishers confessed that Miss Greenaway was inaccessible to them. "We conduct all our business with her by correspondence. I have never seen her personally myself," said a member of the firm.

Bok inwardly decided that two failures in two days were sufficient, and he made up his mind that there should not be a third. He took a bus for the long ride to Hampstead Heath, where the illustrator lived, and finally stood before a picturesque Queen Anne house that one would have recognized at once, with its lower story of red brick, its upper part covered with red tiles, its windows of every size and shape, as the inspiration of Kate Greenaway's pictures. As it turned out later, Miss Greenaway's sister opened the door and told the visitor that Miss Greenaway was not at home.

"But, pardon me, has not Miss Greenaway returned? Is not that she?" asked Bok, as he indicated a figure just coming down the stairs. And as the sister turned to see, Bok stepped into the hall. At least he was inside! Bok had never seen a photograph of Miss Greenaway, he did not know that the figure coming downstairs was the artist; but his instinct had led him right, and good fortune was with him.

He now introduced himself to Kate Greenaway, and explained that one of his objects in coming to London was to see her on behalf of thousands of American children. Naturally there was nothing for the illustrator to do but to welcome her visitor. She took him into the garden, where he saw at once that he was seated under the apple-tree of Miss Greenaway's pictures. It was in full bloom, a veritable picture of spring loveliness. Bok's love for nature pleased the artist and when he recognized the cat that sauntered up, he could see that he was making headway. But when he explained his profession and stated his errand, the atmosphere instantly changed. Miss Greenaway conveyed the unmistakable impression that she had been trapped, and Bok realized at once that he had a long and difficult road ahead.

Still, negotiate it he must and he did! And after luncheon in the garden, with the cat in his lap, Miss Greenaway perceptibly thawed out, and when the editor left late that afternoon he had the promise of the artist that she would do her first magazine work for him. That promise was kept monthly, and for nearly two years her articles appeared, with satisfaction to Miss Greenaway and with great success to the magazine.

The next opposition to Bok's plans arose from the soreness generated by the absence of copyright laws between the United States and Great Britain and Europe. The editor, who had been publishing a series of musical compositions, solicited the aid of Sir Arthur Sullivan. But it so happened that Sir Arthur's most famous composition, "The Lost Chord," had been taken without leave by American music publishers, and sold by the hundreds of thousands with the composer left out on pay-day. Sir Arthur held forth on this injustice, and said further that no accurate copy of "The Lost Chord" had, so far as he knew, ever been printed in the United States. Bok saw his chance, and also an opportunity for a little Americanization.

"Very well, Sir Arthur," suggested Bok; "with your consent, I will rectify both the inaccuracy and the injustice. Write out a correct version of 'The Lost Chord'; I will give it to nearly a million readers, and so render obsolete the incorrect copies; and I shall be only too happy to pay you the first honorarium for an American publication of the song. You can add to the copy the statement that this is the first American honorarium you have ever received, and so shame the American publishers for their dishonesty."

This argument appealed strongly to the composer, who made a correct transcript of his famous song, and published it with the following note:

This is the first and only copy of "The Lost Chord" which has ever been sent by me to an American publisher. I believe all the reprints in America are more or less incorrect. I have pleasure in sending this copy to my friend, Mr. Edward W. Bok, for publication in *The Ladies' Home Journal* for which he gives me an honorarium, the only one I have ever received from an American publisher for this song.

ARTHUR SULLIVAN.

At least, thought Bok, he had healed one man's soreness toward America. But the next day he encountered another. On his way to Paris, he stopped at Amiens to see Jules Verne. Here he found special difficulty in that the aged author could not speak English, and Bok knew only a few words of casual French. Finally a neighbor's servant who knew a handful of English words was commandeered, and a halting three-cornered conversation was begun.

Bok found two grievances here: the author was incensed at the American public because it had insisted on classing his books as juveniles, and accepting them as stories of adventure, whereas he desired them to be recognized as prophetic stories based on scientific facts—an insistence which, as all the world knows, has since been justified. Bok explained, however, that the popular acceptance of the author's books as stories of adventure was by no means confined to America; that even in his own country the same was true. But Jules Verne came back with the rejoinder that if the French were a pack of fools, that was no reason why the Americans should also be.

The argument weighed somewhat with the author,

however, for he then changed the conversation, and pointed out how he had been robbed by American publishers who had stolen his books. So Bok was once more face to face with the old non-copyright conditions; and although he explained the existence then of a new protective law, the old man was not mollified. He did not take kindly to Bok's suggestion for new work, and closed the talk, extremely difficult to all three, by declaring that his writing days were over.

But Bok was by no means through with non-copyright echoes, for he was destined next day to take part in an even stormier interview on the same subject with Alexander Dumas *fils*. Bok had been publishing a series of articles in which authors had told how they had been led to write their most famous books, and he wanted Dumas to tell "How I Came to Write 'Camille.'"

To act as translator this time, Bok took a trusted friend with him, whose services he found were needed, as Dumas was absolutely without knowledge of English. No sooner was the editor's request made known to him than the storm broke. Dumas, hotly excited, denounced the Americans as robbers who had deprived him of his rightful returns on his book and play, and ended by declaring that he would trust no American editor or publisher.

The mutual friend explained the new copyright conditions and declared that Bok intended to treat the author honorably. But Dumas was not to be mollified. He launched forth upon a new arraignment of the Americans; dishonesty was bred in their bones! and they were robbers by instinct. All of this distinctly nettled Bok's Americanism. The interpreting friend finally suggested that the article should be written while Bok was in Paris; that he should be notified when the manuscript was ready, that he should then appear with the actual money in hand in French notes; and that Dumas should give Bok the manuscript when Bok handed Dumas the money.

"After I count it," said Dumas.

This was the last straw!

"Pray ask him," Bok suggested to the interpreter, "what assurance I have that he will deliver the manuscript to me after he has the money." The friend protested against translating this thrust, but Bok insisted, and Dumas, not knowing what was coming, insisted that the message be given him. When it was, the man was a study; he became livid with rage.

"But," persisted Bok, "say to Monsieur Dumas that I have the same privilege of distrusting him as he apparently has of distrusting me."

And Bok can still see the violent gesticulations of the storming French author, his face burning with passionate anger, as the two left him.

Edward Bok now sincerely hoped that his encounters with the absence of a law that has been met were at an end!

Rosa Bonheur, the painter of "The Horse Fair," had been represented to Bok as another recluse who was as inaccessible as Kate Greenaway. He had known of the painter's intimate relations with the ex-Empress Eugénie, and desired to get these reminiscences. Everybody dissuaded him; but again taking a French friend he made the journey to Fontainebleau, where the artist lived in a château in the little village of By.

A group of dogs, great, magnificent tawny creatures, welcomed the two visitors to the château; and the most powerful door that Bok had ever seen, as securely bolted as that of a cell, told of the inaccessibility of the mistress of the house. Two blue-frocked peasants explained how impossible it was for any one to see their mistress, so Bok asked permission to come in and write her a note.

This was granted; and then, as in the case of Kate Greenaway, Rosa Bonheur herself walked into the hall, in a velvet jacket, dressed, as she always was, in man's attire. A delightful smile lighted the strong face, surmounted by a shock of gray hair, cut short at the back; and from the moment of her first welcome there was no doubt of her cordiality to the few who were fortunate enough to work their way into her presence. It was a wonderful afternoon, spent in the painter's studio in the upper part of the château; and Bok carried away with him the promise of Rosa Bonheur to write the story of her life for publication in the magazine.

On his return to London the editor found that Charles Dana Gibson had settled down there for a time. Bok had always wanted Gibson to depict the characters of Dickens; and he felt that this was the opportunity, while the artist was in London and could get the atmosphere for his work. Gibson was as keen for the idea as was Bok, and so the two arranged the series which was subsequently published.

On his way to his steamer to sail for home, Bok visited "Ian Maclaren," whose *Bonnie Brier Bush* stories were then in great vogue, and not only contracted for Doctor Watson's stories of the immediate future, but arranged with him for a series of articles which, for two years thereafter, was published in the magazine.

The editor now sailed for home, content with his assembly of foreign "features."

On the steamer, Bok heard of the recent discovery of some unpublished letters by Louisa May Alcott, written to five girls, and before returning to Philadelphia, he went to Boston, got into touch with the executors of the will of Miss Alcott, brought the letters back with him to read, and upon reaching Philadelphia, wired his acceptance of them for publication.

But the traveller was not at once to enjoy his home. After only a day in Philadelphia he took a train for Indianapolis. Here lived the most thoroughly American writer of the day, in Bok's estimation: James Whitcomb Riley. An arrangement, perfected before his European visit, had secured to Bok practically exclusive rights to all the output of his Chicago friend Eugene Field, and he felt that Riley's work would admirably complement that of Field. This Bok explained to Riley, who readily fell in with the idea, and the editor returned to Philadelphia with a contract to see Riley's next dozen poems. A little later Field passed away. His last poem, "The Dream Ship," and his posthumous story "The Werewolf" appeared in *The Ladies' Home Journal*.

A second series of articles was also arranged for with Mr. Harrison, in which he was to depict, in a personal way, the life of a President of the United States, the domestic life of the White House, and the financial arrangements made by the government for the care of the chief executive and his family. The first series of articles by the former President had been very successful; Bok felt that they had accomplished much in making his women readers familiar with their country and the machinery of its government. After this, which had been undeniably solid reading, Bok reasoned that the supplementary articles, in lighter vein, would serve as a sort of dessert. And so it proved.

Bok now devoted his attention to strengthening the fiction in his magazine. He sought Mark Twain, and bought his two new stories; he secured from Bret Harte a tale which he had just finished; and then ran the gamut of the best fiction writers of the day, and secured their best output. Marion Crawford, Conan Doyle, Sarah Orne Jewett, John Kendrick Bangs, Kate Douglas Wiggin, Hamlin Garland, Mrs. Burton Harrison, Elizabeth Stuart Phelps, Mary E. Wilkins, Jerome K. Jerome, Anthony Hope, Joel Chandler Harris, and others followed in rapid succession.

He next turned for a moment to his religious department, decided that it needed a freshening of interest, and secured Dwight L. Moody, whose evangelical work was then so prominently in the public eye, to conduct "Mr. Moody's Bible Class" in the magazine—practically a study of the stated Bible lesson of the month with explanation in Moody's simple and effective style.

The authors for whom the *Journal* was now publishing attracted the attention of all the writers of the day, and the supply of good material became too great for its capacity. Bok studied the mechanical make-up, and felt that by some method he must find more room in the front portion. He had allotted the first third of the magazine to the general literary contents and the latter two-thirds to departmental features. Toward the close of the number, the departments narrowed down from full pages to single columns with advertisements on each side.

One day Bok was handling a story by Rudyard Kipling which had overrun the space allowed for it in the front. The story had come late, and the rest of the front portion of the magazine had gone to press. The editor was in a quandary what to do with the two remaining columns of the Kipling tale. There were only two pages open, and these were at the back. He remade those pages, and continued the story from pages 6 and 7 to pages 38 and 39.

At once Bok saw that this was an instance where "necessity was the mother of invention." He realized that if he could run some of his front material over to the back he would relieve the pressure at the front, present a more varied contents there, and make his advertisements more valuable by putting them next to the most expensive material in the magazine.

In the next issue he combined some of his smaller departments in the back; and thus, in 1896, he inaugurated the method of "running over into the back" which has now become a recognized principle in the make-up of magazines of larger size. At first, Bok's readers objected, but he explained why he did it; that they were the benefiters by the plan; and, so far as readers can be satisfied with what is, at best, an awkward method of presentation, they were content. To-day the practice is undoubtedly followed to excess, some magazines carrying as much as eighty and ninety columns over from the front to the back; from such abuse it will, of course, free itself either by a return to the original method of make-up or by the adoption of some other less-irritating plan.

In his reading about the America of the past, Bok had been impressed by the unusual amount of interesting personal material that constituted what is termed unwritten history—original events of tremendous personal appeal in which great personalities figured but which had not sufficient historical importance to have been included in American history. Bok determined to please his older readers by harking back to the past and at the same time acquainting the younger generation with the picturesque events which had preceded their time.

He also believed that if he could "dress up" the past, he could arrest the attention of a generation which was too likely to boast of its interest only in the present and the future. He took a course of reading and consulted with Mr. Charles A. Dana, editor of the *New York Sun*, who had become interested in his work and had written him several voluntary letters of commendation. Mr. Dana gave material help in the selection of subjects and writers; and was intensely amused and interested by the manner in which his youthful confrère "dressed up" the titles of what might otherwise have looked like commonplace articles.

"I know," said Bok to the elder editor, "it smacks

a little of the sensational, Mr. Dana, but the purpose I have in mind of showing the young people of to-day that some great things happened before they came on the stage seems to me to make it worth while."

Mr. Dana agreed with this view, supplemented every effort of the Philadelphia editor in several subsequent talks, and in 1897 *The Ladies' Home Journal* began one of the most popular series it ever published. It was called "Great Personal Events," and the picturesque titles explained them. He first pictured the enthusiastic evening "When Jenny Lind Sang in Castle Garden," and, as Bok added to pique curiosity, "when people paid $20 to sit in rowboats to hear the Swedish nightingale."

This was followed by an account of the astonishing episode "When Henry Ward Beecher Sold Slaves in Plymouth Pulpit"; the picturesque journey "When Louis Kossuth Rode Up Broadway"; the triumphant tour "When General Grant Went Round the World"; the forgotten story of "When an Actress Was the Lady of the White House"; the sensational striking of the gold vein in 1849, "When Mackay Struck the Great Bonanza"; the hitherto little-known instance "When Louis Philippe Taught School in Philadelphia"; and even the lesser-known fact of the residence of the brother of Napoleon Bonaparte in America, "When the King of Spain Lived on the Banks of the Schuylkill"; while the story of "When John Wesley Preached in Georgia" surprised nearly every Methodist, as so few had known that the founder of their church had ever visited America. Each month picturesque event followed graphic happening, and never was unwritten history more readily read by the young, or the memories of the older folk more catered to than in this series which won new friends for the magazine on every hand.

CHAPTER XXI

A SIGNAL PIECE OF CONSTRUCTIVE WORK

THE influence of his grandfather and the injunction of his grandmother to her sons that each "should make the world a better or a more beautiful place to live in" now began to be manifest in the grandson. Edward Bok was unconscious that it was this influence. What directly led him to the signal piece of construction in which he engaged was the wretched architecture of small houses. As he travelled through the United States he was appalled by it. Where the houses were not positively ugly, they were, to him, repellently ornate. Money was wasted on useless turrets, filigree work, or machine-made ornamentation. Bok found out that these small householders never employed an architect, but that the houses were put up by builders from their own plans.

Bok felt a keen desire to take hold of the small American house and make it architecturally better. He foresaw, however, that the subject would finally include small gardening and interior decoration. He feared that the subject would become too large for the magazine, which was already feeling the pressure of the material which he was securing. He suggested, therefore, to Mr. Curtis that they purchase a little magazine published in Buffalo, N. Y., called *Country Life*, and develop it into a first-class periodical devoted to the general subject of a better American architecture, gardening, and interior decoration, with special application to the small house. The magazine was purchased, and while Bok was collecting his material for a number of issues ahead, he edited and issued, for copyright purposes, a four-page magazine.

An opportunity now came to Mr. Curtis to purchase *The Saturday Evening Post*, a Philadelphia weekly of honored prestige, founded by Benjamin Franklin. It was apparent at once that the company could not embark upon the development of two magazines at the same time, and as a larger field was seen for *The Saturday Evening Post*, it was decided to leave *Country Life* in abeyance for the present.

Mr. Frank Doubleday, having left the Scribners and started a publishing-house of his own, asked Bok to transfer to him the copyright and good will of *Country Life*—seeing that there was little chance for The Curtis Publishing Company to undertake its publication. Mr. Curtis was willing, but he knew that Bok had set his heart on the new magazine and left it for him to decide. The editor realized, as the Doubleday Company could take up the magazine at once, the unfairness of holding indefinitely the field against them by the publication of a mere copyright periodical. And so, with a feeling as if he were giving up his child to another father, Bok arranged that The Curtis Publishing Company should transfer to the Doubleday, Page Company all rights to the title and periodical of which the present beautiful publication *Country Life* is the outgrowth.

Bok now turned to *The Ladies' Home Journal* as his medium for making the small-house architecture of America better. He realized the limitation of space, but decided to do the best he could under the circumstances. He believed he might serve thousands of his readers if he could make it possible for them to secure, at moderate cost, plans for well-designed houses by the leading domestic architects in the country. He consulted a number of architects, only to find them unalterably opposed to the idea. They disliked the publicity of magazine presentation; prices differed too much in various parts of the country; and they did not care to risk the criticism of their contemporaries. It was "cheapening" their profession!

Bok saw that he should have to blaze the way and demonstrate the futility of these arguments. At last he persuaded one architect to co-operate with him, and in 1895 began the publication of a series of houses which could be built, approximately, for from one thousand five hundred dollars to five thousand dollars. The idea attracted attention at once, and the architect-author was swamped with letters and inquiries regarding his plans.

This proved Bok's instinct to be correct as to the public willingness to accept such designs; upon this proof he succeeded in winning over two additional architects to make plans. He offered his readers full building specifications and plans to scale of the houses with estimates from four builders in different parts of the United States for five dollars a set. The plans and specifications were so complete in every detail that any builder could build the house from them.

A storm of criticism now arose from architects and builders all over the country, the architects claiming that Bok was taking "the bread out of their mouths" by the sale of plans, and local builders vigorously questioned the accuracy of the estimates. But Bok knew he was right and persevered.

Slowly but surely he won the approval of the leading architects, who saw that he was appealing to a class of house-builders who could not afford to pay an architect's fee, and that, with his wide circulation, he might become an influence for better architecture through these small houses. The sets of plans and specifications sold by the thousands. It was not long before the magazine was able to present small-house plans by the foremost architects of the country, whose services the average householder could otherwise never have dreamed of securing.

Bok not only saw an opportunity to better the exterior of the small houses, but he determined that each plan published should provide for two essentials: every servant's room should have two windows to insure cross-ventilation, and contain twice the number of cubic feet usually given to such rooms; and in place of the American parlor, which he considered a useless room, should be substituted either a living-room or a library. He did not point to these improvements; every plan simply presented the larger servant's room and did not present a parlor. It is a singular fact that of the tens of thousands of plans sold, not a purchaser ever noticed the absence of a parlor except one woman in Brookline, Mass., who, in erecting a group of twenty-five "*Journal* houses," discovered after she had built ten that not one contained a parlor!

"*Ladies' Home Journal* houses" were now going up in communities all over the country, and Bok determined to prove that they could be erected for the prices given. Accordingly, he published a prize offer of generous amount for the best set of exterior and interior photographs of a house built after a *Journal* plan within the published price. Five other and smaller prizes were also offered. A legally attested builder's declaration was to accompany each set of photographs. The sets immediately began to come in, until over five thousand had been received. Bok selected the best of these, awarded the prizes, and began the presentation of the houses actually built after the published plans.

Of course this publication gave fresh impetus to the whole scheme; prospective house-builders pointed their builders to the proof given, and additional thousands of sets of plans were sold. The little houses became better and better in architecture as the series went on, and occasionally a plan for a house costing as high as ten thousand dollars was given.

For nearly twenty-five years Bok continued to publish pictures of houses and plans. Entire colonies of "*Ladies' Home Journal* houses" have sprung up, and building promoters have built complete suburban developments with them. How many of these homes have been erected it is, of course, impossible to say; the number certainly runs into the thousands.

It was one of the most constructive and far-reaching pieces of work that Bok did during his editorial career— a fact now recognized by all architects. Shortly before

Stanford White passed away, he wrote: "I firmly believe that Edward Bok has more completely influenced American domestic architecture for the better than any man in this generation. When he began, I was short-sighted enough to discourage him, and refused to co-operate with him. If Bok came to me now, I would not only make plans for him, but I would waive any fee for them in retribution for my early mistake."

Bok then turned to the subject of the garden for the small house, and the development of the grounds around the homes which he had been instrumental in putting on the earth. He encountered no opposition here. The publication of small gardens for small houses finally ran into hundreds of pages, the magazine supplying planting plans and full directions as to when and how to plant— this time without cost.

Next the editor decided to see what he could do for the better and simpler furnishing of the small American home. Here was a field almost limitless in possible improvement, but he wanted to approach it in a new way. The best method baffled him until one day he met a woman friend who told him that she was on her way to a funeral at a friend's home.

"I didn't know you were so well acquainted with Mrs. S——," said Bok.

"I wasn't, as a matter of fact," replied the woman. "I'll be perfectly frank; I am going to the funeral just to see how Mrs. S——'s house is furnished. She was always thought to have great taste, you know, and, whether you know it or not, a woman is always keen to look into another woman's home."

Bok realized that he had found the method of presentation for his interior-furnishing plan if he could secure photographs of the most carefully furnished homes in America. He immediately employed the best available expert, and within six months there came to him an assorted collection of over a thousand photographs of well-furnished rooms. The best were selected, and a series of photographic pages called "Inside of 100 Homes" was begun. The editor's woman friend had correctly pointed the way to him, for this series won for his magazine the enviable distinction of being the first magazine of standing to reach the then marvellous record of a circulation of one million copies a month. The editions containing the series were sold out as fast as they could be printed.

The editor followed this up with another successful series, again pictorial. He realized that to explain good taste in furnishing by text was almost impossible. So he started a series of all-picture pages called "Good Taste and Bad Taste." He presented a chair that was bad in lines and either useless or uncomfortable to sit in, and explained where and why it was bad; and then put a good chair next to it, and explained where and why it was good.

The lesson to the eye was simply and directly effective; the pictures told their story as no printed word could have done, and furniture manufacturers and dealers all over the country, feeling the pressure from their customers, began to put on the market the tables, chairs, divans, bedsteads, and dressing-tables which the magazine was portraying as examples of good taste. It was amazing that, within five years, the physical appearance of domestic furniture in the stores completely changed.

The next undertaking was a systematic plan for improving the pictures on the walls of the American home. Bok was employing the best artists of the day: Edwin A. Abbey, Howard Pyle, Charles Dana Gibson, W. L. Taylor, Albert Lynch, Will H. Low, W. T. Smedley, Irving R. Wiles, and others. As his magazine was rolled to go through the mails, the pictures naturally suffered; Bok therefore decided to print a special edition of each important picture that he published, an edition on plate-paper, without text, and offered to his readers at ten cents a copy. Within a year he had sold nearly one hundred thousand copies, such pictures as W. L. Taylor's "The Hanging of the Crane" and "Home-Keeping Hearts" being particularly popular.

Pictures were difficult to advertise successfully; it was before the full-color press had become practicable for rapid magazine work; and even the large-page black-and-white reproductions which Bok could give in his magazine did not, of course, show the beauty of the original paintings, the majority of which were in full color. He accordingly made arrangements with art publishers to print his pictures in their original colors; then he determined to give the public an opportunity to see what the pictures themselves looked like.

He asked his art editor to select the two hundred and fifty best pictures and frame them. Then he engaged the art gallery of the Philadelphia Art Club, and advertised an exhibition of the original paintings. No admission was charged. The gallery was put into gala attire, and the pictures were well hung. The exhibition, which was continued for two weeks, was visited by over fifteen thousand persons.

His success here induced Bok to take the collection to New York. The galleries of the American Art Association were offered him, but he decided to rent the ballroom of the Hotel Waldorf. The hotel was then new; it was the talk not only of the town but of the country, while the ballroom had been pictured far and wide. It would have a publicity value. He could secure the room for only four days, but he determined to make the most of the short time. The exhibition was well advertised; a "private view" was given the evening before the opening day, and when, at nine o'clock the following morning, the doors of the exhibition were thrown open, over a thousand persons were waiting in line.

The hotel authorities had to resort to a special cordon of police to handle the crowds, and within four days over seventeen thousand persons had seen the pictures. On the last evening it was after midnight before the doors could be closed to the waiting-line. Boston was next visited, and there, at the Art Club Gallery, the previous successes were repeated. Within two weeks over twenty-eight thousand persons visited the exhibition.

Other cities now clamored for a sight of the pictures, and it was finally decided to end the exhibitions by a visit to Chicago. The success here exceeded that in any of the other cities. The banquet-hall of the Auditorium Hotel had been engaged; over two thousand persons were continually in a waiting-line outside, and within a week nearly thirty thousand persons pushed and jostled themselves into the gallery. Over eighty thousand persons in all had viewed the pictures in the four cities.

The exhibition was immediately followed by the publication of a portfolio of the ten pictures that had proved the greatest favorites. These were printed on plate-paper and the portfolio was offered by Bok to his readers for one dollar. The first thousand sets were exhausted within a fortnight. A second thousand were printed, and these were quickly sold out.

Bok's next enterprise was to get his pictures into the homes of the country on a larger scale; he determined to work through the churches. He selected the fifty best pictures, made them into a set and offered first a hundred sets to selected schools, which were at once taken. Then he offered two hundred and fifty sets to churches to sell at their fairs. The managers were to promise to erect a *Ladies' Home Journal* booth (which Bok knew, of course, would be most effective advertising), and the pictures were to sell at twenty-five and fifty cents each, with some at a dollar each. The set was offered to the churches for five dollars: the actual cost of reproduction and expressage. On the day after the publication of the magazine containing the offer, enough telegraphic orders were received to absorb the entire edition. A second edition was immediately printed; and finally ten editions, four thousand sets in all, were absorbed before the demand was filled. By this method, two hundred thousand pictures had been introduced into American homes, and over one hundred and fifty thousand dollars in money had been raised by the churches as their portion.

But all this was simply to lead up to the realization of Bok's cherished dream: the reproduction, in enormous numbers, of the greatest pictures in the world in their original colors. The plan, however, was not for the moment feasible: the cost of the four-color process was at that time prohibitive, and Bok had to abandon it. But he never lost sight of it. He knew the hour would come when he could carry it out, and he bided his time.

It was not until years later that his opportunity came, when he immediately made up his mind to seize it. The magazine had installed a battery of four-color presses; the color-work in the periodical was attracting universal attention, and after all stages of experimentation had been passed, Bok decided to make his dream a reality. He sought the co-operation of the owners of the greatest private art galleries in the country: J. Pierpont Morgan, Henry C. Frick, Joseph E. Widener, George W. Elkins, John G. Johnson, Charles P. Taft, Mrs. John L. Gardner, Charles L. Freer, Mrs. Havemeyer, and the owners of the Benjamin Altman Collection, and sought permission to reproduce their greatest paintings.

Although each felt doubtful of the ability of any process adequately to reproduce their masterpieces, the owners heartily co-operated with Bok. But Bok's co-editors discouraged his plan, since it would involve endless labor, the exclusive services of a corps of photographers and engravers, and the employment of the most careful pressmen available in the United States. The editor realized that the obstacles were numerous and that the expense would be enormous; but he felt sure that the American public was ready for his idea. And early in 1912 he announced his series and began its publication.

The most wonderful Rembrandt, Velasquez, Turner, Hobbema, Van Dyck, Raphael, Frans Hals, Romney, Gainsborough, Whistler, Corot, Mauve, Vermeer, Fragonard, Botticelli, and Titian reproductions followed in such rapid succession as fairly to daze the magazine readers. Four pictures were given in each number, and the faithfulness of the reproductions astonished even their owners. The success of the series was beyond Bok's own best hopes. He was printing and selling one and three-quarter million copies of each issue of his magazine; and before he was through he had presented to American homes throughout the breadth of the country over seventy million reproductions of forty separate masterpieces of art.

The dream of years had come true.

Bok had begun with the exterior of the small American house and made an impression upon it; he had brought the love of flowers into the hearts of thousands of small householders who had never thought they could have an artistic garden within a small area; he had changed the lines of furniture, and he had put better art on the walls of these homes. He had conceived a full-rounded scheme, and he had carried it out.

It was a peculiar satisfaction to Bok that Theodore Roosevelt once summed up this piece of work in these words: "Bok is the only man I ever heard of who changed, for the better, the architecture of an entire nation, and he did it so quickly and yet so effectively that we didn't know it was begun before it was finished. That is a mighty big job for one man to have done."

CHAPTER XXII

AN ADVENTURE IN CIVIC AND PRIVATE ART

EDWARD BOK now turned his attention to those influences of a more public nature which he felt could contribute to elevate the standard of public taste.

He was surprised, on talking with furnishers of homes, to learn to what extent women whose husbands had recently acquired means would refer to certain styles of decoration and hangings which they had seen in the Pullman parlor-cars. He had never seriously regarded the influence of the furnishing of these cars upon the travelling public; now he realized that, in a decorative sense, they were a distinct factor and a very unfortunate one.

For in those days, twenty years ago, the decoration of the Pullman parlor-car was atrocious. Colors were in riotous discord; every foot of wood-panelling was carved and ornamented, nothing being left of the grain of even the most beautiful woods; gilt was recklessly laid on everywhere regardless of its fitness or relation. The hangings in the cars were not only in bad taste, but distinctly unsanitary; the heaviest velvets and showiest plushes were used; mirrors with bronzed and red-plushed frames were the order of the day; cord portières, lambrequins, and tasselled fringes were still in vogue in these cars. It was a veritable riot of the worst conceivable ideas; and it was this standard that these women of the new-money class were accepting and introducing into their homes!

Bok wrote an editorial calling attention to these facts. The Pullman Company paid no attention to it, but the railroad journals did. With one accord they seized the cudgel which Bok had raised, and a series of hammerings began. The Pullman conductors began to report to their division chiefs that the passengers were criticising the cars, and the company at last woke up. It issued a cynical rejoinder; whereupon Bok wrote another editorial, and the railroad journals once more joined in the chorus.

The president of a large Western railroad wrote to Bok that he agreed absolutely with his position, and asked whether he had any definite suggestions to offer for the improvement of some new cars which they were about to order. Bok engaged two of the best architects and decorators in the country, and submitted the results to the officials of the railroad company, who approved of them heartily. The Pullman Company did not take very kindly, however, to suggestions thus brought to them. But a current had been started; the attention of the travelling public had been drawn for the first time to the wretched decoration of the cars; and public sentiment was beginning to be vocal.

The first change came when a new dining-car on the Chicago, Burlington and Quincy Railroad suddenly appeared. It was an artistically treated Flemish-oak-panelled car with longitudinal beams and cross-beams, giving the impression of a ceiling-beamed room. Between the "beams" was a quiet tone of deep yellow.

The sides of the car were wainscoting of plain surface done in a Flemish stain rubbed down to a dull finish. The grain of the wood was allowed to serve as decoration; there was no carv:ng.   The whole tone of the car was that of the rich color of the sunflower.   The effect upon the travelling public was instantaneous.   Every passenger commented favorably on the car.

The Atchison, Topeka and Santa Fé Railroad now followed suit by introducing a new Pullman chair-car. The hideous and germ-laden plush or velvet curtains were gone, and leather hangings of a rich tone took their place.   All the grill-work of a bygone age was missing; likewise the rope curtains.   The woods were left to show the grain; no carving was visible anywhere. The car was a relief to the eye, beautiful and simple, and easy to keep clean.   Again the public observed, and expressed its pleasure.

The Pullman people now saw the drift, and wisely reorganized their decorative department.   Only those who remember the Pullman parlor-car of twenty years ago can realize how long a step it is from the atrociously decorated, unsanitary vehicle of that day to the simple car of to-day.

It was only a step from the Pullman car to the landscape outside, and Bok next decided to see what he could do toward eliminating the hideous bill-board advertisements which defaced the landscape along the lines of the principal roads.   He found a willing ally in this idea in Mr. J. Horace McFarland, of Harrisburg, Pennsylvania, one of the most skilful photographers in the country, and the president of The American Civic

Association. McFarland and Bok worked together; they took innumerable photographs, and began to publish them, calling public attention to the intrusion upon the public eye.

Page after page appeared in the magazine, and after a few months these roused public discussion as to legal control of this class of advertising. Bok meanwhile called the attention of women's clubs and other civic organizations to the question, and urged that they clean their towns of the obnoxious bill-boards. Legislative measures regulating the size, character, and location of bill-boards were introduced in various States, a tax on each bill-board was suggested in other States, and the agitation began to bear fruit.

Bok now called upon his readers in general to help by offering a series of prizes totalling several thousands of dollars for two photographs, one showing a fence, barn, or outbuilding painted with an advertisement or having a bill-board attached to it, or a field with a bill-board in it, and a second photograph of the same spot showing the advertisement removed, with an accompanying affidavit of the owner of the property, legally attested, asserting that the advertisement had been permanently removed. Hundreds of photographs poured in, scores of prizes were awarded, the results were published, and requests came in for a second series of prizes, which were duly awarded.

While Bok did not solve the problem of bill-board advertising, and while in some parts of the country it is a more flagrant nuisance to-day than ever before, he had started the first serious agitation against bill-board advertising of bad design, detrimental, from its location, to landscape beauty. He succeeded in getting rid of a huge bill-board which had been placed at the most picturesque spot at Niagara Falls; and hearing of "the largest advertisement sign in the world" to be placed on the rim of the Grand Canyon of the Colorado, he notified the advertisers that a photograph of the sign, if it was erected, would be immediately published in the magazine and the attention of the women of America called to the defacement of one of the most impressive and beautiful scenes in the world. The article to be advertised was a household commodity, purchased by women; and the owners realized that the proposed advertisement would not be to the benefit of their product. The sign was abandoned.

Of course the advertisers whose signs were shown in the magazine immediately threatened the withdrawal of their accounts from *The Ladies' Home Journal*, and the proposed advertiser at the Grand Canyon, whose business was conspicuous in each number of the magazine, became actively threatening. But Bok contended that the one proposition had absolutely no relation to the other, and that if concerns advertised in the magazine simply on the basis of his editorial policy toward bill-board advertising, it was, to say the least, not a sound basis for advertising. No advertising account was ever actually withdrawn.

In their travels about, Mr. McFarland and Bok began to note the disreputably untidy spots which various municipalities allowed in the closest proximity to the centre of their business life, in the most desirable residential sections, and often adjacent to the most important municipal buildings and parks. It was decided to select a dozen cities, pick out the most flagrant instances of spots which were not only an eyesore and a disgrace from a municipal standpoint, but a menace to health and meant a depreciation of real-estate value.

Lynn, Massachusetts, was the initial city chosen, a number of photographs were taken, and the first of a series of "Dirty Cities" was begun in the magazine. The effect was instantaneous. The people of Lynn rose in protest, and the municipal authorities threatened suit against the magazine; the local newspapers were virulent in their attacks. Without warning, they argued, Bok had held up their city to disgrace before the entire country; the attack was unwarranted; in bad taste; every citizen in Lynn should thereafter cease to buy the magazine, and so the criticisms ran. In answer Bok merely pointed to the photographs; to the fact that the camera could not lie, and that if he had misrepresented conditions he was ready to make amends.

Of course the facts could not be gainsaid; local pride was aroused, and as a result not only were the advertised "dirty spots" cleaned up, but the municipal authorities went out and hunted around for other spots in the city, not knowing what other photographs Bok might have had taken.

Trenton, New Jersey, was the next example, and the same storm of public resentment broke loose—with exactly the same beneficial results in the end to the city. Wilkes-Barre, Pennsylvania, was the third one of America's "dirty cities." Here public anger rose particularly high, the magazine practically being barred from the news-stands. But again the result was to the lasting benefit of the community.

Memphis, Tennessee, came next, but here a different spirit was met. Although some resentment was expressed, the general feeling was that a service had been rendered the city, and that the only wise and practical solution was for the city to meet the situation. · The result here was a group of municipal buildings costing millions of dollars, photographs of which *The Ladies' Home Journal* subsequently published with gratification to itself and to the people of Memphis.

Cities throughout the country now began to look around to see whether they had dirty spots within their limits, not knowing when the McFarland photographers might visit them. Bok received letters from various municipalities calling his attention to the fact that they were cognizant of spots in their cities and were cleaning up, and asking that, if he had photographs of these spots, they should not be published.

It happened that in two such instances Bok had already prepared sets of photographs for publication. These he sent to the mayors of the respective cities, stating that if they would return them with an additional set showing the spots cleaned up there would be no occasion for their publication. In both cases this was done. Atlanta, Georgia; New Haven, Connecticut; Pittsburgh, Cincinnati, and finally Bok's own city of Philadelphia were duly chronicled in the magazine; local storms broke and calmed down—with the spots in every instance improved.

It was an interesting experiment in photographic civics. The pity of it is that more has not been done along this and similar lines.

The time now came when Bok could demonstrate the willingness of his own publishing company to do what it could to elevate the public taste in art. With the increasing circulation of *The Ladies' Home Journal* and of *The Saturday Evening Post* the business of the company had grown to such dimensions that in 1908 plans for a new building were started. For purposes of air and light the vicinity of Independence Square was selected. Mr. Curtis purchased an entire city block facing the square, and the present huge but beautiful publication building was conceived.

Bok strongly believed that good art should find a place in public buildings where large numbers of persons might find easy access to it. The proximity of the proposed new structure to historic Independence Hall and the adjacent buildings would make it a focal point for visitors from all parts of the country and the world. The opportunity presented itself to put good art, within the comprehension of a large public, into the new building, and Bok asked permission of Mr. Curtis to introduce a strong note of mural decoration. The idea commended itself to Mr. Curtis as adding an attraction to the building and a contribution to public art.

The great public dining-room, seating over seven hundred persons, on the top floor of the building, affording unusual lighting facilities, was first selected; and Maxfield Parrish was engaged to paint a series of seventeen panels to fill the large spaces between the windows and

EDWARD BOK AS EDITOR OF "THE LADIES' HOME JOURNAL" IN HIS PHILADELPHIA OFFICE

Pronounced by architects to be one of the most successfully beautiful offices in America

an unusually large wall space at the end of the room. Parrish contracted to give up all other work and devote himself to the commission which attracted him greatly.

For over a year he made sketches, and finally the theme was decided upon: a bevy of youths and maidens in gala costume, on their way through gardens and along terraces to a great fête, with pierrots and dancers and musicians on the main wall space. It was to be a picture of happy youth and sunny gladness. Five years after the conception of the idea the final panel was finished and installed in the dining-room, where the series has since been admired by the thirty to fifty thousand visitors who come to the Curtis Building each year from foreign lands and from every State in America. No other scheme of mural decoration was ever planned on so large a scale for a commercial building, or so successfully carried out.

The great wall space of over one thousand square feet, unobstructed by a single column, in the main foyer of the building was decided upon as the place for the pivotal note to be struck by some mural artist. After looking carefully over the field, Bok finally decided upon Edwin A. Abbey. He took a steamer and visited Abbey in his English home. The artist was working on his canvases for the State capitol at Harrisburg, and it was agreed that the commission for the Curtis Building was to follow the completion of the State work.

"What subject have you in mind?" asked Abbey.

"None," replied Bok. "That is left entirely to you."

The artist and his wife looked at each other in bewilderment.

"Rather unusual," commented Abbey. "You have nothing in mind at all?"

"Nothing, except to get the best piece of work you have ever done," was the assurance.

Poor Abbey! His life had been made so tortuous by suggestions, ideas, yes, demands made upon him in the work of the Harrisburg panels upon which he was engaged, that a commission in which he was to have free scope, his brush full leeway, with no one making suggestions but himself and Mrs. Abbey, seemed like a dream. When he explained this, Bok assured him that was exactly what he was offering him: a piece of work, the subject to be his own selection, with the assurance of absolute liberty to carry out his own ideas. Never was an artist more elated.

"Then, I'll give you the best piece of work of my life," said Abbey.

"Perhaps there is some subject which you have long wished to paint rather than any other," asked Bok, "that might fit our purpose admirably?"

There was: a theme that he had started as a fresco for Mrs. Abbey's bedroom. But it would not answer this purpose at all, although he confessed he would rather paint it than any subject in the realm of all literature and art.

"And the subject?" asked Bok.

"The Grove of Academe," replied Abbey, and the eyes of the artist and his wife were riveted on the editor.

"With Plato and his disciples?" asked Bok.

"The same," said Abbey. "But you see it wouldn't fit."

"Wouldn't fit?" echoed Bok. "Why, it's the very thing."

Abbey and his wife were now like two happy children. Mrs. Abbey fetched the sketches which her husband had begun years ago, and when Bok saw them he was delighted. He realized at once that conditions and choice would conspire to produce Abbey's greatest piece of mural work.

The arrangements were quickly settled; the Curtis architect had accompanied Bok to explain the architectural possibilities to Abbey, and when the artist bade good-by to the two at the railroad station, his last words were:

"Bok, you are going to get the best Abbey in the world."

And Mrs. Abbey echoed the prophecy !

But Fate intervened. On the day after Abbey had stretched his great canvas in Sargent's studio in London, expecting to begin his work the following week, he suddenly passed away, and what would, in all likelihood, have been Edwin Abbey's mural masterpiece was lost to the world.

Assured of Mrs. Abbey's willingness to have another artist take the theme of the Grove of Academe and carry it out as a mural decoration, Bok turned to Howard Pyle. He knew Pyle had made a study of Plato, and believed that, with his knowledge and love of the work of the Athenian philosopher, a good decoration would result. Pyle was then in Italy; Bok telephoned the painter's home in Wilmington, Delaware, to get his address, only to be told that an hour earlier word had been received by the family that Pyle had been fatally stricken the day before.

Once more Bok went over the field of mural art and decided this time that he would go far afield, and present his idea to Boutet de Monvel, the French decorative artist. Bok had been much impressed with some decorative work by De Monvel which had just been exhibited in New York. By letter he laid the proposition in detail before the artist, asked for a subject, and stipulated that if the details could be arranged the artist should visit the building and see the place and surroundings for himself. After a lengthy correspondence, and sketches submitted and corrected, a plan for what promised to be a most unusual and artistically decorative panel was arrived at.

The date for M. de Monvel's visit to Philadelphia was fixed, a final letter from the artist reached Bok on a Monday morning, in which a few remaining details were satisfactorily cleared up, and a cable was sent assuring De Monvel of the entire satisfaction of the company with his final sketches and arrangements. The following morning Bok picked up his newspaper to read that Boutet de Monvel had suddenly passed away in Paris the previous evening!

Bok, thoroughly bewildered, began to feel as if some fatal star hung over his cherished decoration. Three times in succession he had met the same decree of fate.

He consulted six of the leading mural decorators in America, asking whether they would consent, not in competition, to submit each a finished full-color sketch of the subject which he believed fitted for the place in mind; they could take the Grove of Academe or not, as they chose; the subject was to be of their own selection. Each artist was to receive a generous fee for his sketch, whether accepted or rejected. In due time, the six sketches were received; impartial judges were selected, no names were attached to the sketches, several conferences were held, and all the sketches were rejected!

˙ Bok was still exactly where he started, while the building was nearly complete, with no mural for the large place so insistently demanding it.

He now recalled a marvellous stage-curtain entirely of glass mosaic executed by Louis C. Tiffany, of New York, for the Municipal Theatre at Mexico City. The work had attracted universal attention at its exhibition, art critics and connoisseurs had praised it unstintingly, and Bok decided to experiment in that direction.

Just as the ancient Egyptians and Persians had used glazed brick and tile, set in cement, as their form of wall decoration, so Mr. Tiffany had used favrile glass, set in cement. The luminosity was marvellous; the effect of light upon the glass was unbelievably beautiful, and the colorings obtained were a joy to the senses.

Here was not only a new method in wall decoration, but one that was entirely practicable. Glass would not craze like tiles or mosaic; it would not crinkle as will canvas; it needed no varnish. It would retain its color, freshness, and beauty, and water would readily cleanse it from dust.

He sought Mr. Tiffany, who was enthusiastic over the idea of making an example of his mosaic glass of such dimensions which should remain in this country, and gladly offered to co-operate. But, try as he might, Bok could not secure an adequate sketch for Mr. Tiffany to carry out. Then he recalled that one day while at Maxfield Parrish's summer home in New Hampshire the artist had told him of a dream garden which he would like to construct, not on canvas but in reality. Bok suggested to Parrish that he come to New York. He asked him if he could put his dream garden on canvas. The artist thought he could; in fact, was greatly attracted to the idea; but he knew nothing of mosaic work, and was not particularly attracted by the idea of having his work rendered in that medium.

Bok took Parrish to Mr. Tiffany's studio; the two artists talked together, the glass-worker showed the canvas-painter his work, with the result that the two became enthusiastic to co-operate in trying the experiment. Parrish agreed to make a sketch for Mr. Tiffany's approval, and within six months, after a number of conferences and an equal number of sketches, they were ready to begin the work. Bok only hoped that this time both artists would outlive their commissions!

It was a huge picture to be done in glass mosaic. The space to be filled called for over a million pieces of glass, and for a year the services of thirty of the most skilled artisans would be required. The work had to be done from a series of bromide photographs enlarged to a size hitherto unattempted. But at last the decoration was completed; the finished art piece was placed on exhibition in New York and over seven thousand persons came to see it. The leading art critics pronounced the result to be the most amazing instance of the tone capacity of glass-work ever achieved. It was a veritable wonder-piece, far exceeding the utmost expression of paint and canvas.

For six months a group of skilled artisans worked to take the picture apart in New York, transport it and set it into its place in Philadelphia. But at last it was in place: the wonder-picture in glass of which painters have declared that "mere words are only aggravating in describing this amazing picture." Since that day over one hundred thousand visitors to the building have sat in admiration before it.

The Grove of Academe was to become a Dream Garden, but it was only after six years of incessant effort, with obstacles and interventions almost insurmountable, that the dream became true.

CHAPTER XXIII

THEODORE ROOSEVELT'S INFLUENCE

WHEN the virile figure of Theodore Roosevelt swung down the national highway, Bok was one of thousands of young men who felt strongly the attraction of his personality. Colonel Roosevelt was only five years the senior of the editor; he spoke, therefore, as one of his own years. The energy with which he said and did things appealed to Bok. He made Americanism something more real, more stirring than Bok had ever felt it; he explained national questions in a way that caught Bok's fancy and came within his comprehension. Bok's lines had been cast with many of the great men of the day, but he felt that there was something distinctive about the personality of this man: his method of doing things and his way of saying things. Bok observed everything Colonel Roosevelt did and read everything he wrote.

The editor now sought an opportunity to know personally the man whom he admired. It came at a dinner at the University Club, and Colonel Roosevelt suggested that they meet there the following day for a "talkfest." For three hours the two talked together. The fact that Colonel Roosevelt was of Dutch ancestry interested Bok; that Bok was actually of Dutch birth made a strong appeal to the colonel. With his tremendous breadth of interests, Roosevelt, Bok found, had followed him quite closely in his work, and was familiar with "its high points," as he called them. "We must work for the same ends," said the colonel, "you in your way, I in mine. But our lines are bound to cross. You and I can each become good Americans by giving our best to make America better. With the Dutch stock there is in both of us, there's no limit to what we can do. Let's go to it." Naturally that talk left the two firm friends.

Bok felt somehow that he had been given a new draft of Americanism: the word took on a new meaning for him; it stood for something different, something deeper and finer than before. And every subsequent talk with Roosevelt deepened the feeling and stirred Bok's deepest ambitions. "Go to it, you Dutchman," Roosevelt would say, and Bok *would* go to it. A talk with Roosevelt always left him feeling as if mountains were the easiest things in the world to move.

One of Theodore Roosevelt's arguments which made a deep impression upon Bok was that no man had a right to devote his entire life to the making of money. "You are in a peculiar position," said the man of Oyster Bay one day to Bok; "you are in that happy position where you can make money and do good at the same time. A man wields a tremendous power for good or for evil who is welcomed into a million homes and read with confidence. That's fine, and is all right so far as it goes, and in your case it goes very far. Still, there remains more for you to do. The public has built up for you a personality: now give that personality to whatever interests you in contact with your immediate fellow-men: something in your neighborhood, your city, or your State. With one hand work and write to your national audience: let no fads sway you. Hew close to the line. But, with the other hand, swing into the life immediately around you. Think it over."

Bok did think it over. He was now realizing the dream of his life for which he had worked: his means were sufficient to give his mother every comfort; to install her in the most comfortable surroundings wherever she chose to live; to make it possible for her to spend the winters in the United States and the summers in the Netherlands, and thus to keep in touch with her family and friends in both countries. He had for years toiled unceasingly to reach this point: he felt he had now achieved at least one goal.

He had now turned instinctively to the making of a home for himself. After an engagement of four years he had been married, on October 22, 1896, to Mary Louise Curtis, the only child of Mr. and Mrs. Cyrus H. K. Curtis; two sons had been born to them; he had built and was occupying a house at Merion, Pennsylvania, a suburb six miles from the Philadelphia City Hall. When she was in this country his mother lived with him, and also his brother, and, with a strong belief in life insurance, he had seen to it that his family was provided for in case of personal incapacity or of his demise. In other words, he felt that he had put his own house in order; he had carried out what he felt is every man's duty: to be, first of all, a careful and adequate provider for his family. He was now at the point where he could begin to work for another goal, the goal that he felt so few American men saw: the point in his life where he could retire from the call of duty and follow the call of inclination.

At the age of forty he tried to look ahead and plan out his life as far as he could. Barring unforeseen obstacles, he determined to retire from active business when he reached his fiftieth year, and give the remainder of his life over to those interests and influences which he assumed now as part of his life, and which, at fifty, should seem to him best worth while. He realized that in order to do this he must do two things: he must husband his financial resources and he must begin to accumulate a mental reserve.

The wide public acceptance of the periodical which he edited naturally brought a share of financial success to him. He had experienced poverty, and as he subsequently wrote, in an article called "Why I Believe in Poverty," he was deeply grateful for his experience. He had known what it was to be poor; he had seen others dear to him suffer for the bare necessities; there was, in fact, not a single step on that hard road that he had not travelled. He could, therefore, sympathize with the fullest understanding with those similarly situated, could help as one who knew from practice and not from theory. He realized what a marvellous blessing poverty can be; but as a condition to experience, to derive from it poignant lessons, and then to get out of; not as a condition to stay in.

Of course many said to Bok when he wrote the article in which he expressed these beliefs: "That's all very well; easy enough to say, but how can you get out of it?" Bok realized that he could not definitely show any one the way. No one had shown him. No two persons can find the same way out. Bok determined to lift himself out of poverty because his mother was not born in it, did not belong in it, and could not stand it. That gave him the first essential: a purpose. Then he backed up the purpose with effort and an ever-ready willingness to work, and to work at anything that came his way, no matter what it was, so long as it meant "the way out." He did not pick and choose; he took what came, and did it in the best way he knew how; and when he did not like what he was doing he still did it as well as he could while he was doing it, but always with an eye single to the purpose not to do it any longer than was strictly necessary. He used every rung in the ladder as a rung to the one above. He always gave more than his particular position or salary asked for. He never worked by the clock; always by the job; and saw that it was well done regardless of the time it took to do it. This meant effort, of course, untiring, ceaseless, unsparing; and it meant work, hard as nails.

He was particularly careful never to live up to his income; and as his income increased he increased not the percentage of expenditure but the percentage of saving. Thrift was, of course, inborn with him as a Dutchman, but the necessity for it as a prime factor in life was burned into him by his experience with poverty. But he interpreted thrift not as a trait of niggardliness, but as Theodore Roosevelt interpreted it: common sense applied to spending.

At forty, therefore, he felt he had learned the first

essential to carrying out his idea of retirement at fifty.

The second essential—varied interests outside of his business upon which he could rely on relinquishing his duties—he had not cultivated. He had quite naturally, in line with his belief that concentration means success, immersed himself in his business to the exclusion of almost everything else. He felt that he could now spare a certain percentage of his time to follow Theodore Roosevelt's ideas and let the breezes of other worlds blow over him. In that way he could do as Roosevelt suggested and as Bok now firmly believed was right: he could develop himself along broader lines, albeit the lines of his daily work were broadening in and of themselves, and he could so develop a new set of inner resources upon which he could draw when the time came to relinquish his editorial position.

He saw, on every side, the pathetic figures of men who could not let go after their greatest usefulness was past; of other men who dropped before they realized their arrival at the end of the road; and, most pathetic of all, of men who having retired, but because of lack of inner resources did not know what to do with themselves, had become a trial to themselves, their families, and their communities.

Bok decided that, given health and mental freshness, he would say good-by to his public before his public might decide to say good-by to him. So, at forty, he candidly faced the facts of life and began to prepare himself for his retirement at fifty under circumstances that would be of his own making and not those of others.

And thereby Edward Bok proved that he was still,

by instinct, a Dutchman, and had not in his thirty-four years of residence in the United States become so thoroughly Americanized as he believed.

However, it was an American, albeit of Dutch extraction, one whom he believed to be the greatest American in his own day, who had set him thinking and shown him the way.

CHAPTER XXIV

THEODORE ROOSEVELT'S ANONYMOUS EDITORIAL WORK

WHILE Theodore Roosevelt was President of the United States, Bok was sitting one evening talking with him, when suddenly Mr. Roosevelt turned to him and said with his usual emphasis: "Bok, I envy you your power with your public."

The editor was frankly puzzled.

"That is a strange remark from the President of the United States," he replied.

"You may think so," was the rejoinder. "But listen. When do I get the ear of the public? In its busiest moments. My messages are printed in the newspapers and read hurriedly, mostly by men in trolleys or railroad-cars. Women hardly ever read them, I should judge. Now you are read in the evening by the fireside or under the lamp, when the day's work is over and the mind is at rest from other things and receptive to what you offer. Don't you see where you have it on me?"

This diagnosis was keenly interesting, and while the President talked during the balance of the evening, Bok was thinking. Finally, he said: "Mr. President, I should like to share my power with you."

"How?" asked Mr. Roosevelt.

"You recognize that women do not read your messages; and yet no President's messages ever discussed

more ethical questions that women should know about
and get straight in their minds. As it is, some of your
ideas are not at all understood by them; your strenuous-
life theory, for instance, your factory-law ideas, and particularly your race-suicide arguments. Men don't fully
understand them, for that matter; women certainly do
not."

"I am aware of all that," said the President. "What
is your plan to remedy it?"

"Have a department in my magazine, and explain
your ideas," suggested Bok.

"Haven't time for another thing. You know that,"
snapped back the President. "Wish I had."

"Not to write it, perhaps, yourself," returned Bok.
"But why couldn't you find time to do this: select the
writer here in Washington in whose accuracy you have
the most implicit faith; let him talk with you for one
hour each month on one of those subjects; let him write
out your views, and submit the manuscript to you; and
we will have a department stating exactly how the material is obtained and how far it represents your own
work. In that way, with only an hour's work each
month, you can get your views, correctly stated, before
this vast audience when it is not in trolleys or railroad-
cars."

"But I haven't the hour," answered Roosevelt, impressed, however, as Bok saw. "I have only half an
hour, when I am awake, when I am really idle, and that
is when I am being shaved."

"Well," calmly suggested the editor, "why not two
of those half-hours a month, or perhaps one?"

"What?" answered the President, sitting upright, his teeth flashing but his smile broadening. "You Dutchman, you'd make me work while I'm getting shaved, too?"

"Well," was the answer, "isn't the result worth the effort?"

"Bok, you are absolutely relentless," said the President. "But you're right. The result *would* be worth the effort. What writer have you in mind? You seem to have thought this thing through."

"How about O'Brien? You think well of him?"

(Robert L. O'Brien, now editor of the *Boston Herald*, was then Washington correspondent for the *Boston Transcript* and thoroughly in the President's confidence.)

"Fine," said the President. "I trust O'Brien implicitly. All right, if you can get O'Brien to add it on, I'll try it."

And so the "shaving interviews" were begun; and early in 1906 there appeared in *The Ladies' Home Journal* a department called "The President," with the subtitle: "A Department in which will be presented the attitude of the President on those national questions which affect the vital interests of the home, by a writer intimately acquainted and in close touch with him."

O'Brien talked with Mr. Roosevelt once a month, wrote out the results, the President went over the proofs carefully, and the department was conducted with great success for a year.

But Theodore Roosevelt was again to be the editor of a department in *The Ladies' Home Journal;* this time to be written by himself under the strictest possible anonymity, so closely adhered to that, until this revelation, only five persons have known the authorship.

Feeling that it would be an interesting experiment to see how far Theodore Roosevelt's ideas could stand unsupported by the authority of his vibrant personality, Bok suggested the plan to the colonel. It was just after he had returned from his South American trip. He was immediately interested.

"But how can we keep the authorship really anonymous?" he asked.

"Easily enough," answered Bok, "if you're willing to do the work. Our letters about it must be written in long hand addressed to each other's homes; you must write your manuscript in your own hand; I will copy it in mine, and it will go to the printer in that way. I will personally send you the proofs; you mark your corrections in pencil, and I will copy them in ink; the company will pay me for each article, and I will send you my personal check each month. By this means, the identity of the author will be concealed."

Colonel Roosevelt was never averse to hard work if it was necessary to achieve a result that he felt was worth while.

"All right," wrote the colonel finally. "I'll try—with you!—the experiment for a year: 12 articles. . . . I don't know that I can give your readers satisfaction, but I shall try my very best. I am very glad to be associated with you, anyway. At first I doubted the wisdom of the plan, merely because I doubted whether I could give you just that you wished. I never know what an audience wants: I know what it *ought* to want:

and sometimes I can give it, or make it accept what I think it needs—and sometimes I cannot. But the more I thought over your proposal, the more I liked it. . . . Whether the wine will be good enough to attract without any bush I don't know; and besides, in such cases the fault is not in the wine, but in the fact that the consumers decline to have their attention attracted unless there is a bush!"

In the latter part of 1916 an anonymous department called "Men" was begun in the magazine.

The physical work was great. The colonel punctiliously held to the conditions, and wrote manuscript and letters with his own hand, and Bok carried out his part of the agreement. Nor was this simple, for Colonel Roosevelt's manuscript—particularly when, as in this case, it was written on yellow paper with a soft pencil and generously interlined—was anything but legible. Month after month the two men worked each at his own task. To throw the public off the scent, during the conduct of the department, an article or two by Colonel Roosevelt was published in another part of the magazine under his own name, and in the department itself the anonymous author would occasionally quote himself.

It was natural that the appearance of a department devoted to men in a woman's magazine should attract immediate attention. The department took up the various interests of a man's life, such as real efficiency; his duties as an employer and his usefulness to his employees; the employee's attitude toward his employer; the relations of men and women; a father's relations to his sons and daughters; a man's duty to his community;

the public-school system; a man's relation to his church, and kindred topics.

The anonymity of the articles soon took on interest from the positiveness of the opinions discussed; but so thoroughly had Colonel Roosevelt covered his tracks that, although he wrote in his usual style, in not a single instance was his name connected with the department. Lyman Abbott was the favorite "guess" at first; then after various other public men had been suggested, the newspapers finally decided upon former President Eliot of Harvard University as the writer.

All this intensely interested and amused Colonel Roosevelt and he fairly itched with the desire to write a series of criticisms of his own articles to Doctor Eliot. Bok, however, persuaded the colonel not to spend more physical effort than he was already doing on the articles; for, in addition, he was notating answers on the numerous letters received, and those Bok answered "on behalf of the author."

For a year, the department continued. During all that time the secret of the authorship was known to only one man, besides the colonel and Bok, and their respective wives!

When the colonel sent his last article in the series to Bok, he wrote:

Now that the work is over, I wish most cordially to thank you, my dear fellow, for your unvarying courtesy and kindness. I have not been satisfied with my work. This is the first time I ever tried to write precisely to order, and I am not one of those gifted men who can do so to advantage. Generally I find that the 3,000 words is not the right length

A SPECIMEN OF THEODORE ROOSEVELT'S MANUSCRIPT, WHICH EDWARD BOK COPIED FOR HIS ANONYMOUS DEPARTMENT, "MEN"

and that I wish to use 2,000 or 4,000! And in consequence feel as if I had either padded or mutilated the article. And I am not always able to feel that every month I have something worth saying on a given subject.

But I hope that you have not been too much disappointed.

Bok had not been, and neither had his public!

In the meanwhile, Bok had arranged with Colonel Roosevelt for his reading and advising upon manuscripts of special significance for the magazine. In this work, Colonel Roosevelt showed his customary promptness and thoroughness. A manuscript, no matter how long it might be, was in his hands scarcely forty-eight hours, more generally twenty-four, before it was read, a report thereon written, and the article on its way back. His reports were always comprehensive and invariably interesting. There was none of the cut-and-dried flavor of the opinion of the average "reader"; he always put himself into the report, and, of course, that meant a warm personal touch. If he could not encourage the publication of a manuscript, his reasons were always fully given, and invariably without personal bias.

On one occasion Bok sent him a manuscript which he was sure was, in its views, at variance with the colonel's beliefs. The colonel, he knew, felt strongly on the subject, and Bok wondered what would be his criticism. The report came back promptly. He reviewed the article carefully and ended: "Of course, this is all at variance with my own views. I believe thoroughly and completely that this writer is all wrong. And yet, from his side of the case, I am free to say that he makes

SAGAMORE HILL. *April 26ᵗʰ 1916*

This is a really noteworthy story — a profoundly touching story — of the Americanizing of an immigrant girl, who between babyhood and young womanhood leaps over a space which in all cultural and humanizing essentials is far more important than the distance painfully traversed by her forefathers during its preceding thousand years. When we tend to grow disheartened over some of the developments of our American civilization, it is well worth while seeing what this same civilization holds for starved and noble souls who have elsewhere been denied what here we hold to be, as a matter of course, rights free to all — altho we do not, as we should do, make these rights accessible to all who are willing with resolute earnestness to strive for them. I most cordially commend this story.

Theodore Roosevelt

ONE OF THEODORE ROOSEVELT'S "REPORTS" AS A READER OF
SPECIAL MANUSCRIPTS

out the best case I have read anywhere. I think a magazine should present both sides of all questions; and if you want to present this side, I should strongly recommend that you do so with this article."

Not long after, Bok decided to induce Colonel Roosevelt to embark upon an entirely new activity, and negotiations were begun (alas, too late! for it was in the autumn of 1918), which, owing to their tentative character, were never made public. Bok told Colonel Roosevelt that he wanted to invest twenty-five thousand dollars a year in American boyhood—the boyhood that he felt twenty years hence would be the manhood of America, and that would actually solve the problems with which we were now grappling.

Although, all too apparently, he was not in his usual vigorous health, Colonel Roosevelt was alert in a moment.

"Fine!" he said, with his teeth gleaming. "Couldn't invest better anywhere. How are you going to do it?"

"By asking you to assume the active headship of the National Boy Scouts of America, and paying you that amount each year as a fixed salary."

The colonel looked steadily ahead for a moment, without a word, and then with the old Roosevelt smile wreathing his face and his teeth fairly gleaming, he turned to his "tempter," as he called him, and said:

"Do you know that was very well put? Yes, sir, very well put."

"Yes?" answered Bok. "Glad you think so. But how about your acceptance of the idea?"

"That's another matter; quite another matter. How about the organization itself? There are men in it that don't approve of me at all, you know," he said.

Bok explained that the organization knew nothing of his offer; that it was entirely unofficial. It was

purely a personal thought. He believed the Boy
Scouts of America needed a leader; that the colonel
was the one man in the United States fitted by every
natural quality to be that leader; that the Scouts would
rally around him, and that, at his call, instead of four
hundred thousand Scouts, as there were then, the organization would grow into a million and more. Bok
further explained that he believed his connection with
the national organization was sufficient, if Colonel Roosevelt would favorably consider such a leadership, to warrant him in presenting it to the national officers; and
he was inclined to believe they would welcome the opportunity. He could not assure the colonel of this!
He had no authority for saying they would; but was
Colonel Roosevelt receptive to the idea?

At first, the colonel could not see it. But he went
over the ground as thoroughly as a half-hour talk permitted; and finally the opportunity for doing a piece of
constructive work that might prove second to none that
he had ever done, made its appeal.

"You mean for me to be the active head?" asked the
colonel.

"Could you be anything else, colonel?" answered
Bok.

"Quite so," said the colonel. "That's about right.
Do you know," he pondered, "I think Edie (Mrs. Roosevelt) might like me to do something like that. She
would figure it would keep me out of mischief in 1920,"
and the colonel's smile spread over his face.

"Bok," he at last concluded, "do you know, after
all, I think you've said something! Let's think it over.

Let's see how I get along with this trouble of mine. I am not sure, you know, how far I can go in the future. Not at all sure, you know—not at all. That last trip of mine to South America was a bit too much. Shouldn't have done it, you know. I know it now. Well, as I say, let's both think it over and through; I will, gladly and most carefully. There's much in what you say; it's a great chance; I'd love doing it. By Jove! it would be wonderful to rally a million boys for real Americanism, as you say. It looms up as I think it over. Suppose we let it simmer for a month or two."

And so it was left—for "a month or two." It was to be forever—unfortunately. Edward Bok has always felt that the most worth-while idea that ever came to him had, for some reason he never could understand, come too late. He felt, as he will always feel, that the boys of America had lost a national leader that might have led them—where *would* have been the limit?

CHAPTER XXV

THE PRESIDENT AND THE BOY

ONE of the incidents connected with Edward Bok that Theodore Roosevelt never forgot was when Bok's eldest boy chose the colonel as a Christmas present. And no incident better portrays the wonderful character of the colonel than did his remarkable response to the compliment.

A vicious attack of double pneumonia had left the heart of the boy very weak—and Christmas was close by! So the father said:

"It's a quiet Christmas for you this year, boy. Suppose you do this: think of the one thing in the world that you would rather have than anything else and I'll give you that, and that will have to be your Christmas."

"I know now," came the instant reply.

"But the world is a big place, and there are lots of things in it, you know."

"I know that," said the boy, "but this is something I have wanted for a long time, and would rather have than anything else in the world." And he looked as if he meant it.

"Well, out with it, then, if you're so sure."

And to the father's astonished ears came this request:

"Take me to Washington as soon as my heart is all

right, introduce me to President Roosevelt, and let me shake hands with him."

"All right," said the father, after recovering from his surprise. "I'll see whether I can fix it." And that morning a letter went to the President saying that he had been chosen as a Christmas present. Naturally, any man would have felt pleased, no matter how high his station, and for Theodore Roosevelt, father of boys, the message had a special appeal.

The letter had no sooner reached Washington than back came an answer, addressed not to the father but to the boy! It read:

The White House, Washington.
November 13th, 1907.

DEAR CURTIS:
Your father has just written me, and I want him to bring you on and shake hands with me as soon as you are well enough to travel. Then I am going to give you, myself, a copy of the book containing my hunting trips since I have been President; unless you will wait until the new edition, which contains two more chapters, is out. If so, I will send it to you, as this new edition probably won't be ready when you come on here.

Give my warm regards to your father and mother.

Sincerely yours,
THEODORE ROOSEVELT.

Here was joy serene! But the boy's heart had acted queerly for a few days, and so the father wrote, thanked the President, and said that as soon as the heart moderated a bit the letter would be given the boy. It was a rare bit of consideration that now followed. No sooner had the father's letter reached the White House than an answer came back by first post—this time with a special-delivery stamp on it. It was Theodore Roosevelt, the father, who wrote this time; his mind and time filled with affairs of state, and yet full of tender thoughtfulness for a little boy:

DEAR MR. BOK:—

I have your letter of the 16th instant. I hope the little fellow will soon be all right. Instead of giving him my letter, give him a message from me based on the letter, if that will be better for him. Tell Mrs. Bok how deeply Mrs. Roosevelt and I sympathize with her. We know just how she feels.

Sincerely yours,

THEODORE ROOSEVELT.

"That's pretty fine consideration," said the father. He got the letter during a business conference and he read it aloud to the group of business men. Some there were in that group who keenly differed with the President on national issues, but they were all fathers, and two of the sturdiest turned and walked to the window as they said: "Yes, that *is* fine!"

Then came the boy's pleasure when he was handed the letter; the next few days were spent inditing an answer to "my friend, the President." At last the momentous epistle seemed satisfactory, and off to the busy presidential desk went the boyish note, full of thanks and assurances that he would come just as soon as he could, and that Mr. Roosevelt must not get impatient!

The "soon as he could" time, however, did not come as quickly as all had hoped!—a little heart pumped for days full of oxygen and accelerated by hypodermic injections is slow to mend. But the President's framed letter, hanging on the spot on the wall first seen in the morning, was a daily consolation.

Then, in March, although four months after the promise—and it would not have been strange, in his busy life, for the President to have forgotten or at least overlooked it—on the very day that the book was published came a special "large-paper" copy of *The Outdoor Pastimes of an American Hunter*, and on the fly-leaf there greeted the boy, in the President's own hand:

To MASTER CURTIS BOK,
    With the best wishes of his friend,
                              THEODORE ROOSEVELT.
March 11, 1908.

The boy's cup was now full, and so said his letter to the President.   And the President wrote back to the father: "I am really immensely amused and interested, and shall be mighty glad to see the little fellow."

In the spring, on a beautiful May day, came the great moment.   The mother had to go along, the boy insisted, to see the great event, and so the trio found themselves shaking the hand of the President's secretary at the White House.

"Oh, the President is looking for you, all right," he said to the boy, and then the next moment the three were in a large room.   Mr. Roosevelt, with beaming face, was already striding across the room, and with a "Well, well, and so this is my friend Curtis!" the two stood looking into each other's faces, each fairly wreathed in smiles, and each industriously shaking the hand of the other.

"Yes, Mr. President, I'm mighty glad to see you!" said the boy.

"I am glad to see you, Curtis," returned Mr. Roosevelt.

Then there came a white rose from the presidential desk for the mother, but after that father and mother might as well have faded away. Nobody existed save the President and the boy. The anteroom was full; in the Cabinet-room a delegation waited to be addressed. But affairs of state were at a complete standstill as, with boyish zeal, the President became oblivious to all but the boy before him.

"Now, Curtis, I've got some pictures here of bears that a friend of mine has just shot. Look at that whopper, fifteen hundred pounds—that's as much as a horse weighs, you know. Now, my friend shot him" —and it was a toss-up who was the more keenly interested, the real boy or the man-boy, as picture after picture came out and bear adventure crowded upon the heels of bear adventure.

"Gee, he's a corker, all right!" came from the boy at one point, and then, from the President: "That's right, he *is* a corker. Now you see his head here"— and then both were off again.

The private secretary came in at this point and whispered in the President's ear.

"I know, I know. I'll see him later. Say that I am very busy now." And the face beamed with smiles.

"Now, Mr. President—" began the father.

"No, sir; no, sir; not at all. Affairs can wait. This is a long-standing engagement between Curtis and me, and that must come first. Isn't that so, Curtis?"

Of course the boy agreed.

Suddenly the boy looked around the room and said:

"Where's your gun, Mr. President?   Got it here?"

"No," laughingly came from the President, "but I'll tell you"—and then the two heads were together again.

A moment for breath-taking came, and the boy said:

"Aren't you ever afraid of being shot?"

"You mean while I am hunting?"

"Oh, no.   I mean as President."

"No," replied the smiling President.   "I'll tell you, Curtis; I'm too busy to think about that.   I have too many things to do to bother about anything of that sort.   When I was in battle I was always too anxious to get to the front to think about the shots.   And here—well, here I'm too busy too.   Never think about it. But I'll tell you, Curtis, there are some men down there," pointing out of the window in the direction of the capitol, "called the Congress, and if they would only give me the four battleships I want, I'd be perfectly willing to have any one take a crack at me."   Then, for the first time recognizing the existence of the parents, the President said: "And I don't know but if they did pick me off I'd be pretty well ahead of the game."

Just in that moment only did the boy-knowing President get a single inch above the boy-interest.   It was astonishing to see the natural accuracy with which the man gauged the boy-level.

"Now, how would you like to see a bear, Curtis?" came next.   "I know where there's a beauty, twelve hundred pounds."

"Must be some bear!" interjected the boy.

"That's what it is," put in the President.   "Regular

cinnamon-brown type"—and then off went the talk to the big bear at the Washington "Zoo" where the President was to send the boy.

Then, after a little: "Now, Curtis, see those men over there in that room. They've travelled from all parts of the country to come here at my invitation, and I've got to make a little speech to them, and I'll do that while you go off to see the bear."

And then the hand came forth to say good-by. The boy put his in it, each looked into the other's face, and on neither was there a place big enough to put a ten-cent piece that was not wreathed in smiles. "He certainly is all right," said the boy to the father, looking wistfully after the President.

Almost to the other room had the President gone when he, too, instinctively looked back to find the boy following him with his eyes. He stopped, wheeled around, and then the two instinctively sought each other again. The President came back, the boy went forward. This time each held out both hands, and as each looked once more into the other's eyes a world of complete understanding was in both faces, and every looker-on smiled with them.

"Good-by, Curtis," came at last from the President.

"Good-by, Mr. President," came from the boy.

Then, with another pump-handly shake and with a "Gee, but he's great, all right!" the boy went out to see the cinnamon-bear at the "Zoo," and to live it all over in the days to come.

Two boy-hearts had met, although one of them belonged to the President of the United States.

CHAPTER XXVI

THE LITERARY BACK-STAIRS

HIS complete absorption in the magazine work now compelled Bok to close his newspaper syndicate in New York and end the writing of his weekly newspaper literary letter. He decided, however, to transfer to the pages of his magazine his idea of making the American public more conversant with books and authors. Accordingly, he engaged Robert Bridges (the present editor of *Scribner's Magazine*) to write a series of conversational book-talks under his nom de plume of "Droch." Later, this was supplemented by the engagement of Hamilton W. Mabie, who for years reviewed the newest books.

In almost every issue of the magazine there appeared also an article addressed to the literary novice. Bok was eager, of course, to attract the new authors to the magazine; but, particularly, he had in mind the correction of the popular notion, then so prevalent (less so to-day, fortunately, but still existent), that only the manuscripts of famous authors were given favorable reading in editorial offices; that in these offices there really existed a clique, and that unless the writer knew the literary back-stairs he had a slim chance to enter and be heard.

In the minds of these misinformed writers, these back-stairs are gained by "knowing the editor" or through "having some influence with him." These writers have conclusively settled two points in their own minds: first, that an editor is antagonistic to the struggling writer; and, second, that a manuscript sent in the ordinary manner to an editor never reaches him. Hence, some "influence" is necessary, and they set about to secure it.

Now, the truth is, of course, that there are no "literary back-stairs" to the editorial office of the modern magazine. There cannot be. The making of a modern magazine is a business proposition; the editor is there to make it pay. He can do this only if he is of service to his readers, and that depends on his ability to obtain a class of material essentially the best of its kind and varied in its character.

The "best," while it means good writing, means also that it shall say something. The most desired writer in the magazine office is the man who has something to say, and knows how to say it. Variety requires that there shall be many of these writers, and it is the editor's business to ferret them out. It stands to reason, therefore, that there can be no such thing as a "clique"; limitation by the editor of his list of authors would mean being limited to the style of the few and the thoughts of a handful. And with a public that easily tires even of the best where it continually comes from one source, such an editorial policy would be suicidal.

Hence, if the editor is more keenly alert for one thing than for another, it is for the new writer. The frequency of the new note in his magazine is his salvation; for just in proportion as he can introduce that new note is his success with his readers. A successful magazine is exactly like a successful store: it must keep its wares constantly fresh and varied to attract the eye and hold the patronage of its customers.

With an editor ever alive to the new message, the new note, the fresh way of saying a thing, the new angle on a current subject, whether in article or story—since fiction is really to-day only a reflection of modern thought—the foolish notion that an editor must be approached through "influence," by a letter of introduction from some friend or other author, falls of itself. There is no more powerful lever to open the modern magazine door than a postage-stamp on an envelope containing a manuscript that says something. No influence is needed to bring that manuscript to the editor's desk or to his attention. That he will receive it the sender need not for a moment doubt; his mail is too closely scanned for that very envelope.

The most successful authors have "broken into" the magazines very often without even a letter accompanying their first manuscript. The name and address in the right-hand corner of the first page; some "return" stamps in the left corner, and all that the editor requires is there. The author need tell nothing about the manuscript; if what the editor wants is in it he will find it. An editor can stand a tremendous amount of letting alone. If young authors could be made to realize how simple is the process of "breaking into" the modern magazine, which apparently gives them such needless heartburn, they would save themselves infinite pains, time, and worry.

Despite all the rubbish written to the contrary, manuscripts sent to the magazines of to-day are, in every case, read, and frequently more carefully read than the author imagines. Editors know that, from the standpoint of good business alone, it is unwise to return a manuscript unread. Literary talent has been found in many instances where it was least expected.

This does not mean that every manuscript received by a magazine is read from first page to last. There is no reason why it should be, any more than that all of a bad egg should be eaten to prove that it is bad. The title alone sometimes decides the fate of a manuscript. If the subject discussed is entirely foreign to the aims of the magazine, it is simply a case of misapplication on the author's part; and it would be a waste of time for the editor to read something which he knows from its subject he cannot use.

This, of course, applies more to articles than to other forms of literary work, although unsuitability in a poem is naturally as quickly detected. Stories, no matter how unpromising they may appear at the beginning, are generally read through, since gold in a piece of fiction has often been found almost at the close. This careful attention to manuscripts in editorial offices is fixed by rules, and an author's indorsement or a friend's judgment never affects the custom.

At no time does the fallacy hold in a magazine office that "a big name counts for everything and an unknown name for nothing." There can be no denial of the fact that where a name of repute is attached to a meritorious story or article the combination is ideal. But as between an indifferent story and a well-known name and a good story with an unknown name the editor may be depended upon to accept the latter. Editors are very careful nowadays to avoid the public impatience that invariably follows upon publishing material simply on account of the name attached to it. Nothing so quickly injures the reputation of a magazine in the estimation of its readers. If a person, taking up a magazine, reads a story attracted by a famous name, and the story disappoints, the editor has a doubly disappointed reader on his hands: a reader whose high expectations from the name have not been realized and who is disappointed with the story.

It is a well-known fact among successful magazine editors that their most striking successes have been made by material to which unknown names were attached, where the material was fresh, the approach new, the note different. That is what builds up a magazine; the reader learns to have confidence in what he finds in the periodical, whether it bears a famous name or not.

Nor must the young author believe that the best work in modern magazine literature "is dashed off at white heat." What is dashed off *reads dashed off*, and one does not come across it in the well-edited magazine, because it is never accepted. Good writing is laborious writing, the result of revision upon revision. The work of masters such as Robert Louis Stevenson and Rudyard Kipling represents never less than eight or ten revisions, and often a far greater number. It was Stevenson who once said to Edward Bok, after a laborious correction of certain proofs: "My boy, I could be a healthy man, I think, if I did something else than writing. But to write, as I try to write, takes every ounce of my vitality." Just as the best "impromptu" speeches are those most carefully prepared, so do the simplest articles and stories represent the hardest kind of work; the simpler the method seems and the easier the article reads, the harder, it is safe to say, was the work put into it.

But the author must also know when to let his material alone. In his excessive regard for style even so great a master as Robert Louis Stevenson robbed his work of much of the spontaneity and natural charm found, for example, in his *Vailima Letters*. The main thing is for a writer to say what he has to say in the best way, natural to himself, in which he can say it, and then let it alone—always remembering that, provided he has made himself clear, the message itself is of greater import than the manner in which it is said. Up to a certain point only is a piece of literary work an artistic endeavor. A readable, lucid style is far preferable to what is called a "literary style"—a foolish phrase, since it often means nothing except a complicated method of expression which confuses rather than clarifies thought. What the public wants in its literature is human nature, and that human nature simply and forcibly expressed. This is fundamental, and this is why true literature has no fashion and knows no change, despite the cries of the modern weaklings who affect weird forms. The clarity of Shakespeare is the clarity of to-day and will be that of to-morrow.

CHAPTER XXVII

WOMEN'S CLUBS AND WOMAN SUFFRAGE

EDWARD BOK was now jumping from one sizzling frying-pan into another. He had become vitally interested in the growth of women's clubs as a power for good, and began to follow their work and study their methods. He attended meetings; he had his editors attend others and give him reports; he collected and read the year-books of scores of clubs, and he secured and read a number of the papers that had been presented by members at these meetings. He saw at once that what might prove a wonderful power in the civic life of the nation was being misdirected into gatherings of pseudo-culture, where papers ill-digested and mostly copied from books were read and superficially discussed. Apparently the average club thought nothing of disposing of the works of the Victorian poets in one afternoon; the Italian Renaissance was "fully treated and most ably discussed," according to one programme, at a single meeting; Rembrandt and his school were likewise disposed of in one afternoon, and German literature was "adequately treated" at one session "in able papers."

Bok gathered a mass of this material, and then paid his respects to it in the magazine. He recited his evidence and then expressed his opinion of it. He realized that his arraignment of the clubs would cost the magazine hundreds of friends; but, convinced of the great power of the woman's club with its activities rightly directed, he concluded that he could afford to risk incurring displeasure if he might point the way to more effective work. The one was worth the other.

The displeasure was not slow in making itself manifest. It came to maturity overnight, as it were, and expressed itself in no uncertain terms. Every club flew to arms, and Bok was intensely interested to note that the clubs whose work he had taken as "horrible examples," although he had not mentioned their names, were the most strenuous in their denials of the methods outlined in the magazine, and that the members of those clubs were particularly heated in their attacks upon him.

He soon found that he had stirred up quite as active a hornet's nest as he had anticipated. Letters by the hundred poured in attacking and reviling him. In nearly every case the writers fell back upon personal abuse, ignoring his arguments altogether. He became the subject of heated debates at club meetings, at conventions, in the public press; and soon long petitions demanding his removal as editor began to come to Mr. Curtis. These petitions were signed by hundreds of names. Bok read them with absorbed interest, and bided his time for action. Meanwhile he continued his articles of criticism in the magazine, and these, of course, added fuel to the conflagration.

Former President Cleveland now came to Bok's side, and in an article in the magazine went even further than Bok had ever thought of going in his criticism of women's clubs. This article deflected the criticism from Bok momentarily, and Mr. Cleveland received a grilling to which his experiences in the White House were "as child's play," as he expressed it. The two men, the editor and the former President, were now bracketed as copartners in crime in the eyes of the club-women, and nothing too harsh could be found to say or write of either.

Meanwhile Bok had been watching the petitions for his removal which kept coming in. He was looking for an opening, and soon found it. One of the most prominent women's clubs sent a protest condemning his attitude and advising him by resolutions, which were enclosed, that unless he ceased his attacks, the members of the —— Woman's Club had resolved "to unitedly and unanimously boycott *The Ladies' Home Journal* and had already put the plan into effect with the current issue."

Bok immediately engaged counsel in the city where the club was situated, and instructed his lawyer to begin proceedings, for violation of the Sherman Act, against the president and the secretary of the club, and three other members; counsel to take particular pains to choose, if possible, the wives of three lawyers.

Within forty-eight hours Bok heard from the husbands of the five wives, who pointed out to him that the women had acted in entire ignorance of the law, and suggested a reconsideration of his action. Bok replied by quoting from the petition which set forth that it was signed "by the most intelligent women of —— who were thoroughly versed in civic and national affairs";

and if this were true, Bok argued, it naturally followed that they must have been cognizant of a legislative measure so well known and so widely discussed as the Sherman Act. He was basing his action, he said, merely on their declaration.

Bok could easily picture to himself the chagrin and wrath of the women, with the husbands laughing up their sleeves at the turn of affairs. "My wife never could see the humor in the situation," said one of these husbands to Bok, when he met him years later. Bok capitulated, and then apparently with great reluctance, only when the club sent him an official withdrawal of the protest and an apology for "its ill-considered action." It was years after that one of the members of the club, upon meeting Bok, said to him: "Your action did not increase the club's love for you, but you taught it a much-needed lesson which it never forgot."

Up to this time, Bok had purposely been destructive in his criticism. Now, he pointed out a constructive plan whereby the woman's club could make itself a power in every community. He advocated less of the cultural and more of the civic interest, and urged that the clubs study the numerous questions dealing with the life of their communities. This seems strange, in view of the enormous amount of civic work done by women's clubs to-day. But at that time, when the woman's club movement was unformed, these civic matters found but a small part in the majority of programmes; in a number of cases none at all.

Of course, the clubs refused to accept or even to consider his suggestions; they were quite competent to decide for themselves the particular subjects for their meetings, they argued; they did not care to be tutored or guided, particularly by Bok. They were much too angry with him even to admit that his suggestions were practical and in order. But he knew, of course, that they would adopt them of their own volition—under cover, perhaps, but that made no difference, so long as the end was accomplished. One club after another, during the following years, changed its programme, and soon the supposed cultural interest had yielded first place to the needful civic questions.

For years, however, the clubwomen of America did not forgive Bok. They refused to buy or countenance his magazine, and periodically they attacked it or made light of it. But he knew he had made his point, and was content to leave it to time to heal the wounds. This came years afterward, when Mrs. Pennypacker became president of the General Federation of Women's Clubs and Mrs. Rudolph Blankenburg, vice-president.

Those two far-seeing women and Bok arranged that an official department of the Federation should find a place in *The Ladies' Home Journal*, with Mrs. Pennypacker as editor and Mrs. Blankenburg, who lived in Philadelphia, as the resident consulting editor. The idea was arranged agreeably to all three; the Federation officially endorsed its president's suggestion, and for several years the department was one of the most successful in the magazine.

The breach had been healed; two powerful forces were working together, as they should, for the mutual good of the American woman. No relations could have been pleasanter than those between the editor-in-chief of the magazine and the two departmental editors. The report was purposely set afloat that Bok had withdrawn from his position of antagonism (?) toward women's clubs, and this gave great satisfaction to thousands of women club-members and made everybody happy!

At this time the question of suffrage for women was fast becoming a prominent issue, and naturally Bok was asked to take a stand on the question in his magazine. No man sat at a larger gateway to learn the sentiments of numbers of women on any subject. He read his vast correspondence carefully. He consulted women of every grade of intelligence and in every station in life. Then he caused a straw-vote to be taken among a selected list of thousands of his subscribers in large cities and in small towns. The result of all these inquiries was most emphatic and clear: by far the overwhelming majority of the women approached either were opposed to the ballot or were indifferent to it. Those who desired to try the experiment were negligible in number. So far as the sentiment of any wide public can be secured on any given topic, this seemed to be the dominant opinion.

Bok then instituted a systematic investigation of conditions in those states where women had voted for years; but he could not see, from a thoughtful study of his investigations, that much had been accomplished. The results certainly did not measure up to the prophecies constantly advanced by the advocates of a nation-wide equal suffrage.

The editor now carefully looked into the speeches of the suffragists, examined the platform of the National body in favor of woman suffrage, and talked at length with such leaders in the movement as Susan B. Anthony, Julia Ward Howe, Anna Howard Shaw, and Jane Addams.

All this time Bok had kept his own mind open. He was ready to have the magazine, for whose editorial policy he was responsible, advocate that side of the issue which seemed for the best interests of the American woman.

The arguments that a woman should not have a vote because she was a woman; that it would interfere with her work in the home; that it would make her more masculine; that it would take her out of her own home; that it was a blow at domesticity and an actual menace to the home life of America—these did not weigh with him. There was only one question for him to settle: Was the ballot something which, in its demonstrated value or in its potentiality, would serve the best interests of American womanhood?

After all his investigations of both sides of the question, Bok decided upon a negative answer. He felt that American women were not ready to exercise the privilege intelligently and that their mental attitude was against it.

Forthwith he said so in his magazine. And the storm broke. The denunciations brought down upon him by his attitude toward woman's clubs was as nothing compared to what was now let loose. The attacks were bitter. His arguments were ignored; and the suffragists evidently decided to concentrate their criticisms upon the youthful years of the editor. They regarded this as a most vulnerable point of attack, and reams of paper were used to prove that the opinion of a man so young in years and so necessarily unformed in his judgment was of no value.

Unfortunately, the suffragists did not know, when they advanced this argument, that it would be over-thrown by the endorsement of Bok's point of view by such men and women of years and ripe judgment as Doctor Eliot, then president of Harvard University, former President Cleveland, Lyman Abbott, Margaret Deland, and others. When articles by these opponents to suffrage appeared, the argument of youth hardly held good; and the attacks of the suffragists were quickly shifted to the ground of "narrow-mindedness and old-fashioned fogyism."

The article by former President Cleveland particularly stirred the ire of the attacking suffragists, and Miss Anthony hurled a broadside at the former President in a newspaper interview. Unfortunately for her best judgment, and the strength of her argument, the attack became intensely personal; and of course, nullified its force. But it irritated Mr. Cleveland, who called Bok to his Princeton home and read him a draft of a proposed answer for publication in Bok's magazine.

Those who knew Mr. Cleveland were well aware of the force that he could put into his pen when he chose, and in this proposed article he certainly chose! It would have made very unpleasant reading for Miss Anthony in particular, as well as for her friends. Bok argued strongly against the article. He reminded Mr. Cleveland that it would be undignified to make such an answer; that it was always an unpopular thing to attack a woman in public, especially a woman who was old and ill; that she would again strive for the last word; that there would be no point to the controversy and nothing gained by it. He pleaded with Mr. Cleveland to meet Miss Anthony's attack by a dignified silence.

These arguments happily prevailed. In reality, Mr. Cleveland was not keen to attack Miss Anthony or any other woman; such a thought was foreign to his nature. He summed up his feeling to Bok when he tore up the draft of his article and smilingly said: "Well, I've got it off my chest, that is the main thing. I wanted to get it out of my system, and talking it over has driven it out. It is better in the fire," and he threw the torn paper into the open grate.

As events turned out, it was indeed fortunate that the matter had been so decided; for the article would have appeared in the number of Bok's magazine published on the day that Miss Anthony passed away. It would have been a most unfortunate moment, to say the least, for the appearance of an attack such as Mr. Cleveland had in mind.

This incident, like so many instances that might be adduced, points with singular force to the value of that editorial discrimination which the editor often makes between what is wise or unwise for him to publish. Bok realized that had he encouraged Mr. Cleveland to publish the article, he could have exhausted any edition he might have chosen to print. Times without number, editors make such decisions directly against what would be of temporary advantage to their publications. The public never hears of these incidents.

More often than not the editor hears "stories" that, if printed, would be a "scoop" which would cause his publication to be talked about from one end of the country to the other. The public does not give credit to the editor, particularly of the modern newspaper, for the high code of honor which constantly actuates him in his work. The prevailing notion is that an editor prints all that he knows, and much that he does not know. Outside of those in the inner government circles, no group of men, during the Great War, had more information of a confidential nature constantly given or brought to them, and more zealously guarded it, than the editors of the newspapers of America. Among no other set of professional men is the code of honor so high; and woe betide the journalist who, in the eyes of his fellow-workers, violates, even in the slightest degree, that code of editorial ethics. Public men know how true is this statement; the public at large, however, has not the first conception of it. If it had, it would have a much higher opinion of its periodicals and newspapers.

At this juncture, Rudyard Kipling unconsciously came into the very centre of the suffragists' maelstrom of attack when he sent Bok his famous poem: "The Female of the Species." The suffragists at once took the argument in the poem as personal to themselves, and now Kipling got the full benefit of their vitriolic abuse. Bok sent a handful of these criticisms to Kipling, who was very gleeful about them. "I owe you a good laugh over the clippings," he wrote. "They were delightful. But what a quantity of spare time some people in this world have to burn!"

It was a merry time; and the longer it continued the more heated were the attacks. The suffragists now had a number of targets, and they took each in turn and proceeded to riddle it. That Bok was publishing articles explaining both sides of the question, presenting arguments by the leading suffragists as well as known anti-suffragists, did not matter in the least. These were either conveniently overlooked, or, when referred to at all, were considered in the light of "sops" to the offended women.

At last Bok reached the stage where he had exhausted all the arguments worth printing, on both sides of the question, and soon the storm calmed down.

It was always a matter of gratification to him that the woman who had most bitterly assailed him during the suffrage controversy, Anna Howard Shaw, became in later years one of his stanchest friends, and was an editor on his pay-roll. When the United States entered the Great War, Bok saw that Doctor Shaw had undertaken a gigantic task in promising, as chairman, to direct the activities of the National Council for Women. He went to see her in Washington, and offered his help and that of the magazine. Doctor Shaw, kindliest of women in her nature, at once accepted the offer; Bok placed the entire resources of the magazine and of its Washington editorial force at her disposal; and all through America's participation in the war, she successfully conducted a monthly department in *The Ladies' Home Journal.*

"Such help," she wrote at the close, "as you and your associates have extended me and my co-workers;

such unstinted co-operation and such practical guidance I never should have dreamed possible. You made your magazine a living force in our work; we do not see now how we would have done without it. You came into our activities at the psychological moment, when we most needed what you could give us, and none could have given with more open hands and fuller hearts."

So the contending forces in a bitter word-war came together and worked together, and a mutual regard sprang up between the woman and the man who had once so radically differed.

CHAPTER XXVIII

GOING HOME WITH KIPLING, AND AS A LECTURER

It was in June, 1899, when Rudyard Kipling, after the loss of his daughter and his own almost fatal illness from pneumonia in America, sailed for his English home on the White Star liner, *Teutonic*. The party consisted of Kipling, his wife, his father J. Lockwood Kipling, Mr. and Mrs. Frank N. Doubleday, and Bok. It was only at the last moment that Bok decided to join the party, and the steamer having its full complement of passengers, he could only secure one of the officers' large rooms on the upper deck. Owing to the sensitive condition of Kipling's lungs, it was not wise for him to be out on deck except in the most favorable weather. The atmosphere of the smoking-room was forbidding, and as the rooms of the rest of the party were below deck, it was decided to make Bok's convenient room the headquarters of the party. Here they assembled for the best part of each day; the talk ranged over literary and publishing matters of mutual interest, and Kipling promptly labelled the room "The Hatchery,"—from the plans and schemes that were hatched during these discussions.

It was decided on the first day out that the party, too active-minded to remain inert for any length of time, should publish a daily newspaper to be written on large sheets of paper and to be read each evening to the group.

It was called *The Teuton Tonic;* Mr. Doubleday was appointed publisher and advertising manager; Mr. Lockwood Kipling was made art editor to embellish the news; Rudyard Kipling was the star reporter, and Bok was editor.

Kipling, just released from his long confinement, like a boy out of school, was the life of the party—and when, one day, he found a woman aboard reading a copy of *The Ladies' Home Journal* his joy knew no bounds; he turned in the most inimitable "copy" to the *Tonic,* describing the woman's feelings as she read the different departments in the magazine. Of course, Bok, as editor of the *Tonic,* promptly pigeon-holed the reporter's "copy"; then relented, and, in a fine spirit of large-mindedness, "printed" Kipling's pæans of rapture over Bok's subscriber. The preparation of the paper was a daily joy: it kept the different members busy, and each evening the copy was handed to "the large circle of readers"—the two women of the party—to read aloud. At the end of the sixth day, it was voted to "suspend publication," and the daily of six issues was unanimously bequeathed to the little daughter of Mr. Lockwood de Forest, a close friend of the Kipling family—a choice bit of Kiplingania.

One day it was decided by the party that Bok should be taught the game of poker, and Kipling at once offered to be the instructor! He wrote out a list of the "hands" for Bok's guidance, which was placed in the centre of the table, and the party, augmented by the women, gathered to see the game.

A baby had been born that evening in the steerage,

and it was decided to inaugurate a small "jack-pot" for the benefit of the mother. All went well until about the fourth hand, when Bok began to bid higher than had been originally planned. Kipling questioned the beginner's knowledge of the game and his tactics, but Bok retorted it was his money that he was putting into the pot and that no one was compelled to follow his bets if he did not choose to do so. Finally, the jack-pot assumed altogether too large dimensions for the party, Kipling "called" and Bok, true to the old idea of "beginner's luck" in cards, laid down a royal flush! This was too much, and poker, with Bok in it, was taboo from that moment. Kipling's version of this card-playing does not agree in all particulars with the version here written. "Bok learned the game of poker," Kipling says; "had the deck stacked on him, and on hearing that there was a woman aboard who read *The Ladies' Home Journal* insisted on playing after that with the cabin-door carefully shut." But Kipling's art as a reporter for *The Tonic* was not as reliable as the art of his more careful book work.

Bok derived special pleasure on this trip from his acquaintance with Father Kipling, as the party called him. Rudyard Kipling's respect for his father was the tribute of a loyal son to a wonderful father.

"What annoys me," said Kipling, speaking of his father one day, "is when the pater comes to America to have him referred to in the newspapers as 'the father of Rudyard Kipling.' It is in India where they get the relation correct: there I am always 'the son of Lockwood Kipling.'"

Father Kipling was, in every sense, a choice spirit: gentle, kindly, and of a most remarkably even temperament. His knowedge of art, his wide reading, his extensive travel, and an interest in every phase of the world's doings, made him a rare conversationalist, when inclined to talk, and an encyclopædia of knowledge as extensive as it was accurate. It was very easy to grow fond of Father Kipling, and he won Bok's affection as few men ever did.

Father Kipling's conversation was remarkable in that he was exceedingly careful of language and wasted few words.

One day Kipling and Bok were engaged in a discussion of the Boer problem, which was then pressing. Father Kipling sat by listening, but made no comment on the divergent views, since, Kipling holding the English side of the question and Bok the Dutch side, it followed that they could not agree. Finally Father Kipling arose and said: "Well, I will take a stroll and see if I can't listen to the water and get all this din out of my ears."

Both men felt gently but firmly rebuked and the discussion was never again taken up.

Bok tried on one occasion to ascertain how the father regarded the son's work.

"You should feel pretty proud of your son," remarked Bok.

"A good sort," was the simple reply.

"I mean, rather, of his work. How does that strike you?" asked Bok.

"Which work?"

"His work as a whole," explained Bok.

"Creditable," was the succinct answer.

"No more than that?" asked Bok.

"Can there be more?" came from the father.

"Well," said Bok, "the judgment seems a little tame as applied to one who is generally regarded as a genius."

'By whom?"

"The critics, for instance," replied Bok.

"There are no such," came the answer.

"No such what, Mr. Kipling?" asked Bok.

"Critics."

"No critics?"

"No," and for the first time the pipe was removed for a moment. "A critic is one who only exists as such in his own imagination."

"But surely you must consider that Rud has done some great work?" persisted Bok.

"Creditable," came once more.

"You think him capable of great work, do you not?" asked Bok. For a moment there was silence. Then:

"He has a certain grasp of the human instinct. That, some day, I think, will lead him to write a great work."

There was the secret: the constant holding up to the son, apparently, of something still to be accomplished; of a goal to be reached; of a higher standard to be attained. Rudyard Kipling was never in danger of unintelligent laudation from his safest and most intelligent reader.

During the years which intervened until his passing away, Bok sought to keep in touch with Father Kipling, and received the most wonderful letters from him.

One day he enclosed in a letter a drawing which he had made showing Sakia Muni sitting under the bo-tree with two of his disciples, a young man and a young woman, gathered at his feet. It was a piece of exquisite drawing. "I like to think of you and your work in this way," wrote Mr. Kipling, "and so I sketched it for you." Bok had the sketch enlarged, engaged John La Farge to translate it into glass, and inserted it in a window in the living-room of his home at Merion.

After Father Kipling had passed away, the express brought to Bok one day a beautiful plaque of red clay, showing the elephant's head, the lotus, and the swastika, which the father had made for the son. It was the original model of the insignia which, as a watermark, is used in the pages of Kipling's books and on the cover of the subscription edition.

"I am sending with this for your acceptance," wrote Kipling to Bok, "as some little memory of my father to whom you were so kind, the original of one of the plaques that he used to make for me. I thought it being the swastika would be appropriate for *your* swastika. May it bring you even more good fortune."

To those who knew Lockwood Kipling, it is easier to understand the genius and the kindliness of the son. For the sake of the public's knowledge, it is a distinct loss that there is not a better understanding of the real sweetness of character of the son. The public's only idea of the great writer is naturally one derived from writers who do not understand him, or from reporters whom he refused to see, while Kipling's own slogan is expressed in his own words: "I have always managed

If.

If you can keep your head when all about you
  Are losing theirs and blaming it on you,
If you can trust yourself when all men doubt you,
  But make allowance for their doubting too;
If you can wait and not grow tired by waiting,
  Or, being lied about, don't deal in lies,
Or, being hated, don't give way to hating,
  And yet don't look too good or talk too wise;

If you can dream and not make dreams your master;
  If you can think and not make thoughts your aim,
If you can meet with Triumph and Disaster,
  And treat those two impostors just the same;
If you can stand to hear the truth you've spoken
  Twisted by knaves to make a trap for fools,
Or watch the work you've given your life to, broken,
  And stoop and build it up with worn-out tools;

If you can make one pile of all your winnings
  And risk it at one game of pitch-and-toss,
And lose, and start again from your beginnings
  And never breathe a word about your loss;
If you can force your heart and nerve and sinew
  To serve your turn long after they are gone,
And so hold on, though there is nothing in you
  Except the will that says to them, "Hold on!"

If you can talk to crowds and keep your virtue,
  And walk with kings nor lose the common touch,
If neither foes nor loving friends can hurt you,
  If all men count with you, but none too much;
If you can fill the unforgiving minute
  With sixty seconds worth of distance run,
Yours is the Earth and everything that's in it,
And — which is more — you'll be a Man, my son!

Copied out from memory by   Rudyard Kipling.
                          Batemans: Sep. 1913.
                     for . E. W. Bok on his 50th Birthday.

to keep clear of 'personal' things as much as possible."

It was on Bok's fiftieth birthday that Kipling sent him a copy of " If." Bok had greatly admired this poem, but knowing Kipling's distaste for writing out his own work, he had resisted the strong desire to ask him for a copy of it. It is significant of the author's remarkable memory that he wrote it, as he said, "from memory," years after its publication, and yet a comparison of the copy with the printed form, corrected by Kipling, fails to discover the difference of a single word.

The lecture bureaus now desired that Edward Bok should go on the platform. Bok had never appeared in the role of a lecturer, but he reasoned that through the medium of the rostrum he might come in closer contact with the American public, meet his readers personally, and secure some first-hand constructive criticism of his work. This last he was always encouraging. It was a naïve conception of a lecture tour, but Bok believed it and he contracted for a tour beginning at Richmond, Virginia, and continuing through the South and Southwest as far as Saint Joseph, Missouri, and then back home by way of the Middle West.

Large audiences greeted him wherever he went, but he had not gone far on his tour when he realized that he was not getting what he thought he would. There was much entertaining and lionizing, but nothing to help him in his work by pointing out to him where he could better it. He shrank from the pitiless publicity that was inevitable; he became more and more self-

conscious when during the first five minutes on the
stage he felt the hundreds of opera-classes levelled at
him, and he and Mrs. Bok, who accompanied him, had
not a moment to themselves from early morning to
midnight. Yet his large correspondence was following
him from the office, and the inevitable invitations in
each city had at least to be acknowledged. Bok realized he had miscalculated the benefits of a lecture tour
to his work, and began hopefully to wish for the ending
of the circuit.

One afternoon as he was returning with his manager from a large reception, the "impresario" said to
him: "I don't like these receptions. They hurt the
house."

"The house?" echoed Bok.

"Yes, the attendance."

"But you told me the house for this evening was sold
out?" said the lecturer.

"That is true enough. House, and even the stage.
Not a seat unsold. But hundreds just come to see you
and not to hear your lecture, and this exposure of a lecturer at so crowded a reception as this, before the talk,
satisfies the people without their buying a ticket. My
rule is that a lecturer should not be seen in public before his lecture, and I wish you would let me enforce the
rule with you. It wears you out, anyway, and no receptions until afterward will give you more time for
yourself and save your vitality for the talk."

Bok was entirely acquiescent. He had no personal
taste for the continued round of functions, but he had
accepted it as part of the game.

The idea from this talk that impressed Bok, however, with particular force, was that the people who crowded his houses came to see him and not to hear his lecture. Personal curiosity, in other words. This was a new thought. He had been too busy to think of his personality; now he realized a different angle to the situation. And, much to his manager's astonishment, two days afterwards Bok refused to sign an agreement for another tour later in the year. He had had enough of exhibiting himself as a curiosity. He continued his tour; but before its conclusion fell ill—a misfortune with a pleasant side to it, for three of his engagements had to be cancelled.

The Saint Joseph engagement could not be cancelled. The house had been oversold; it was for the benefit of a local charity which besought Bok by wire after wire to keep a postponed date. He agreed, and he went. He realized that he was not well, but he did not realize the extent of his mental and physical exhaustion until he came out on the platform and faced the crowded auditorium. Barely sufficient space had been left for him and for the speaker's desk; the people on the stage were close to him, and he felt distinctly uncomfortable.

Then, to his consternation, it suddenly dawned upon him that his tired mind had played a serious trick on him. He did not remember a line of his lecture; he could not even recall how it began! He arose, after his introduction, in a bath of cold perspiration. The applause gave him a moment to recover himself, but not a word came to his mind. He sparred for time by some informal prefatory remarks expressing regret at his illness and that he had been compelled to disappoint his audience a few days before, and then he stood helpless! In sheer desperation he looked at Mrs. Bok sitting in the stage box, who, divining her husband's plight, motioned to the inside pocket of his coat. He put his hand there and pulled out a copy of his lecture which she had placed there! The whole tragic comedy had happened so quickly that the audience was absolutely unaware of what had occurred, and Bok went on and practically read his lecture. But it was not a successful evening for his audience or for himself, and the one was doubtless as glad when it was over as the other.

When he reached home, he was convinced that he had had enough of lecturing! He had to make a second short tour, however, for which he had contracted with another manager before embarking on the first. This tour took him to Indianapolis, and after the lecture, James Whitcomb Riley gave him a supper. There were some thirty men in the party; the affair was an exceedingly happy one; the happiest that Bok had attended. He said this to Riley on the way to the hotel.

"Usually," said Bok, "men, for some reason or other, hold aloof from me on these lecture tours. They stand at a distance and eye me, and I see wonder on their faces rather than a desire to mix."

"You've noticed that, then?" smilingly asked the poet.

"Yes, and I can't quite get it. At home, my friends are men. Why should it be different in other cities?"

"I'll tell you," said Riley. "Five or six of the men you met to-night were loath to come. When I pinned them down to their reason, it was as I thought: they regard you as an effeminate being, a sissy."

"Good heavens!" interrupted Bok.

"Fact," said Riley, "and you can't wonder at it nor blame them. You have been most industriously paragraphed, in countless jests, about your penchant for pink teas, your expert knowledge of tatting, crocheting, and all that sort of stuff. Look what Eugene Field has done in that direction. These paragraphs have, doubtless, been good advertising for your magazine, and, in a way, for you. But, on the other hand, they have given a false impression of you. Men have taken these paragraphs seriously and they think of you as the man pictured in them. It's a fact; I know. It's all right after they meet you and get your measure. The joke then is on them. Four of the men I fairly dragged to the dinner this evening said this to me just before I left. That is one reason why I advise you to keep on lecturing. Get around and show yourself, and correct this universal impression. Not that you can't stand what men think of you, but it's unpleasant."

It was unpleasant, but Bok decided that the solution as found in lecturing was worse than the misconception. From that day to this he never lectured again.

But the public conception of himself, especially that of men, awakened his interest and amusement. Some of his friends on the press were still busy with their paragraphs, and he promptly called a halt and asked them to desist. "Enough was as good as a feast," he told them, and explained why.

One day Bok got a distinctly amusing line on himself

from a chance stranger.   He was riding from Washington to Philadelphia in the smoking compartment, when the newsboy stuck his head in the door and yelled: "*Ladies' Home Journal*, out to-day."   He had heard this many times before; but on this particular day, upon hearing the title of his own magazine yelled almost in his ears, he gave an involuntary start.

Opposite to him sat a most companionable young fellow, who, noticing Bok's start, leaned over and with a smile said: "I know, I know just how you feel.   That's the way I feel whenever I hear the name of that damned magazine.   Here, boy," he called to the retreating magazine-carrier, "give me a copy of that *Ladies' Home Disturber:* I might as well buy it here as in the station."

Then to Bok: "Honest, if I don't bring home that sheet on the day it is out, the wife is in a funk.   She runs her home by it literally.   Same with you?"

"The same," answered Bok.   "As a matter of fact, in our family, we live by it, on it, and from it."

Bok's neighbor, of course, couldn't get the real point of this, but he thought he had it.

"Exactly," he replied.   "So do we.   That fellow Bok certainly has the women buffaloed for good.   Ever see him?"

"Oh, yes," answered Bok.

"Live in Philadelphia?"

"Yes."

"There's where the thing is published, all right. What does Bok look like?"

"Oh," answered Bok carelessly, "just like, well, like all of us.   In fact, he looks something like me."

"Does he, now?" echoed the man. "Shouldn't think it would make you very proud!"

And, the train pulling in at Baltimore, Bok's genial neighbor sent him a hearty good-bye and ran out with the much-maligned magazine under his arm!

He had an occasion or two now to find out what women thought of him!

He was leaving the publication building one evening after office hours when just as he opened the front door, a woman approached. Bok explained that the building was closed.

"Well, I am sorry," said the woman in a dejected tone, "for I don't think I can manage to come again."

"Is there anything I can do?" asked Bok. "I am employed here."

"No-o," said the woman. "I came to see Mr. Curtis on a personal matter."

"I shall see him this evening," suggested Bok, "and can give him a message for you if you like."

"Well, I don't know if you can. I came to complain to him about Mr. Bok," announced the woman.

"Oh, well," answered Bok, with a slight start at the matter-of-fact announcement, "that is serious; quite serious. If you will explain your complaint, I will surely see that it gets to Mr. Curtis."

Bok's interest grew.

"Well, you see," said the woman, "it is this way. I live in a three-family flat. Here is my name and card," and a card came out of a bag. "I subscribe to *The Ladies' Home Journal*. It is delivered at my house each month by Mr. Bok. Now I have told that man three times over that when he delivers the magazine, he must ring the bell twice. But he just persists in ringing once and then that cat who lives on the first floor gets my magazine, reads it, and keeps it sometimes for three days before I get it! Now, I want Mr. Curtis to tell Mr. Bok that he must do as I ask and ring the bell twice. Can you give him that message for me? There's no use talking to Mr. Bok; I've done that, as I say."

And Bok solemnly assured his subscriber that he would!

Bok's secretary told him one day that there was in the outer office the most irate woman he had ever tried to handle; that he had tried for half an hour to appease her, but it was of no use. She threatened to remain until Bok admitted her, and see him she would, and tell him exactly what she thought of him. The secretary looked as if he had been through a struggle. "It's hopeless," he said. "Will you see her?"

"Certainly," said Bok. "Show her in."

The moment the woman came in, she began a perfect torrent of abuse. Bok could not piece out, try as he might, what it was all about. But he did gather from the explosion that the woman considered him a hypocrite who wrote one thing and did another; that he was really a thief, stealing a woman's money, and so forth. There was no chance of a word for fully fifteen minutes and then, when she was almost breathless, Bok managed to ask if his caller would kindly tell him just what he had done.

Another torrent of incoherent abuse came forth, but after a while it became apparent that the woman's complaint was that she had sent a dollar for a subscription to *The Ladies' Home Journal;* had never had a copy of the magazine, had complained, and been told there was no record of the money being received. And as she had sent her subscription to Bok personally, he had purloined the dollar!

It was fully half an hour before Bok could explain to the irate woman that he never remembered receiving a letter from her; that subscriptions, even when personally addressed to him, did not come to his desk, etc.; that if she would leave her name and address he would have the matter investigated. Absolutely unconvinced that anything would be done, and unaltered in her opinion about Bok, the woman finally left.

Two days later a card was handed in to the editor with a note asking him to see for a moment the husband of his irate caller. When the man came in, he looked sheepish and amused in turn, and finally said:

"I hardly know what to say, because I don't know what my wife said to you. But if what she said to me is any index of her talk with you, I want to apologize for her most profoundly. She isn't well, and we shall both have to let it go at that. As for her subscription, you, of course, never received it, for, with difficulty, I finally extracted the fact from her that she pinned a dollar bill to a postal card and dropped it in a street postal box. And she doesn't yet see that she has done anything extraordinary, or that she had a faith in Uncle Sam that I call sublime."

The Journal had been calling the attention of its

readers to the defacement of the landscape by billboard advertisers. One day on his way to New York he found himself sitting in a sleeping-car section opposite a woman and her daughter.

The mother was looking at the landscape when suddenly she commented:

"There are some of those ugly advertising signs that Mr. Bok says are such a defacement to the landscape. I never noticed them before, but he is right, and I am going to write and tell him so."

"Oh, mamma, don't," said the girl. "That man is pampered enough by women. Don't make him worse. Ethel says he is now the vainest man in America."

Bok's eyes must have twinkled, and just then the mother looked at him, caught his eye; she gave a little gasp, and Bok saw that she had telepathically discovered him!

He smiled, raised his hat, presented his card to the mother, and said: "Excuse me, but I do want to defend myself from that last statement, if I may. I couldn't help overhearing it."

The mother, a woman of the world, read the name on the card quickly and smiled, but the daughter's face was a study as she leaned over and glanced at the card. She turned scarlet and then white.

"Now, do tell me," asked Bok of the daughter, "who 'Ethel' is, so that I may try at least to prove that I am not what she thinks."

The daughter was completely flustered. For the rest of the journey, however, the talk was informal; the girl became more at ease, and Bok ended by dining with the mother and daughter at their hotel that evening.

But he never found out "Ethel's" other name!

There were curiously amusing sides to a man's editorship of a woman's magazine!

CHAPTER XXIX

AN EXCURSION INTO THE FEMININE NATURE

THE strangling hold which the Paris couturiers had secured on the American woman in their absolute dictation as to her fashions in dress, had interested Edward Bok for some time. As he studied the question, he was constantly amazed at the audacity with which these French dressmakers and milliners, often themselves of little taste and scant morals, cracked the whip, and the docility with which the American woman blindly and unintelligently danced to their measure. The deeper he went into the matter, too, the more deceit and misrepresentation did he find in the situation. It was inconceivable that the American woman should submit to what was being imposed upon her if she knew the facts. He determined that she should. The process of Americanization going on within him decided him to expose the Paris conditions and advocate and present American-designed fashions for women.

The Journal engaged the best-informed woman in Paris frankly to lay open the situation to the American women; she proved that the designs sent over by the so-called Paris arbiters of fashion were never worn by the French-woman of birth and good taste; that they were especially designed and specifically intended for "the bizarre American trade," as one polite Frenchman called it; and that the only women in Paris who wore these grotesque and often immoderate styles were of the demimonde.

This article was the opening gun of the campaign, and this was quickly followed by a second equally convincing—both articles being written from the inside of the gilded circles of the couturiers' shops. Madame Sarah Bernhardt was visiting the United States at the time, and Bok induced the great actress to verify the statements printed. She went farther and expressed amazement at the readiness with which the American woman had been duped; and indicated her horror on seeing American women of refined sensibilities and position dressed in the gowns of the *déclassé* street-women of Paris. The somewhat sensational nature of the articles attracted the attention of the American newspapers, which copied and commented on them; the gist of them was cabled over to Paris, and, of course, the Paris couturiers denied the charges. But their denials were in general terms; and no convincing proof of the falsity of the charges was furnished. The French couturier simply resorted to a shrug of the shoulder and a laugh, implying that the accusations were beneath his notice.

Bok now followed the French models of dresses and millinery to the United States, and soon found that for every genuine Parisian model sold in the large cities at least ten were copies, made in New York shops, but with the labels of the French dressmakers and milliners sewed on them. He followed the labels to their source, and discovered a firm one of whose specialties was the making of these labels bearing the names of the leading French designers. They were manufactured by the gross, and sold in bundles to the retailers. Bok secured a list of the buyers of these labels and found that they represented some of the leading merchants throughout the country. All these facts he published. The retailers now sprang up in arms and denied the charges, but again the denials were in general terms. Bok had the facts and they knew it. These facts were too specific and too convincing to be controverted.

The editor had now presented a complete case before the women of America as to the character of the Paris-designed fashions and the manner in which women were being hoodwinked in buying imitations.

Meanwhile, he had engaged the most expert designers in the world of women's dress and commissioned them to create American designs. He sent one of his editors to the West to get first-hand *motifs* from Indian costumes and adapt them as decorative themes for dress embroideries. Three designers searched the Metropolitan Museum for new and artistic ideas, and he induced his company to install a battery of four-color presses in order that the designs might be given in all the beauty of their original colors. For months designers and artists worked; he had the designs passed upon by a board of judges composed of New York women who knew good clothes, and then he began their publication.

The editor of *The New York Times* asked Bok to conduct for that newspaper a prize contest for the best American-designed dresses and hats, and edit a special supplement presenting them in full colors, the prizes to be awarded by a jury of six of the leading New York women best versed in matters of dress. Hundreds of designs were submitted, the best were selected, and the supplement issued under the most successful auspices.

In his own magazine, Bok published pages of American-designed fashions: their presence in the magazine was advertised far and wide; conventions of dressmakers were called to consider the salability of domestic-designed fashions; and a campaign with the slogan "American Fashions for American Women" was soon in full swing.

But there it ended. The women looked the designs over with interest, as they did all designs of new clothes, and paid no further attention to them. The very fact that they were of American design prejudiced the women against them. America never had designed good clothes, they argued: she never would. Argument availed naught. The Paris germ was deep-rooted in the feminine mind of America: the women acknowledged that they were, perhaps, being hoodwinked by spurious French dresses and hats; that the case presented by Bok seemed convincing enough, but the temptation to throw a coat over a sofa or a chair to expose a Parisian label to the eyes of some other woman was too great; there was always a gambling chance that her particular gown, coat, or hat was an actual Paris creation.

Bok called upon the American woman to come out from under the yoke of the French couturiers, show her patriotism, and encourage American design. But it was of no use. He talked with women on every hand; his mail was full of letters commending him for his stand; but as for actual results, there were none. One of his most intelligent woman-friends finally summed up the situation for him:

"You can rail against the Paris domination all you like; you can expose it for the fraud that it is, and we know that it is; but it is all to no purpose, take my word. When it comes to the question of her personal adornment, a woman employs no reason; she knows no logic. She knows that the adornment of her body is all that she has to match the other woman and outdo her, and to attract the male, and nothing that you can say will influence her a particle. I know this all seems incomprehensible to you as a man, but that is the feminine nature. You are trying to fight something that is unfightable."

"Has the American woman no instinct of patriotism, then?" asked Bok.

"Not the least," was the answer, "when it comes to her adornment. What Paris says, she will do, blindly and unintelligently if you will, but she will do it. She will sacrifice her patriotism; she will even justify a possible disregard of the decencies. Look at the present Parisian styles. They are absolutely indecent. Women know it, but they follow them just the same, and they will. It is all very unpleasant to say this, but it is the truth and you will find it out. Your effort, fine as it is, will bear no fruit."

Wherever Bok went, women upon whose judgment he felt he could rely, told him, in effect, the same thing. They were all regretful, in some cases ashamed of their sex, universally apologetic; but one and all declared that such is "the feminine nature," and Bok would only have his trouble for nothing.

And so it proved. For a period, the retail shops were more careful in the number of genuine French models of gowns and hats which they exhibited, and the label firm confessed that its trade had fallen off. But this was only temporary. Within a year after *The Journal* stopped the campaign, baffled and beaten, the trade in French labels was greater than ever, hundreds of French models were sold that had never crossed the ocean, the American woman was being hoodwinked on every hand, and the reign of the French couturier was once more supreme.

There was no disguising the fact that the case was hopeless, and Bok recognized and accepted the inevitable. He had, at least, the satisfaction of having made an intelligent effort to awaken the American woman to her unintelligent submission. But she refused to be awakened. She preferred to be a tool: to be made a fool of.

Bok's probe into the feminine nature had been keenly disappointing. He had earnestly tried to serve the American woman, and he had failed. But he was destined to receive a still greater and deeper disappointment on his next excursion into the feminine nature, although, this time, he was to win.

During his investigations into women's fashions, he had unearthed the origin of the fashionable aigrette, the most desired of all the feathered possessions of womankind. He had been told of the cruel torture of the mother-heron, who produced the beautiful aigrette only in her period of maternity and who was cruelly slaughtered, usually left to die slowly rather than killed, leaving her whole nest of baby-birds to starve while they awaited the return of the mother-bird.

Bok was shown the most heart-rending photographs portraying the butchery of the mother and the starvation of her little ones. He collected all the photographs that he could secure, had the most graphic text written to them, and began their publication. He felt certain that the mere publication of the frightfully convincing photographs would be enough to arouse the mother-instinct in every woman and stop the wearing of the so-highly prized feather. But for the second time in his attempt to reform the feminine nature he reckoned beside the mark.

He published a succession of pages showing the frightful cost at which the aigrette was secured. There was no challenging the actual facts as shown by the photographic lens: the slaughter of the mother-bird, and the starving baby-birds; and the importers of the feather wisely remained quiet, not attempting to answer Bok's accusations. Letters poured in upon the editor from Audubon Society workers; from lovers of birds, and from women filled with the humanitarian instinct. But Bok knew that the answer was not with those few: the solution lay with the larger circle of American womanhood from which he did not hear.

He waited for results. They came. But they were not those for which he had striven. After four months of his campaign, he learned from the inside of the importing-houses which dealt in the largest stocks of aigrettes in the

United States that the demand for the feather had more than quadrupled! Bok was dumbfounded! He made inquiries in certain channels from which he knew he could secure the most reliable information, and after all the importers had been interviewed, the conviction was unescapable that just in proportion as Bok had dwelt upon the desirability of the aigrette as the hallmark of wealth and fashion, upon its expense, and the fact that women regarded it as the last word in feminine adornment, he had by so much made these facts familiar to thousands of women who had never before known of them, and had created the desire to own one of the precious feathers.

Bok could not and would not accept these conclusions. It seemed to him incredible that women would go so far as this in the question of personal adornment. He caused the increased sales to be traced from wholesaler to retailer, and from retailer to customer, and was amazed at the character and standing of the latter. He had a number of those buyers who lived in adjacent cities, privately approached and interviewed, and ascertained that, save in two instances, they were all his readers, had seen the gruesome pictures he had presented, and then had deliberately purchased the coveted aigrette.

Personally again he sought the most intelligent of his woman-friends, talked with scores of others, and found himself facing the same trait in feminine nature which he had encountered in his advocacy of American fashions. But this time it seemed to Bok that the facts he had presented went so much deeper.

"It will be hard for you to believe," said one of his most trusted woman-friends. "I grant your arguments:

there is no gainsaying them. But you are fighting the same thing again that you do not understand: the feminine nature that craves outer adornment will secure it at any cost, even at the cost of suffering."

"Yes," argued Bok. "But if there is one thing above everything else that we believe a woman feels and understands, it is the mother-instinct. Do you mean to tell me that it means nothing to her that these birds are killed in their period of motherhood, and that a whole nest of starving baby-birds is the price of every aigrette?"

"I won't say that this does not weigh with a woman. It does, naturally. But when it comes to her possession of an ornament of beauty, as beautiful as the aigrette, it weighs with her, but it doesn't tip the scale against her possession of it. I am sorry to have to say this to you, but it is a fact. A woman will regret that the mother-bird must be tortured and her babies starve, but she *will* have the aigrette. She simply trains herself to forget the origin.

"Take my own case. You will doubtless be shocked when I tell you that I was perfectly aware of the conditions under which the aigrette is obtained before you began your exposure of the method. But did it prevent my purchase of one? Not at all. Why? Because I am a woman: I realize that no head ornament will set off my hair so well as an aigrette. Say I am cruel if you like. I wish the heron-mother didn't have to be killed or the babies starve, but, Mr. Bok, I *must* have my beautiful aigrette!"

Bok was frankly astounded: he had certainly probed

deep this time into the feminine nature. With every desire and instinct to disbelieve the facts, the deeper his inquiries went, the stronger the evidence rolled up: there was no gainsaying it; no sense in a further disbelief of it.

But Bok was determined that this time he would not fail. His sense of justice and protection to the motherbird and her young was now fully aroused. He resolved that he would, by compulsion, bring about what he had failed to do by persuasion. He would make it impossible for women to be untrue to their most sacred instinct. He sought legal talent, had a bill drawn up making it a misdemeanor to import, sell, purchase, or wear an aigrette. Armed with this measure, and the photographs and articles which he had published, he sought and obtained the interest and promise of support of the most influential legislators in several States. He felt a sense of pride in his own sex that he had no trouble in winning the immediate interest of every legislator with whom he talked.

Where he had failed with women, he was succeeding with men! The outrageous butchery of the birds and the circumstances under which they were tortured appealed with direct force to the sporting instinct in every man, and aroused him. Bok explained to each that he need expect no support for such a measure from women save from the members of the Audubon Societies, and a few humanitarian women and bird-lovers. Women, as a whole, he argued from his experiences, while they would not go so far as openly to oppose such a measure, for fear of public comment, would do nothing to further its passage, for in their hearts they preferred failure to success for the legislation. They had frankly told him so: he was not speaking from theory.

In one State after another Bok got into touch with legislators. He counselled, in each case, a quiet passage for the measure instead of one that would draw public attention to it.

Meanwhile, a strong initiative had come from the Audubon Societies throughout the country, and from the National Association of Audubon Societies, at New York. This latter society also caused to be introduced bills of its own to the same and in various legislatures, and here Bok had a valuable ally. It was a curious fact that the Audubon officials encountered their strongest resistance in Bok's own State: Pennsylvania. But Bok's personal acquaintance with legislators in his Keystone State helped here materially.

The demand for the aigrette constantly increased and rose to hitherto unknown figures. In one State where Bok's measure was pending before the legislature, he heard of the coming of an unusually large shipment of aigrettes to meet this increased demand. He wired the legislator in charge of the measure apprising him of this fact, of what he intended to do, and urging speed in securing the passage of the bill. Then he caused the shipment to be seized at the dock on the ground of illegal importation.

The importing firm at once secured an injunction restraining the seizure. Bok replied by serving a writ setting the injunction aside. The lawyers of the importers got busy, of course, but meanwhile the legislator had taken advantage of a special evening session, had the bill passed, and induced the governor to sign it, the act taking effect at once.

This was exactly what Bok had been playing for. The aigrettes were now useless; they could not be reshipped to another State, they could not be offered for sale. The suit was dropped, and Bok had the satisfaction of seeing the entire shipment, valued at $160,000, destroyed. He had not saved the lives of the mother-birds, but, at least, he had prevented hundreds of American women from wearing the hallmark of torture.

State after State now passed an aigrette-prohibition law until fourteen of the principal States, including practically all the large cities, fell into line.

Later, the National Association of Audubon Societies had introduced into the United States Congress and passed a bill prohibiting the importation of bird-feathers into the country, thus bringing a Federal law into existence.

Bok had won his fight, it is true, but he derived little satisfaction from the character of his victory. His ideal of womanhood had received a severe jolt. Women had revealed their worst side to him, and he did not like the picture. He had appealed to what he had been led to believe was the most sacred instinct in a woman's nature. He received no response. Moreover, he saw the deeper love for personal vanity and finery absolutely dominate the mother-instinct. He was conscious that something had toppled off its pedestal which could never be replaced.

He was aware that his mother's words, when he accepted his editorial position, were coming terribly true: "I am sorry you are going to take this position. It will cost you the high ideal you have always held of your mother's sex. But a nature, as is the feminine nature, wholly swayed inwardly by emotion, and outwardly influenced by an insatiate love for personal adornment, will never stand the analysis you will give it."

He realized that he was paying a high price for his success. Such experiences as these—and, unfortunately, they were only two of several—were doubtless in his mind when, upon his retirement, the newspapers clamored for his opinions of women. "No, thank you," he said to one and all, "not a word."

He did not give his reasons.

He never will.

CHAPTER XXX

CLEANING UP THE PATENT–MEDICINE AND OTHER EVILS

IN 1892 *The Ladies' Home Journal* announced that it would thereafter accept no advertisements of patent medicines for its pages. It was a pioneer stroke. During the following two years, seven other newspapers and periodicals followed suit. The American people were slaves to self-medication, and the patent-medicine makers had it all their own way. There was little or no legal regulation as to the ingredients in their nostrums; the mails were wide open to their circulars, and the pages of even the most reputable periodicals welcomed their advertisements. The patent-medicine business in the United States ran into the hundreds of millions of dollars annually. The business is still large; then it was enormous.

Into this army of deceit and spurious medicines, *The Ladies' Home Journal* fired the first gun. Neither the public nor the patent-medicine people paid much attention to the first attacks. But as they grew, and the evidence multiplied, the public began to comment and the nostrum makers began to get uneasy.

The magazine attacked the evil from every angle. It aroused the public by showing the actual contents of some of their pet medicines, or the absolute worthlessness of them. The Editor got the Women's Christian

Temperance Union into action against the periodicals for publishing advertisements of medicines containing as high as forty per cent alcohol. He showed that the most confidential letters written by women with private ailments were opened by young clerks of both sexes, laughed at and gossiped over, and that afterward their names and addresses, which they had been told were held in the strictest confidence, were sold to other lines of business for five cents each. He held the religious press up to the scorn of church members for accepting advertisements which the publishers knew and which he proved to be not only fraudulent, but actually harmful. He called the United States Post Office authorities to account for accepting and distributing obscene circular matter.

He cut an advertisement out of a newspaper which ended with the statement:

Mrs. Pinkham, in her laboratory at Lynn, Massachusetts, is able to do more for the ailing women of America than the family physician. Any woman, therefore, is responsible for her own suffering who will not take the trouble to write to Mrs. Pinkham for advice.

Next to this advertisement representing Mrs. Lydia Pinkham as "in her laboratory," Bok simply placed the photograph of Mrs. Pinkham's tombstone in Pine Grove Cemetery, at Lynn, showing that Mrs. Pinkham had passed away twenty-two years before!

It was one of the most effective pieces of copy that the magazine used in the campaign. It told its story with absolute simplicity, but with deadly force.

The proprietors of "Mrs. Winslow's Soothing Syrup" had strenuously denied the presence of morphine in their preparation. Bok simply bought a bottle of the syrup in London, where, under the English Pharmacy Act, the authorities compelled the proprietors of the syrup to affix the following declaration on each bottle: "This preparation, containing, among other valuable ingredients, a small amount of morphine is, in accordance with the Pharmacy Act, hereby labelled 'Poison!'" The magazine published a photograph of the label, and it told its own convincing story. It is only fair to say that the makers of this remedy now publish their formula.

Bok now slipped a cog in his machinery. He published a list of twenty-seven medicines, by name, and told what they contained. One preparation, he said, contained alcohol, opium, and digitalis. He believed he had been extremely careful in this list. He had consulted the highest medical authorities, physicians, and chemists. But in the instance of the one preparation referred to above he was wrong.

The analysis had been furnished by the secretary of the State Board of Health of Massachusetts; a recognized expert, who had taken it from the analysis of a famous German chemist. It was in nearly every standard medical authority, and was accepted by the best medical authorities. Bok accepted these authorities as final. Nevertheless, the analysis and the experts were wrong. A suit for two hundred thousand dollars was brought by the patent-medicine company against The Curtis Publishing Company, and, of course, it was decided in favor of the former. But so strong a public sentiment had been created against the whole business of patent medicines by this time that the jury gave a verdict of only sixteen thousand dollars, with costs, against the magazine.

Undaunted, Bok kept on. He now engaged Mark Sullivan, then a young lawyer in downtown New York, induced him to give up his practice, and bring his legal mind to bear upon the problem. It was the beginning of Sullivan's subsequent journalistic career, and he justified Bok's confidence in him. He exposed the testimonials to patent medicines from senators and congressmen then so widely published, showed how they were obtained by a journalist in Washington who made a business of it. He charged seventy-five dollars for a senator's testimonial, forty dollars for that of a congressman, and accepted no contract for less than five thousand dollars.

Sullivan next exposed the disgraceful violation of the confidence of women by these nostrum vendors in selling their most confidential letters to any one who would buy them. Sullivan himself bought thousands of these letters and names, and then wrote about them in the magazine. One prominent firm indignantly denied the charge, asserting that whatever others might have done, their names were always held sacred. In answer to this declaration Sullivan published an advertisement of this righteous concern offering fifty thousand of their names for sale.

Bok had now kept up the fight for over two years, and the results were apparent on every hand. Reputable newspapers and magazines were closing their pages to the advertisements of patent medicines; legislation was appearing in several States; the public had been awakened to the fraud practised upon it, and a Federal Pure Food and Drug Act was beginning to be talked about.

Single-handed, *The Ladies' Home Journal* kept up the fight until Mark Sullivan produced an unusually strong article, but too legalistic for the magazine. He called the attention of Norman Hapgood, then editor of *Collier's Weekly*, to it, who accepted it at once, and, with Bok's permission, engaged Sullivan, who later succeeded Hapgood as editor of *Collier's*. Robert J. Collier now brought Samuel Hopkins Adams to Bok's attention and asked the latter if he should object if *Collier's Weekly* joined him in his fight. The Philadelphia editor naturally welcomed the help of the weekly, and Adams began his wonderfully effective campaign.

The weekly and the monthly now pounded away together; other periodicals and newspapers, seeing success ahead, and desiring to be part of it and share the glory, came into the conflict, and it was not long before so strong a public sentiment had been created as to bring about the passage of the United States Food and Drug Act, and the patent-medicine business of the United States had received a blow from which it has never recovered. To-day the pages of every newspaper and periodical of recognized standing are closed to the advertisements of patent medicines; the Drug Act regulates the ingredients, and post office officials scan the literature sent through the United States mails.

There are distinct indications that the time has come once more to scan the patent-medicine horizon carefully, but the conditions existing in 1920 are radically different from those prevailing in 1904.

One day when Bok was at luncheon with Doctor Lyman Abbott, the latter expressed the wish that Bok would take up the subject of venereal disease as he had the patent-medicine question.

"Not our question," answered Bok.

"It is most decidedly your question," was the reply.

Bok cherished the highest regard for Doctor Abbott's opinion and judgment, and this positive declaration amazed him.

"Read up on the subject," counselled Doctor Abbott, "and you will find that the evil has its direct roots in the home with the parents. You will agree with me before you go very far that it *is* your question."

Bok began to read on the unsavory subject. It was exceedingly unpleasant reading, but for two years Bok persisted, only to find that Doctor Abbott was right. The root of the evil lay in the reticence of parents with children as to the mystery of life; boys and girls were going out into the world blind-folded as to any knowledge of their physical selves; "the bloom must not be rubbed off the peach," was the belief of thousands of parents, and the results were appalling. Bok pursued his investigations from books direct into the "Homes of Refuge," "Doors of Hope," and similar institutions, and unearthed a condition, the direct results of the false modesty of parents, that was almost unbelievable.

Bok had now all his facts, but realized that for his

magazine, of all magazines, to take up this subject would be like a bolt from the blue in tens of thousands of homes. But this very fact, the unquestioned position of the magazine, the remarkable respect which its readers had for it, and the confidence with which parents placed the periodical on their home tables—all this was, after all, Bok thought, the more reason why he should take up the matter and thresh it out. He consulted with friends, who advised against it; his editors were all opposed to the introduction of the unsavory subject into the magazine.

"But it isn't unsavory," argued Bok. "That is just it. We have made it so by making it mysterious, by surrounding it with silence, by making it a forbidden topic. It is the most beautiful story in life."

Mr. Curtis, alone, encouraged his editor. Was he sure he was right? If he was, why not go ahead? Bok called his attention to the fact that a heavy loss in circulation was a foregone conclusion; he could calculate upon one hundred thousand subscribers, at least, stopping the magazine. "It is a question of right," answered the publisher, "not of circulation."

And so, in 1906, with the subject absolutely prohibited in every periodical and newspaper of standing, never discussed at a public gathering save at medical meetings, Bok published his first editorial.

The readers of his magazine fairly gasped; they were dumb with astonishment! *The Ladies' Home Journal*, of all magazines, to discuss such a subject! When they had recovered from their astonishment, the parents began to write letters, and one morning Bok was confronted with a large waste-basket full brought in by his two office boys.

"Protests," laconically explained one of his editors. "More than that, the majority threaten to stop their subscription unless you stop."

"All right, that proves I am right," answered Bok. "Write to each one and say that what I have written is nothing as compared in frankness to what is coming, and that we shall be glad to refund the unfulfilled part of their subscriptions."

Day after day, thousands of letters came in. The next issue contained another editorial, stronger than the first. Bok explained that he would not tell the actual story of the beginning of life in the magazine—that was the prerogative of the parents, and he had no notion of taking it away from either; but that he meant to insist upon putting their duty squarely up to them, that he realized it was a long fight, hence the articles to come would be many and continued; and that those of his readers who did not believe in his policy had better stop the magazine at once. But he reminded them that no solution of any question was ever reached by running away from it. This question had to be faced some time, and now was as good a time as any.

Thousands of subscriptions were stopped; advertisements gave notice that they would cancel their accounts; the greatest pressure was placed upon Mr. Curtis to order his editor to cease, and Bok had the grim experience of seeing his magazine, hitherto proclaimed all over the land as a model advocate of the virtues, refused admittance into thousands of homes, and saw his own

friends tear the offending pages out of the periodical before it was allowed to find a place on their home-tables.

But *The Journal* kept steadily on. Number after
number contained some article on the subject, and
finally such men and women as Jane Addams, Cardinal
Gibbons, Margaret Deland, Henry van Dyke, President Eliot, the Bishop of London, braved the public
storm, came to Bok's aid, and wrote articles for his magazine heartily backing up his lonely fight.

The public, seeing this array of distinguished opinion
expressing itself, began to wonder "whether there might
not be something in what Bok was saying, after all."
At the end of eighteen months, inquiries began to take
the place of protests; and Bok knew then that the fight
was won. He employed two experts, one man and one
woman, to answer the inquiries, and he had published
a series of little books, each written by a different author
on a different aspect of the question.

This series was known as *The Edward Bok Books*.
They sold for twenty-five cents each, without profit to
either editor or publisher. The series sold into the
tens of thousands. Information was, therefore, to be
had, in authoritative form, enabling every parent to tell
the story to his or her child. Bok now insisted that
every parent should do this, and announced that he
intended to keep at the subject until the parents did.
He explained that the magazine had lost about seventy-
five thousand subscribers, and that it might just as well
lose some more; but that the insistence should go on.

Slowly but surely the subject became a debatable one.
Where, when Bok began, the leading prophylactic

society in New York could not secure five speaking dates for its single lecturer during a session, it was now put to it to find open dates for over ten speakers. Mothers' clubs, women's clubs, and organizations of all kinds clamored for authoritative talks; here and there a much-veiled article apologetically crept into print, and occasionally a progressive school board or educational institution experimented with a talk or two.

The Ladies' Home Journal published a full-page editorial declaring that seventy of every one hundred special surgical operations on women were directly or indirectly the result of one cause; that sixty of every one hundred new-born blinded babies were blinded soon after birth from this same cause; and that every man knew what this cause was!

Letters from men now began to pour in by the hundreds. With an oath on nearly every line, they told him that their wives, daughters, sisters, or mothers had demanded to know this cause, and that they had to tell them. Bok answered these heated men and told them that was exactly why the *Journal* had published the editorial, and that in the next issue there would be another for those women who might have missed his first. He insisted that the time had come when women should learn the truth, and that, so far as it lay in his power, he intended to see that they did know.

The tide of public opinion at last turned toward *The Ladies' Home Journal* and its campaign. Women began to realize that it had a case; that it was working for their best interests and for those of their children, and they decided that the question might as well be faced.

Bok now felt that his part in the work was done. He had started something well on its way; the common sense of the public must do the rest. He had taken the question of natural life, and stripped it of its false mystery in the minds of hundreds of thousands of young people; had started their inquiring minds; had shown parents the way; had made a forbidden topic a debatable subject, discussed in open gatherings, by the press, an increasing number of books, and in schools and colleges. He dropped the subject, only to take up one that was more or less akin to it.

That was the public drinking-cup. Here was a distinct menace that actual examples and figures showed was spreading the most loathsome diseases among innocent children. In 1908, he opened up the subject by ruthlessly publishing photographs that were unpleasantly but tremendously convincing. He had now secured the confidence of his vast public, who listened attentively to him when he spoke on an unpleasant topic; and having learned from experience that he would simply keep on until he got results, his readers decided that this time they would act quickly. So quick a result was hardly ever achieved in any campaign. Within six months legislation all over the country was introduced or enacted prohibiting the common drinking-cup in any public gathering-place, park, store, or theatre, and substituting the individual paper cup. Almost over night, the germ-laden common drinking-cup, which had so widely spread disease, disappeared; and in a number of States, the common towel, upon Bok's insistence, met the same fate. Within a year, one of the worst menaces to American life had been wiped out by public sentiment.

Bok was now done with health measures for a while, and determined to see what he could do with two or three civic questions that he felt needed attention.

CHAPTER XXXI

ADVENTURES IN CIVICS

THE electric power companies at Niagara Falls were beginning to draw so much water from above the great Horseshoe Falls as to bring into speculation the question of how soon America's greatest scenic asset would be a coal-pile with a thin trickle of water crawling down its vast cliffs. Already companies had been given legal permission to utilize one-quarter of the whole flow, and additional companies were asking for further grants. Permission for forty per cent of the whole volume of water had been granted. J. Horace McFarland, as President of the American Civic Association, called Bok's attention to the matter, and urged him to agitate it through his magazine so that restrictive legislation might be secured.

Bok went to Washington, conferred with President Roosevelt, and found him cognizant of the matter in all its aspects.

"I can do nothing," said the President, "unless there is an awakened public sentiment that compels action. Give me that, and I'll either put the subject in my next message to Congress or send a special message. I'm from Missouri on this point," continued the President. "Show me that the American people want their Falls preserved, and I'll do the rest. But I've got to be shown." Bok assured the President he could demonstrate this to him.

The next number of his magazine presented a graphic picture of the Horseshoe Falls as they were and the same Falls as they would be if more water was allowed to be taken for power: a barren coal-pile with a tiny rivulet of water trickling down its sides. The editorial asked whether the American women were going to allow this? If not, each, if an American, should write to the President, and, if a Canadian, to Earl Grey, then Governor-General of Canada. Very soon after the magazine had reached its subscribers' hands, the letters began to reach the White House; not by dozens, as the President's secretary wrote to Bok, but by the hundreds and then by the thousands. "Is there any way to turn this spigot off?" telegraphed the President's secretary. "We are really being inundated."

Bok went to Washington and was shown the huge pile of letters.

"All right," said the President. "That's all I want. You've proved it to me that there is a public sentiment."

The clerks at Rideau Hall, at Ottawa, did not know what had happened one morning when the mail quadrupled in size and thousands of protests came to Earl Grey. He wired the President, the President exchanged views with the governor-general, and the great international campaign to save Niagara Falls had begun. The American Civic Association and scores of other civic and patriotic bodies had joined in the clamor.

The attorney-general and the secretary of state were instructed by the President to look into the legal and diplomatic aspects of the question, and in his next message to Congress President Roosevelt uttered a clarion call to that body to restrict the power-grabbing companies.

The Ladies' Home Journal urged its readers to write to their congressmen and they did by the thousands. Every congressman and senator was overwhelmed. As one senator said: "I have never seen such an avalanche. But thanks to *The Ladies' Home Journal*, I have received these hundreds of letters from my constituents; they have told me what they want done, and they are mostly from those of my people whose wishes I am bound to respect."

The power companies, of course, promptly sent their attorneys and lobbyists to Washington; but the public sentiment aroused was too strong to be disregarded, and on June 29, 1906, the President signed the Burton Bill restricting the use of the water of Niagara Falls.

The matter was then referred to the secretary of war, William Howard Taft, to grant the use of such volume of water as would preserve the beauty of the Falls. McFarland and Bok wanted to be sure that Secretary Taft felt the support of public opinion, for his policy was to be conservative, and tremendous pressure was being brought upon him from every side to permit a more liberal use of water. Bok turned to his readers and asked them to write to Secretary Taft and assure him of the support of the American women in his attitude of conservatism.

The flood of letters that descended upon the secretary almost taxed even his genial nature; and when Mr. McFarland, as the editorial representative of *The Ladies' Home Journal*, arose to speak at the public hearing in

Washington, the secretary said: "I can assure you that you don't have to say very much. Your case has already been pleaded for you by, I should say at the most conservative estimate, at least one hundred thousand women. Why, I have had letters from even my wife and my mother."

Secretary Taft adhered to his conservative policy, Sir Wilfred Laurier, premier of Canada, met the overtures of Secretary of State Root, a new international document was drawn up, and Niagara Falls had been saved to the American people.

In 1905 and in previous years the casualties resulting from fireworks on the Fourth of July averaged from five to six thousand each year. The humorous weekly *Life* and *The Chicago Tribune* had been for some time agitating a restricted use of fireworks on the national fête day, but nevertheless the list of casualties kept creeping to higher figures. Bok decided to help by arousing the parents of America, in whose hands, after all, lay the remedy. He began a series of articles in the magazine, showing what had happened over a period of years, the criminality of allowing so many young lives to be snuffed out, and suggested how parents could help by prohibiting the deadly firecrackers and cannon, and how organizations could assist by influencing the passing of city ordinances. Each recurring January, *The Journal* returned to the subject, looking forward to the coming Fourth. It was a deep-rooted custom to eradicate, and powerful influences, in the form of thousands of small storekeepers, were at work upon local officials to pay no heed to the agitation. Gradually public opinion changed.

The newspapers joined in the cry; women's organizations insisted upon action from local municipal bodies.

Finally, the civic spirit in Cleveland, Ohio, forced the passage of a city ordinance prohibiting the sale or use of fireworks on the Fourth. The following year when Cleveland reported no casualties as compared to an ugly list for the previous Fourth, a distinct impression was made upon other cities. Gradually, other municipalities took action, and year by year the list of Fourth of July casualties grew perceptibly shorter. New York City was now induced to join the list of prohibitive cities, by a personal appeal made to its mayor by Bok, and on the succeeding Fourth of July the city authorities, on behalf of the people of New York City, conferred a gold medal upon Edward Bok for his services in connection with the birth of the new Fourth in that city.

There still remains much to be done in cities as yet unawakened; but a comparison of the list of casualties of 1920 with that of 1905 proves the growth in enlightened public sentiment in fifteen years to have been steadily increasing. It is an instance not of Bok taking the initiative—that had already been taken— but of throwing the whole force of the magazine with those working in the field to help. It is the American woman who is primarily responsible for the safe and sane Fourth, so far as it already exists in this country to-day, and it is the American woman who can make it universal.

Mrs. Pennypacker, as president of The Federation of Women's Clubs, now brought to Bok's attention the conditions under which the average rural school-teacher lived; the suffering often entailed on her in having to walk miles to the schoolhouse in wintry weather; the discomfort she had to put up with in the farm-houses where she was compelled to live, with the natural result, under those conditions, that it was almost impossible to secure the services of capable teachers, or to have good teaching even where efficient teachers were obtained.

Mrs. Pennypacker suggested that Bok undertake the creation of a public sentiment for a residence for the teacher in connection with the schoolhouse. The parson was given a parsonage; why not the teacher a "teacherage"? *The Journal* co-operated with Mrs. Pennypacker and she began the agitation of the subject in the magazine. She also spoke on the subject wherever she went, and induced women's clubs all over the country to join the magazine in its advocacy of the "teacherage."

By personal effort, several "teacherages" were established in connection with new schoolhouses; photographs of these were published and sent personally to school-boards all over the country; the members of women's clubs saw to it that the articles were brought to the attention of members of their local school-boards; and the now-generally accepted idea that a "teacherage" must accompany a new schoolhouse was well on its way to national recognition.

It only remains now for communities to install a visiting nurse in each of these "teacherages" so that the teacher need not live in solitary isolation, and that the health of the children at school can be looked after at first hand. Then the nurse shall be at the call of every small

American community—particularly to be available in
cases of childbirth, since in these thinly settled districts
it is too often impossible to obtain the services of a
physician, with the result of a high percentage of fatali-
ties to mothers that should not be tolerated by a wealthy
and progressive people. No American mother, at childbirth, should be denied the assistance of professional
skill, no matter how far she may live from a physician.
And here is where a visiting nurse in every community
can become an institution of inestimable value.

Just about this time a group of Philadelphia physicians, headed by Doctor Samuel McClintock Hamill,
which had formed itself into a hygienic committee for
babies, waited upon Bok to ask him to join them in the
creation of a permanent organization devoted to the
welfare of babies and children. Bok found that he was
dealing with a company of representative physicians,
and helped to organize "The Child Federation," an
organization "to do good on a business basis."

It was to go to the heart of the problem of the baby
in the congested districts of Philadelphia, and do a piece
of intensive work in the ward having the highest infant
mortality, establishing the first health centre in the
United States actively managed by competent physicians
and nurses. This centre was to demonstrate to the city
authorities that the fearful mortality among babies,
particularly in summer, could be reduced.

Meanwhile, there was created a "Baby Saving Show,"
a set of graphic pictures conveying to the eye methods
of sanitation and other too often disregarded essentials
of the wise care and feeding of babies; and this travelled,

like a theatrical attraction, to different parts of the city. "Little Mothers' Leagues" were organized to teach the little girl of ten or twelve, so often left in charge of a family of children when the mother is at work during the day, and demonstrations were given in various parts of the city.

The Child Federation now undertook one activity after the other. Under its auspices, the first municipal Christmas tree ever erected in Philadelphia was shown in the historic Independence Square, and with two bands of music giving concerts every day from Christmas to New Year's Day, attracted over two hundred thousand persons. A pavilion was erected in City Hall Square, the most central spot in the city, and the "Baby Saving Show" was permanently placed there and visited by over one hundred thousand visitors from every part of the country on their way to and from the Pennsylvania Station at Broad Street.

A searching investigation of the Day Nurseries of Philadelphia—probably one of the most admirable pieces of research work ever made in a city—changed the methods in vogue and became a standard guide for similar institutions throughout the country. So successful were the Little Mothers' Leagues that they were introduced into the public schools of Philadelphia, and are to-day a regular part of the curriculum. The Health Centre, its success being proved, was taken over by the city Board of Health, and three others were established.

To-day The Child Federation is recognized as one of the most practically conducted child welfare agencies in Philadelphia, and its methods have been followed by similar organizations all over the country. It is now rapidly becoming the central medium through which the other agencies in Philadelphia are working, thus avoiding the duplication of infant welfare work in the city. Broadening its scope, it is not unlikely to become one of the greatest indirect influences in the welfare work of Philadelphia and the vicinity, through which other organizations will be able to work.

Bok's interest and knowledge in civic matters had now peculiarly prepared him for a personal adventure into community work. Merion, where he lived, was one of the most beautiful of the many suburbs that surround the Quaker City; but, like hundreds of similar communities, there had been developed in it no civic interest. Some of the most successful business men of Philadelphia lived in Merion; they had beautiful estates, which they maintained without regard to expense, but also without regard to the community as a whole. They were busy men; they came home tired after a day in the city; they considered themselves good citizens if they kept their own places sightly, but the idea of devoting their evenings to the problems of their community had never occurred to them before the evening when two of Bok's neighbors called to ask his help in forming a civic association.

A canvass of the sentiment of the neighborhood revealed the unanimous opinion that the experiment, if attempted, would be a failure,—an attitude not by any means confined to the residents of Merion! Bok decided to test it out; he called together twenty of his neighbors, put the suggestion before them and asked for two thousand dollars as a start, so that a paid secretary might be engaged, since the men themselves were too busy to attend to the details of the work. The amount was immediately subscribed, and in 1913 The Merion Civic Association applied for a charter and began its existence.

The leading men in the community were elected as a Board of Directors, and a salaried secretary was engaged to carry out the directions of the Board. The association adopted the motto: "To be nation right, and State right, we must first be community right." Three objectives were selected with which to attract community interest and membership: safety to life, in the form of proper police protection; safety to property, in the form of adequate hydrant and fire-engine service; and safety to health, in careful supervision of the water and milk used in the community.

"The three S's," as they were called, brought an immediate response. They were practical in their appeal, and members began to come in. The police force was increased from one officer at night and none in the day, to three at night and two during the day, and to this the Association added two special night officers of its own. Private detectives were intermittently brought in to "check up" and see that the service was vigilant. A fire hydrant was placed within seven hundred feet of every house, with the insurance rates reduced from twelve and one-half to thirty per cent; the services of three fire-engine companies was arranged for. Fire-gongs were introduced into the community to guard against danger from interruption of telephone service.

The water supply was chemically analyzed each month and the milk supply carefully scrutinized. One hundred and fifty new electric-light posts specially designed, and pronounced by experts as the most beautiful and practical road lamps ever introduced into any community. were erected, making Merion the best-lighted community in its vicinity.

At every corner was erected an artistically designed cast-iron road sign; instead of the unsightly wooden ones, cast-iron automobile warnings were placed at every dangerous spot; community bulletin-boards, preventing the display of notices on trees and poles, were placed at the railroad station; litter-cans were distributed over the entire community; a new railroad station and post-office were secured; the station grounds were laid out as a garden by a landscape architect; new roads of permanent construction, from curb to curb, were laid down; uniform tree-planting along the roads was introduced; bird-houses were made and sold, so as to attract bird-life to the community; toll-gates were abolished along the two main arteries of travel; the removal of all telegraph and telephone poles was begun; an efficient Boy Scout troop was organized, and an American Legion post; the automobile speed limit was reduced from twenty-four to fifteen miles as a protection to children; roads were regularly swept, cleaned, and oiled, and uniform sidewalks advocated and secured.

Within seven years so efficiently had the Association functioned that its work attracted attention far beyond its own confines and that of Philadelphia, and caused Theodore Roosevelt voluntarily to select it as a subject for a special magazine article in which he declared it to "stand as a model in civic matters." To-day it may be conservatively said of The Merion Civic Association that it is pointed out as one of the most successful suburban civic efforts in the country; as Doctor Lyman Abbott said in *The Outlook*, it has made "Merion a model suburb, which may standardize ideal suburban life, certainly for Philadelphia, possibly for the United States."

When the armistice was signed in November, 1918, the Association immediately canvassed the neighborhood to erect a suitable Tribute House, as a memorial to the eighty-three Merion boys who had gone into the Great War: a public building which would comprise a community centre, with an American Legion Post room, a Boy Scout house, an auditorium, and a meeting-place for the civic activities of Merion. A subscription was raised, and plans were already drawn for the Tribute House, when Mr. Eldridge R. Johnson, president of the Victor Talking Machine Company, one of the strong supporters of The Merion Civic Association, presented his entire estate of twelve acres, the finest in Merion, to the community, and agreed to build a Tribute House at his own expense. The grounds represented a gift of two hundred thousand dollars, and the building a gift of two hundred and fifty thousand dollars. This building, now about to be erected, will be one of the most beautiful and complete community centres in the United States.

Perhaps no other suburban civic effort proves the efficiency of community co-operation so well as does the seven years' work of The Merion Civic Association. It is a practical demonstration of what a community can do for itself by concerted action. It preached, from the very start, the gospel of united service; it translated into actual practice the doctrine of being one's brother's keeper, and it taught the invaluable habit of collective action. The Association has no legal powers; it rules solely by persuasion; it accomplishes by the power of combination; by a spirit of the community for the community.

When The Merion Civic Association was conceived, the spirit of local pride was seemingly not present in the community. As a matter of fact, it was there as it is in practically every neighborhood; it was simply dormant; it had to be awakened, and its value brought vividly to the community consciousness.

CHAPTER XXXII

A BEWILDERED BOK

ONE of the misfortunes of Edward Bok's training, which he realized more clearly as time went on, was that music had little or no place in his life. His mother did not play; and aside from the fact that his father and mother were patrons of the opera during their residence in The Netherlands, the musical atmosphere was lacking in his home. He realized how welcome an outlet music might be in his now busy life. So what he lacked himself and realized as a distinct omission in his own life he decided to make possible for others.

The Ladies' Home Journal began to strike a definite musical note. It first caught the eye and ear of its public by presenting the popular new marches by John Philip Sousa; and when the comic opera of "Robin Hood" became the favorite of the day, it secured all the new compositions by Reginald de Koven. Following these, it introduced its readers to new compositions by Sir Arthur Sullivan, Tosti, Moscowski, Richard Strauss, Paderewski, Josef Hofmann, Edouard Strauss, and Mascagni. Bok induced Josef Hofmann to give a series of piano lessons in his magazine, and Madame Marchesi a series of vocal lessons. *The Journal* introduced its readers to all the great instrumental and vocal artists of the day through articles; it offered prizes for the best piano and vocal compositions; it had the leading critics of New York, Boston, and Chicago write articles explanatory of orchestral music and how to listen to music.

Bok was early attracted by the abilities of Josef Hofmann. In 1898, he met the pianist, who was then twenty-two years old. Of his musical ability Bok could not judge, but he was much impressed by his unusual mentality, and soon both learned and felt that Hofmann's art was deeply and firmly rooted. Hofmann had a wider knowledge of affairs than other musicians whom Bok had met; he had not narrowed his interests to his own art. He was striving to achieve a position in his art, and, finding that he had literary ability, Bok asked him to write a reminiscent article on his famous master, Rubinstein.

This was followed by other articles; the publication of his new mazurka; still further articles; and then, in 1907, Bok offered him a regular department in the magazine and a salaried editorship on his staff.

Bok's musical friends and the music critics tried to convince the editor that Hofmann's art lay not so deep as Bok imagined; that he had been a child prodigy, and would end where all child prodigies invariably end—opinions which make curious reading now in view of Hofmann's commanding position in the world of music. But while Bok lacked musical knowledge, his instinct led him to adhere to his belief in Hofmann; and for twelve years, until Bok's retirement as editor, the pianist was a regular contributor to the magazine. His success was, of course, unquestioned. He answered hundreds of questions sent him by his readers, and these answers furnished such valuable advice for piano students that two volumes were made in book form and are to-day used by piano teachers and students as authoritative guides.

Meanwhile, Bok's marriage had brought music directly into his domestic circle. Mrs. Bok loved music, was a pianist herself, and sought to acquaint her husband with what his former training had omitted. Hofmann and Bok had become strong friends outside of the editorial relation, and the pianist frequently visited the Bok home. But it was some time, even with these influences surrounding him, before music began to play any real part in Bok's own life.

He attended the opera occasionally; more or less under protest, because of its length, and because his mind was too practical for the indirect operatic form. He could not remain patient at a recital; the effort to listen to one performer for an hour and a half was too severe a tax upon his restless nature. The Philadelphia Orchestra gave a symphony concert each Saturday evening, and Bok dreaded the coming of that evening in each week for fear of being taken to hear music which he was convinced was "over his head."

Like many men of his practical nature, he had made up his mind on this point without ever having heard such a concert. The word "symphony" was enough; it conveyed to him a form of the highest music quite beyond his comprehension. Then, too, in the back of his mind there was the feeling that, while he was perfectly willing to offer the best that the musical world afforded in his magazine, his readers were primarily women, and the appeal of music, after all, he felt was largely, if not wholly, to the feminine nature. It was very satisfying to him to hear his wife play in the evening; but when it came to public concerts, they were not for his masculine nature. In other words, Bok shared the all too common masculine notion that music is for women and has little place in the lives of men.

One day Josef Hofmann gave Bok an entirely new point of view. The artist was rehearsing in Philadelphia for an appearance with the orchestra, and the pianist was telling Bok and his wife of the desire of Leopold Stokowski, who had recently become conductor of the Philadelphia Orchestra, to eliminate encores from his symphonic programmes; he wanted to begin the experiment with Hofmann's appearance that week. This was a novel thought to Bok: why eliminate encores from any concert? If he liked the way any performer played, he had always done his share to secure an encore. Why should not the public have an encore if it desired it, and why should a conductor or a performer object? Hofmann explained to him the entity of a symphonic programme; that it was made up with one composition in relation to the others as a sympathetic unit, and that an encore was an intrusion, disturbing the harmony of the whole.

"I wish you would let Stokowski come out and explain to you what he is trying to do," said Hofmann. "He knows what he wants, and he is right in his efforts; but he doesn't know how to educate the public. There is where you could help him."

But Bok had no desire to meet Stokowski. He mentally pictured the conductor: long hair; feet never touching the earth; temperament galore; he knew them! And he had no wish to introduce the type into his home life.

Mrs. Bok, however, ably seconded Josef Hofmann, and endeavored to dissipate Bok's preconceived notion, with the result that Stokowksi came to the Bok home.

Bok was not slow to see that Stokowski was quite the reverse of his mental picture, and became intensely interested in the youthful conductor's practical way of looking at things. It was agreed that the encore "bull" was to be taken by the horns that week; that no matter what the ovation to Hofmann might be, however the public might clamor, no encore was to be forthcoming; and Bok was to give the public an explanation during the following week. The next concert was to present Mischa Elman, and his co-operation was assured so that continuity of effort might be counted upon.

In order to have first-hand information, Bok attended the concert that Saturday evening. The symphony, Dvořák's "New World Symphony," amazed Bok by its beauty; he was more astonished that he could so easily grasp any music in symphonic form. He was equally surprised at the simple beauty of the other numbers on the programme, and wondered not a little at his own perfectly absorbed attention during Hofmann's playing of a rather long concerto.

The pianist's performance was so beautiful that the audience was uproarious in its approval; it had calculated, of course, upon an encore, and recalled the pianist again and again until he had appeared and bowed his thanks several times. But there was no encore;

the stage hands appeared and moved the piano to one side, and the audience relapsed into unsatisfied and rather bewildered silence.

Then followed Bok's publicity work in the newspapers, beginning the next day, exonerating Hofmann and explaining the situation. The following week, with Mischa Elman as soloist, the audience once more tried to have its way and its cherished encore, but again none was forthcoming. Once more the newspapers explained; the battle was won, and the no-encore rule has prevailed at the Philadelphia Orchestra concerts from that day to this, with the public entirely resigned to the idea and satisfied with the reason therefor.

But the bewildered Bok could not make out exactly what had happened to his preconceived notion about symphonic music. He attended the following Saturday evening concert; listened to a Brahms symphony that pleased him even more than had "The New World," and when, two weeks later, he heard the Tschaikowski "Pathetique" and later the "Unfinished" symphony, by Schubert, and a Beethoven symphony, attracted by each in turn, he realized that his prejudice against the whole question of symphonic music had been both wrongly conceived and baseless.

He now began to see the possibility of a whole world of beauty which up to that time had been closed to him, and he made up his mind that he would enter it. Somehow or other, he found the appeal of music did not confine itself to women; it seemed to have a message for men. Then, too, instead of dreading the approach of Saturday evenings, he was looking forward to them, and invariably so arranged his engagements that they might not interfere with his attendance at the orchestra concerts.

After a busy week, he discovered that nothing he had ever experienced served to quiet him so much as these end-of-the-week concerts. They were not too long, an hour and a half at the utmost; and, above all, except now and then, when the conductor would take a flight into the world of Bach, he found he followed him with at least a moderate degree of intelligence; certainly with personal pleasure and inner satisfaction.

Bok concluded he would not read the articles he had published on the meaning of the different "sections" of a symphony orchestra, or the books issued on that subject. He would try to solve the mechanism of an orchestra for himself, and ascertain as he went along the relation that each portion bore to the other. When, therefore, in 1913, the president of the Philadelphia Orchestra Association asked him to become a member of its Board of Directors, his acceptance was a natural step in the gradual development of his interest in orchestral music.

The public support given to orchestras now greatly interested Bok. He was surprised to find that every symphony orchestra had a yearly deficit. This he immediately attributed to faulty management; but on investigating the whole question he learned that a symphony orchestra could not possibly operate, at a profit or even on a self-sustaining basis, because of its weekly change of programme, the incessant rehearsals required, and the limited number of times it could actually play within a contracted season. An annual deficit was inevitable.

He found that the Philadelphia Orchestra had a small but faithful group of guarantors who each year made good the deficit in addition to paying for its concert seats. This did not seem to Bok a sound business plan; it made of the orchestra a necessarily exclusive organization, maintained by a few; and it gave out this impression to the general public, which felt that it did not "belong," whereas the true relation of public and orchestra was that of mutual dependence. Other orchestras, he found, as, for example, the Boston Symphony and the New York Philharmonic had their deficits met by one individual patron in each case. This, to Bok's mind, was an even worse system, since it entirely excluded the public, making the orchestra dependent on the continued interest and life of a single man.

In 1916 Bok sought Mr. Alexander Van Rensselaer, the president of the Philadelphia Orchestra Association, and proposed that he, himself, should guarantee the deficit of the orchestra for five years, provided that during that period an endowment fund should be raised, contributed by a large number of subscribers, and sufficient in amount to meet, from its interest, the annual deficit. It was agreed that the donor should remain in strict anonymity, an understanding which has been adhered to until the present writing.

The offer from the "anonymous donor," presented by the president, was accepted by the Orchestra Association. A subscription to an endowment fund was shortly afterward begun; and the amount had been brought to eight hundred thousand dollars when the Great War interrupted any further additions. In the autumn of 1919, however, a city-wide campaign for an addition of one million dollars to the endowment fund was launched. The amount was not only secured, but over-subscribed. Thus, instead of a guarantee fund, contributed by thirteen hundred subscribers, with the necessity for annual collection, an endowment fund of one million eight hundred thousand dollars, contributed by fourteen thousand subscribers, has been secured; and the Philadelphia Orchestra has been promoted from a privately maintained organization to a public institution in which fourteen thousand residents of Philadelphia feel a proprietary interest. It has become in fact, as well as in name, "our orchestra."

CHAPTER XXXIII

HOW MILLIONS OF PEOPLE ARE REACHED

THE success of *The Ladies' Home Journal* went steadily forward. The circulation had passed the previously unheard-of figure for a monthly magazine of a million and a half copies per month; it had now touched a million and three-quarters.

And not only was the figure so high, but the circulation itself was absolutely free from "water." The public could not obtain the magazine through what are known as clubbing-rates, since no subscriber was permitted to include any other magazine with it; years ago it had abandoned the practice of offering premiums or consideration of any kind to induce subscriptions; and the newsdealers were not allowed to return unsold copies of the periodical. Hence every copy was either purchased by the public at the full price at a newsstand, or subscribed for at its stated subscription price. It was, in short, an authoritative circulation. And on every hand the question was being asked: "How is it done? How is such a high circulation obtained?"

Bok's invariable answer was that he gave his readers the very best of the class of reading that he believed would interest them, and that he spared neither effort nor expense to obtain it for them. When Mr. Howells once asked him how he classified his audience, Bok replied: "We appeal to the intelligent American woman rather than to the intellectual type." And he gave her the best he could obtain. As he knew her to be fond of the personal type of literature, he gave her in succession Jane Addams's story of "My Fifteen Years at Hull House," and the remarkable narration of Helen Keller's "Story of My Life"; he invited Henry Van Dyke, who had never been in the Holy Land, to go there, camp out in a tent, and then write a series of sketches, "Out of Doors in the Holy Land"; he induced Lyman Abbott to tell the story of "My Fifty Years as a Minister." He asked Gene Stratton Porter to tell of her bird-experiences in the series: "What I Have Done with Birds"; he persuaded Dean Hodges to turn from his work of training young clergymen at the Episcopal Seminary, at Cambridge, and write one of the most successful series of Bible stories for children ever printed; and then he supplemented this feature for children by publishing Rudyard Kipling's "Just So" stories and his "Puck of Pook's Hill." He induced F. Hopkinson Smith to tell the best stories he had ever heard in his wide travels in "The Man in the Arm Chair"; he got Kate Douglas Wiggin to tell a country church experience of hers in "The Old Peabody Pew"; and Jean Webster her knowledge of almshouse life in "Daddy Long Legs."

The readers of *The Ladies' Home Journal* realized that it searched the whole field of endeavor in literature and art to secure what would interest them, and they responded with their support.

Another of Bok's methods in editing was to do the common thing in an uncommon way. He had the faculty of putting old wine in new bottles and the public liked it. His ideas were not new; he knew there were no new ideas, but he presented his ideas in such a way that they seemed new. It is a significant fact, too, that a large public will respond more quickly to an idea than it will to a name.

This *The Ladies' Home Journal* proved again and again. Its most pronounced successes, from the point of view of circulation, were those in which the idea was the sole and central appeal. For instance, when it gave American women an opportunity to look into a hundred homes and see how they were furnished, it added a hundred thousand copies to the circulation. There was nothing new in publishing pictures of rooms and, had it merely done this, it is questionable whether success would have followed the effort. It was the way in which it was done. The note struck entered into the feminine desire, reflected it, piqued curiosity, and won success.

Again, when *The Journal* decided·to show good taste and bad taste in furniture, in comparative pictures, another hundred thousand circulation came to it. There was certainly nothing new in the comparative idea; but applied to a question of taste, which could not be explained so clearly in words, it seemed new.

Had it simply presented masterpieces of art as such, the series might have attracted little attention. But when it announced that these masterpieces had always been kept in private galleries, and seen only by the favored few; that the public had never been allowed to get any closer to them than to read of the fabulous prices paid by their millionaire owners; and that now the magazine would open the doors of those exclusive galleries and let the public in—public curiosity was at once piqued, and over one hundred and fifty thousand persons who had never before bought the magazine were added to the list.

In not one of these instances, nor in the case of other successful series, did the appeal to the public depend upon the names of contributors; there were none: it was the idea which the public liked and to which it responded.

The editorial Edward Bok enjoyed this hugely; the real Edward Bok did not. The one was bottled up in the other. It was a case of absolute self-effacement. The man behind the editor knew that if he followed his own personal tastes and expressed them in his magazine, a limited audience would be his instead of the enormous clientele that he was now reaching. It was the man behind the editor who had sought expression in the idea of *Country Life*, the magazine which his company sold to Doubleday, Page & Company, and which he would personally have enjoyed editing.

It was in 1913 that the real Edward Bok, bottled up for twenty-five years, again came to the surface. The majority stockholders of *The Century Magazine* wanted to dispose of their interest in the periodical. Overtures were made to The Curtis Publishing Company, but its hands were full, and the matter was presented for Bok's personal consideration. The idea interested him, as he saw in *The Century* a chance for his self-expression. He entered into negotiations, looked carefully into the property itself and over the field which such a magazine might fill, decided to buy it, and install an active editor while he, as a close adviser, served as the propelling power.

Bok figured out that there was room for one of the trio of what was, and still is, called the standard-sized magazines, namely *Scribner's*, *Harper's*, and *The Century*. He believed, as he does to-day, that any one of these magazines could be so edited as to preserve all its traditions and yet be so ingrafted with the new progressive, modern spirit as to dominate the field and constitute itself the leader in that particular group. He believed that there was a field which would produce a circulation in the neighborhood of a quarter of a million copies a month for one of those magazines, so that it would be considered not, as now, one of three, but *the* one.

What Bok saw in the possibilities of the standard illustrated magazine has been excellently carried out by Mr. Ellery Sedgwick in *The Atlantic Monthly;* every tradition has been respected, and yet the new progressive note introduced has given it a position and a circulation never before attained by a non-illustrated magazine of the highest class.

As Bok studied the field, his confidence in the proposition, as he saw it, grew. For his own amusement, he made up some six issues of *The Century* as he visualized it, and saw that the articles he had included were all obtainable. He selected a business manager and publisher who would relieve him of the manufacturing problems; but before the contract was actually closed Bok, naturally, wanted to consult Mr. Curtis, who was just returning from abroad, as to this proposed sharing of his editor.

For one man to edit two magazines inevitably meant a distribution of effort, and this Mr. Curtis counselled against. He did not believe that any man could successfully serve two masters; it would also mean a division of public association; it might result in Bok's physical undoing, as already he was overworked. Mr. Curtis's arguments, of course, prevailed; the negotiations were immediately called off, and for the second time—for some wise reason, undoubtedly—the real Edward Bok was subdued. He went back into the bottle!

A cardinal point in Edward Bok's code of editing was not to commit his magazine to unwritten material, or to accept and print articles or stories simply because they were the work of well-known persons. And as his acquaintance with authors multiplied, he found that the greater the man the more willing he was that his work should stand or fall on its merit, and that the editor should retain his prerogative of declination—if he deemed it wise to exercise it.

Rudyard Kipling was, and is, a notable example of this broad and just policy. His work is never imposed upon an editor; it is invariably submitted, in its completed form, for acceptance or declination. "Wait until it's done," said Kipling once to Bok as he outlined a story to him which the editor liked, "and see whether you want it. You can't tell until then." (What a difference from the type of author who insists that an editor must take his or her story before a line is written!)

"I told Watt to send you," he writes to Bok, "the first four of my child stories (you see I hadn't forgotten my promise), and they may serve to amuse you for a while personally, even if you don't use them for publication. Frankly, I don't myself see how they can be used for the L. H. J.; but they're part of a scheme of mine for trying to give children *not* a notion of history, but a notion of the time sense which is at the bottom of all knowledge of history; and history, rightly understood, means the love of one's fellow-men and the land one lives in."

James Whitcomb Riley was another who believed that an editor should have the privilege of saying "No" if he so elected. When Riley was writing a series of poems for Bok, the latter, not liking a poem which the Hoosier poet sent him, returned it to him. He wondered how Riley would receive a declination—naturally a rare experience. But his immediate answer settled the question:

Thanks equally for your treatment of both poems, [he wrote], the one accepted and the other returned. Maintain your own opinions and respect, and my vigorous esteem for you shall remain "deep-rooted in the fruitful soil." No occasion for apology whatever. In my opinion, you are wrong; in your opinion, you are right; therefore, you *are* right,—at least righter than wronger. It is seldom that I drop other work for logic, but when I do, as my grandfather was wont to sturdily remark, "it is to some purpose, I can promise you."

Am goin' to try mighty hard to send you the dialect work you've so long wanted; in few weeks at furthest. "Patience and shuffle the cards."

I am really, just now, stark and bare of one common-

sense idea. In the writing line, I was never so involved before and see no end to the ink-(an humorous voluntary pro-
vocative, I trust of much merriment)-creasing pressure of
it all. Even the hope of waking to find myself famous is
denied me, since I haven't time in which to fall asleep. Therefore, very drowsily and yawningly indeed, I am your

JAMES WHITCOMB RILEY.

Neither did the President of the United States consider himself above a possible declination of his material
if it seemed advisable to the editor. In 1916 Woodrow
Wilson wrote to Bok:

Sometime ago you kindly intimated to me that you would
like to publish an article from me. At first, it seemed impossible for me to undertake anything of the kind, but I have found
a little interval in which I have written something on Mexico
which I hope you will think worthy of publication. If not,
will you return it to me?

The President, too, acted as an intermediary in turning authors in Bok's direction, when the way opened.
In a letter written not on the official White House letter-
head, but on his personal "up-stairs" stationery, as it
is called, he asks:

Will you do me the favor of reading the enclosed to see if
it is worthy of your acceptance for the *Journal*, or whether
you think it indicates that the writer, with a few directions
and suggestions, might be useful to you?

It was written by ——. She is a woman of great refine-
ment, of a very unusually broad social experience, and of
many exceptional gifts, who thoroughly knows what she is
writing about, whether she has yet discovered the best way
to set it forth or not. She is one of the most gifted and re-

sourceful hostesses I have known, but has now fallen upon hard times.

Among other things that she really knows, she really does thoroughly know old furniture and all kinds of china worth knowing.

Pardon me if I have been guilty of an indiscretion in sending this direct to you. I am throwing myself upon your indulgence in my desire to help a splendid woman.

She has a great collection of recipes which housekeepers would like to have. Does a serial cook-book sound like nonsense?

A further point in his editing which Bok always kept in view was his rule that the editor must always be given the privilege of revising or editing a manuscript. Bok's invariable rule was, of course, to submit his editing for approval, but here again the bigger the personality back of the material, the more willing the author was to have his manuscript "blue pencilled," if he were convinced that the deletions or condensations improved or at least did not detract from his arguments. It was the small author who ever resented the touch of the editorial pencil upon his precious effusions.

As a matter of fact there are few authors who cannot be edited with advantage, and it would be infinitely better for our reading if this truth was applied to some of the literature of to-day.

Bok had once under his hand a story by Mark Twain, which he believed contained passages that should be deleted. They represented a goodly portion of the manuscript. They were, however, taken out, and the result submitted to the humorist. The answer was curious. Twain evidently saw that Bok was right, for he wrote: "Of course, I want every single line and word of it left out," and then added: "Do me the favor to call the next time you are again in Hartford. I want to say things which—well, I want to argue with you." Bok never knew what those "things" were, for at the next meeting they were not referred to.

It is, perhaps, a curious coincidence that all the Presidents of the United States whose work Bok had occasion to publish were uniformly liberal with regard to having their material edited.

Colonel Roosevelt was always ready to concede improvement: "Fine," he wrote; "the changes are much for the better. I never object to my work being improved, where it needs it, so long as the sense is not altered."

William Howard Taft wrote, after being subjected to editorial revision: "You have done very well by my article. You have made it much more readable by your rearrangement."

Mr. Cleveland was very likely to let his interest in a subject run counter to the space exigencies of journalism; and Bok, in one instance, had to reduce one of his articles considerably. He explained the reason and enclosed the revision.

"I am entirely willing to have the article cut down as you suggest," wrote the former President. "I find sufficient reason for this in the fact that the matter you suggest for elimination has been largely exploited lately. And in looking the matter over carefully, I am inclined to think that the article expurgated as you suggest will gain in unity and directness. At first, I feared it would appear a little 'bobbed' off, but you are a much better judge of that than I. . . . I leave it altogether to you."

It was always interesting to Bok, as a study of mental processes, to note how differently he and some author with whom he would talk it over would see the method of treating some theme. He was discussing the growing unrest among American women with Rudyard Kipling at the latter's English home; and expressed the desire that the novelist should treat the subject and its causes.

They talked until the early hours, when it was agreed that each should write out a plan, suggest the best treatment, and come together the next morning. When they did so, Kipling had mapped out the scenario of a novel; Bok had sketched out the headings of a series of analytical articles. Neither one could see the other's viewpoint, Kipling contending for the greater power of fiction and Bok strongly arguing for the value of the direct essay. In this instance, the point was never settled, for the work failed to materialize in any form!

If the readers of *The Ladies' Home Journal* were quick to support its editor when he presented an idea that appealed to them, they were equally quick to tell him when he gave them something of which they did not approve. An illustration of this occurred during the dance-craze that preceded the Great War. In 1914, America was dance-mad, and the character of the dances rapidly grew more and more offensive. Bok's readers, by the hundreds, urged him to come out against the tendency.

The editor looked around and found that the country's terpsichorean idols were Mr. and Mrs. Vernon Castle;

he decided that, with their cooperation, he might, by thus going to the fountainhead, effect an improvement through the introduction, by the Castles, of better and more decorous new dances. Bok could see no reason why the people should not dance, if they wanted to, so long as they kept within the bounds of decency.

He found the Castles willing and eager to cooperate, not only because of the publicity it would mean for them, but because they were themselves not in favor of the new mode. They had little sympathy for the elimination of the graceful dance by the introduction of what they called the "shuffle" or the "bunny-hug," "turkey-trot," and other ungraceful and unworthy dances. It was decided that the Castles should, through Bok's magazine and their own public exhibitions, revive the gavotte, the polka, and finally the waltz. They would evolve these into new forms and Bok would present them pictorially. A series of three double-page presentations was decided upon, allowing for large photographs so that the steps could be easily seen and learned from the printed page.

The magazine containing the first "lesson" was no sooner published than protests began to come in by the hundreds. Bok had not stated his object, and the public misconstrued his effort and purpose into an acknowledgment that he had fallen a victim to the prevailing craze. He explained in letters, but to no purpose. Try as he might, Bok could not rid the pages of the savor of the cabaret. He published the three dances as agreed, but he realized he had made a mistake, and was as much disgusted as were his readers.

Nor did he, in the slightest degree, improve the dance situation. The public refused to try the new Castle dances, and kept on turkey-trotting and bunny-hugging.

The Ladies' Home Journal followed the Castle lessons with a series of the most beautiful dances of Madam Pavlowa, the Russian dancer, hoping to remove the unfavorable impression of the former series. But it was only partially successful. Bok had made a mistake in recognizing the craze at all; he should have ignored it, as he had so often in the past ignored other temporary, superficial hysterics of the public. *The Journal* readers knew the magazine had made a mistake and frankly said so.

Which shows that, even after having been for over twenty-five years in the editorial chair, Edward Bok was by no means infallible in his judgment of what the public wanted or would accept.

No man is, for that matter.

CHAPTER XXXIV

A WAR MAGAZINE AND WAR ACTIVITIES

When, early in 1917, events began so to shape themselves as directly to point to the entrance of the United States into the Great War, Edward Bok set himself to formulate a policy for *The Ladies' Home Journal*. He knew that he was in an almost insurmountably difficult position. The huge edition necessitated going to press fully six weeks in advance of publication, and the preparation of material fully four weeks previous to that. He could not, therefore, get much closer than ten weeks to the date when his readers received the magazine. And he knew that events, in war time, had a way of moving rapidly.

Late in January he went to Washington, consulted those authorities who could indicate possibilities to him better than any one else, and found, as he had suspected, that the entry of the United States into the war was a practical certainty; it was only a question of time.

Bok went South for a month's holiday to get ready for the fray, and in the saddle and on the golf links he formulated a policy. The newspapers and weeklies would send innumerable correspondents to the front, and obviously, with the necessity for going to press so far in advance, *The Journal* could not compete with them. They would depict every activity in the field. There was but one logical thing for him to do: ignore the "front" entirely, refuse all the offers of correspondents, men and women, who wanted to go with the armies for his magazine, and cover fully and practically the results of the war as they would affect the women left behind. He went carefully over the ground to see what these would be, along what particular lines women's activities would be most likely to go, and then went home and back to Washington.

It was now March. He conferred with the President, had his fears confirmed, and offered all the resources of his magazine to the government. His diagnosis of the situation was verified in every detail by the authorities whom he consulted. *The Ladies' Home Journal* could best serve by keeping up the morale at home and by helping to meet the problems that would confront the women; as the President said: "Give help in the second line of defense."

A year before, Bok had opened a separate editorial office in Washington and had secured Dudley Harmon, the Washington correspondent for *The New York Sun*, as his editor-in-charge. The purpose was to bring the women of the country into a clearer understanding of their government and a closer relation with it. This work had been so successful as to necessitate a force of four offices and twenty stenographers. Bok now placed this Washington office on a war-basis, bringing it into close relation with every department of the government that would be connected with the war activities. By this means, he had an editor and an organized force on the spot, devoting full time to the preparation of war material, with Mr. Harmon in daily conference with the department chiefs to secure the newest developments.

Bok learned that the country's first act would be to recruit for the navy, so as to get this branch of the service into a state of preparedness. He therefore secured Franklin D. Roosevelt, assistant secretary of the navy, to write an article explaining to mothers why they should let their boys volunteer for the Navy and what it would mean to them.

He made arrangements at the American Red Cross Headquarters for an official department to begin at once in the magazine, telling women the first steps that would be taken by the Red Cross and how they could help. He secured former President William Howard Taft, as chairman of the Central Committee of the Red Cross, for the editor of this department.

He cabled to Viscount Northcliffe and Ian Hay for articles showing what the English women had done at the outbreak of the war, the mistakes they had made, what errors the American women should avoid, the right lines along which English women had worked and how their American sisters could adapt these methods to transatlantic conditions.

And so it happened that when the first war issue of *The Journal* appeared on April 20th, only three weeks after the President's declaration, it was the only monthly that recognized the existence of war, and its pages had already begun to indicate practical lines along which women could help.

The President planned to bring the Y. M. C. A. into the service by making it a war-work body, and Bok immediately made arrangements for a page to appear each month under the editorship of John R. Mott, general secretary of the International Y. M. C. A. Committee.

The editor had been told that the question of food would come to be of paramount importance; he knew that Herbert Hoover had been asked to return to America as soon as he could close his work abroad, and he cabled over to his English representative to arrange that the proposed Food Administrator should know, at first hand, of the magazine and its possibilities for the furtherance of the proposed Food Administration work.

The Food Administration was no sooner organized than Bok made arrangements for an authoritative department to be conducted in his magazine, reflecting the plans and desires of the Food Administration, and Herbert Hoover's first public declaration as food administrator to the women of America was published in *The Ladies' Home Journal.* Bok now placed all the resources of his four-color press-work at Mr. Hoover's disposal; and the Food Administration's domestic experts, in conjunction with the full culinary staff of the magazine, prepared the new war dishes and presented them appetizingly in full colors under the personal endorsement of Mr. Hoover and the Food Administration. From six to sixteen articles per month were now coming from Mr. Hoover's department alone.

The Department of Agriculture was laid under contribution by the magazine for the best ideas for the raising of food from the soil in the creation of war-gardens.

Doctor Anna Howard Shaw had been appointed chairman of the National Committee of the Women's Council of National Defence, and Bok arranged at once with her that she should edit a department page in his magazine, setting forth the plans of the committee and how the women of America could co-operate therewith.

The magazine had thus practically become the semi-official mouthpiece of all the various government war bureaus and war-work bodies. James A. Flaherty, supreme knight of the Knights of Columbus, explained the proposed work of that body; Commander Evangeline Booth presented the plans of the Salvation Army, and Mrs. Robert E. Speer, president of the National Board of the Young Women's Christian Association, reflected the activities of her organization; while the President's daughter, Miss Margaret Wilson, discussed her work for the opening of all schoolhouses as community war-centres.

The magazine reflected in full-color pictures the life and activities of the boys in the American camps, and William C. Gorgas, surgeon-general of the United States, was the spokesman in the magazine for the health of the boys.

Secretary of the Treasury McAdoo interpreted the first Liberty Loan "drive" to the women; the President of the United States, in a special message to women, wrote in behalf of the subsequent Loan; Bernard Baruch, as chairman of the War Industries Board, made clear the need for war-time thrift; the recalled ambassador to Germany, James W. Gerard, told of the ingenious plans resorted to by German women which American women could profitably copy; and Elizabeth, Queen of the Belgians, explained the plight of the babies and children of Belgium, and made a plea to the women of the magazine to help. So straight to the point did the Queen write, and so well did she present her case that within six months there had been sent to her, through *The Ladies' Home Journal*, two hundred and forty-eight thousand cans of condensed milk, seventy-two thousand cans of pork and beans, five thousand cans of infants' prepared food, eighty thousand cans of beef soup, and nearly four thousand bushels of wheat, purchased with the money donated by the magazine readers.

On the coming of the coal question, the magazine immediately reflected the findings and recommendations of the Fuel Administration, and Doctor H. A. Garfield, as fuel administrator, placed the material of his Bureau at the disposal of the magazine's Washington editor.

The Committee on Public Information now sought the magazine for the issuance of a series of official announcements explanatory of matters to women.

When the "meatless" and the "wheatless" days were inaugurated, the women of America found that the magazine had anticipated their coming; and the issue appearing on the first of these days, as publicly announced by the Food Administration, presented pages of substitutes in full colors.

Of course, miscellaneous articles on the war there were, without number. Before the war was ended, the magazine did send a representative to the front in Catherine Van Dyke, who did most effective work for the magazine in articles of a general nature. The full-page battle pictures, painted from data furnished by those who took actual part, were universally commended and exhausted even the largest editions that could be printed. A source of continual astonishment was the number of copies of the magazine found among the boys in France; it became the third in the official War Department list of the most desired American periodicals, evidently representing a tie between the boys and their home folks. But all these "war" features, while appreciated and desirable, were, after all, but a side-issue to the more practical economic work of the magazine. It was in this service that the magazine excelled, it was for this reason that the women at home so eagerly bought it, and that it was impossible to supply each month the editions called for by the extraordinary demand.

Considering the difficulties to be surmounted, due to the advance preparation of material, and considering that, at the best, most of its advance information, even by the highest authorities, could only be in the nature of surmise, the comprehensive manner in which *The Ladies' Home Journal* covered every activity of women during the Great War, will always remain one of the magazine's most noteworthy achievements. This can be said without reserve here, since the credit is due to no single person; it was the combined, careful work of its entire staff, weighing every step before it was taken, looking as clearly into the future as circumstances made possible, and always seeking the most authoritative sources of information.

Bok merely directed. Each month, before his magazine went to press, he sought counsel and vision from at least one of three of the highest sources; and upon this guidance, as authoritative as anything could be in times of war when no human vision can actually foretell what the next day will bring forth, he acted. The result, as one now looks back upon it, was truly amazing; an uncanny timeliness would often color material on publication day. Of course, much of this was due to the close government co-operation, so generously and painstakingly given.

With the establishment of the various war boards in Washington, Bok received overtures to associate himself exclusively with them and move to the capital. He sought the best advice and with his own instincts pointing in the same way, he decided that he could give his fullest service by retaining his editorial position and adding to that such activities as his leisure allowed. He undertook several private commissions for the United States Government, and then he was elected vice-president of the Philadelphia Belgian Relief Commission.

With the Belgian consul-general for the United States, Mr. Paul Hagemans, as the president of the Commission, and guided by his intimate knowledge of the Belgian people, Bok selected a committee of the ablest buyers and merchants in the special lines of foods which he would have to handle. The Commission raised hundreds of thousands of dollars, with which it purchased foods and chartered ships. The quantities of food ran into prodigious figures; Bok felt that he was feeding the world; and yet when the holds of the ships began to take in the thousands of crates of canned goods, the bags of peas and beans, and the endless tins of condensed milk, it was amazing how the piled-up

boxes melted from the piers and the ship-holds yawned
for more.   Flour was sent in seemingly endless hundreds
of barrels.

Each line of goods was bought by a specialist on the
Committee at the lowest quantity prices; and the result was that the succession of ships leaving the port of
Philadelphia was a credit to the generosity of the people
of the city and the commonwealth. The Commission
delegated one of its members to go to Belgium and
personally see that the food actually reached the needy
Belgian people.

In September, 1917, word was received from John
R. Mott that Bok had been appointed State chairman
for the Y. M. C. A. War Work Council for Pennsylvania;
that a country-wide campaign for twenty-five million
dollars would be launched six weeks hence, and that
Pennsylvania's quota was three millions of dollars.
He was to set up an organization throughout the State,
conduct the drive from Philadelphia, speak at various
centres in Pennsylvania, and secure the allocated quota.
Bok knew little or nothing about the work of the Y. M.
C. A.; he accordingly went to New York headquarters
and familiarized himself with the work being done and
proposed; and then began to set up his State machinery.
The drive came off as scheduled, Pennsylvania doubled
its quota, subscribing six instead of three millions of
dollars, and of this was collected five million eight hundred and twenty-nine thousand dollars—almost one
hundred per cent.

Bok, who was now put on the National War Work
Council of the Y. M. C. A. at New York, was asked to

take part in the creation of the machinery necessary for the gigantic piece of work that the organization had been called upon by the President of the United States to do. It was a herculean task; practically impossible with any large degree of efficiency in view of the almost insurmountable obstacles to be contended with. But step by step the imperfect machinery was set up, and it began to function in the home camps. Then the overseas work was introduced by the first troops going to France, and the difficulties increased a hundredfold.

But Bok's knowledge of the workings of the government departments at Washington, the war boards, and the other war-work organizations soon convinced him that the Y. M. C. A. was not the only body, asked to set up an organization almost overnight, that was staggering under its load and falling down as often as it was functioning.

The need for Y. M. C. A. secretaries overseas and in the camps soon became acute, and Bok was appointed chairman of the Philadelphia Recruiting Committee. As in the case of his Belgian relief work, he at once surrounded himself with an able committee: this time composed of business and professional men trained in a knowledge of human nature in the large, and of wide acquaintance in the city. Simultaneously, Bok secured the release of one of the ablest men in the Y. M. C. A. service in New York, Edward S. Wilkinson, who became the permanent secretary of the Philadelphia Committee. Bok organized a separate committee composed of automobile manufacturers to recruit for chauffeurs and mechanicians; another separate committee recruited for physical directors, and later a third committee recruited for women.

The work was difficult because the field of selection was limited. No men between the military ages could be recruited; the War Boards at Washington had drawn heavily upon the best men of the city; the slightest physical defect barred out a man, on account of the exposure and strain of the Y. M. C. A. work; the residue was not large.

It was scarcely to be wondered at that so many incompetent secretaries had been passed and sent over to France. How could it have been otherwise with the restricted selection? But the Philadelphia Committee was determined, nevertheless, that its men should be of the best, and it decided that to get a hundred men of unquestioned ability would be to do a greater job than to send over two hundred men of indifferent quality. The Committee felt that enough good men were still in Philadelphia and the vicinity, if they could be pried loose from their business and home anchorages, and that it was rather a question of incessant work than an impossible task.

Bok took large advertising spaces in the Philadelphia newspapers, asking for men of exceptional character to go to France in the service of the Y. M. C. A.; and members of the Committee spoke before the different commercial bodies at their noon luncheons. The applicants now began to come, and the Committee began its discriminating selection. Each applicant was carefully questioned by the secretary before he appeared before the Committee, which held sittings twice a week.

Hence of over twenty-five hundred applicants, only three hundred appeared before the Committee, of whom two hundred and fifty-eight were passed and sent overseas.

The Committee's work was exceptionally successful; it soon proved of so excellent a quality as to elicit a cabled request from Paris headquarters to send more men of the Philadelphia type. The secret of this lay in the sterling personnel of the Committee itself, and its interpretation of the standards required; and so well did it work that when Bok left for the front to be absent from Philadelphia for ten weeks, his Committee, with Thomas W. Hulme, of the Pennsylvania Railroad, acting as Chairman, did some of its best work.

The after-results, according to the report of the New York headquarters, showed that no Y. M. C. A. recruiting committee had equalled the work of the Philadelphia committee in that its men, in point of service, had proved one hundred per cent secretaries. With two exceptions, the entire two hundred and fifty-eight men passed, brought back one hundred per cent records, some of them having been placed in the most important posts abroad and having given the most difficult service. The work of the other Philadelphia committees, particularly that of the Women's Committee, was equally good.

To do away with the multiplicity of "drives," rapidly becoming a drain upon the efforts of the men engaged in them, a War Chest Committee was now formed in Philadelphia and vicinity to collect money for all the war-work agencies. Bok was made a member of the

Executive Committee, and chairman of the Publicity Committee. In May, 1918, a campaign for twenty millions of dollars was started; the amount was subscribed, and although much of it had to be collected after the armistice, since the subscriptions were in twelve monthly payments, a total of fifteen and a half million dollars was paid in and turned over to the different agencies.

Bok, who had been appointed one of the Boy Scout commissioners in his home district of Merion, saw the possibilities of the Boy Scouts in the Liberty Loan and other campaigns. Working in co-operation with the other commissioners, and the scoutmaster of the Merion Troop, Bok supported the boys in their work in each campaign as it came along. Although there were in the troop only nine boys, in ages ranging from twelve to fourteen years—Bok's younger son was one of them— so effectively did these youngsters work under the inspiration of the scoutmaster, Thomas Dun Belfield, that they soon attracted general attention and acquired distinction as one of the most efficient troops in the vicinity of Philadelphia. They won nearly all the prizes offered in their vicinity, and elicited the special approval of the Secretary of the Treasury.

Although only "gleaners" in most of the campaigns —that is, working only in the last three days after the regular committees had scoured the neighborhood— these Merion Boy Scouts sold over one million four hundred thousand dollars in Liberty Bonds, and raised enough money in the Y. M. C. A. campaign to erect one of the largest huts in France for the army boys, and a Y. M. C. A. gymnasium at the League Island Navy Yard accommodating two thousand sailor-boys.

In the summer of 1918, the eight leading war-work agencies, excepting the Red Cross, were merged, for the purpose of one drive for funds, into the United War Work Campaign, and Bok was made chairman for Pennsylvania. In November a country-wide campaign was launched, the quota for Pennsylvania being twenty millions of dollars—the largest amount ever asked of the commonwealth. Bok organized a committee of the representative men of Pennsylvania, and proceeded to set up the machinery to secure the huge sum. He had no sooner done this, however, than he had to sail for France, returning only a month before the beginning of the campaign.

But the efficient committee had done its work; upon his return Bok found the organization complete. On the first day of the campaign, the false rumor that an armistice had been signed made the raising of the large amount seem almost hopeless; furthermore, owing to the influenza raging throughout the commonwealth, no public meetings had been permitted or held. Still, despite all these obstacles, not only was the twenty millions subscribed but oversubscribed to the extent of nearly a million dollars; and in face of the fact that every penny of this large total had to be collected after the signing of the armistice, twenty millions of dollars was paid in and turned over to the war agencies.

It is indeed a question whether any single war act on the part of the people of Pennsylvania redounds so highly to their credit as this marvellous evidence of patriotic generosity. It was one form of patriotism to subscribe so huge a sum while the war was on and the guns were firing; it was quite another and a higher patriotism to subscribe and pay such a sum after the war was over!

Bok's position as State chairman of the United War Work Campaign made it necessary for him to follow authoritatively and closely the work of each of the eight different organizations represented in the fund. Because he felt he had to know what the Knights of Columbus, the Salvation Army, the Y. W. C. A., and the others were doing with the money he had been instrumental in collecting, and for which he felt, as chairman, responsible to the people of Pennsylvania, he learned to know their work just as thoroughly as he knew what the Y. M. C. A. was doing.

He had now seen and come into personal knowledge of the work of the Y. M. C. A. from his Philadelphia point of vantage, with his official connection with it at New York headquarters; he had seen the work as it was done in the London and Paris headquarters; and he had seen the actual work in the American camps, the English rest-camps, back of the French lines, in the trenches, and as near the firing-line as he had been permitted to go.

He had, in short, seen the Y. M. C. A. function from every angle, but he had also seen the work of the other organizations in England and France, back of the lines and in the trenches. He found them all faulty—necessarily so. Each had endeavored to create an organization within an incredibly short space of time and in the face of adverse circumstances. Bok saw at once that the charge that the Y. M. C. A. was "falling down" in its work was as false as that the Salvation Army was doing "a marvellous work" and that the K. of C. was "efficient where others were incompetent," and that the Y. W. C. A. was "nowhere to be seen."

The Salvation Army was unquestionably doing an excellent piece of work within a most limited area; it could not be on a wider scale, when one considered the limited personnel it had at its command. The work of the K. of C. was not a particle more or less efficient than the work of the other organizations. What it did, it strove to do well, but so did the others. The Y. W. C. A. made little claim about its work in France, since the United States Government would not, until nearly at the close of the war, allow women to be sent over in the uniforms of any of the war-work organizations. But no one can gainsay for a single moment the efficient service rendered by the Y. W. C. A. in its hostess-house work in the American camps; that work alone would have entitled it to the support of the American people. That of the Y. M. C. A. was on so large a scale that naturally its inefficiency was often in proportion to its magnitude.

Bok was in France when the storm of criticism against the Y. M. C. A. broke out, and, as State chairman for Pennsylvania, it was his duty to meet the outcry when it came over to the United States. That the work of the Y. M. C. A. was faulty no one can deny. Bok saw the "holes" long before they were called to the attention of the public, but he also saw the almost impossible task, in face of prevailing difficulties, of caulking them up. No one who was not in France can form any conception of the practically insurmountable obstacles against which all the war-work organizations worked; and the larger the work the greater were the obstacles, naturally. That the Y. M. C. A. and the other similar agencies made mistakes is not the wonder so much as that they did not make more. The real marvel is that they did so much efficient work. For after we get a little farther away from the details and see the work of these agencies in its broader aspects, when we forget the lapses—which, after all, though irritating and regrettable, were not major—the record as a whole will stand as a most signal piece of volunteer service.

What was actually accomplished was nothing short of marvellous; and it is this fact that must be borne in mind; not the omissions, but the commissions. And when the American public gets that point of view—as it will, and, for that matter, is already beginning to do—the work of the American Y. M. C. A. will no longer suffer for its omissions, but will amaze and gladden by its accomplishments. As an American officer of high rank said to Bok at Chaumont headquarters: "The mind cannot take in what the war would have been without the 'Y.'" And that, in time, will be the universal American opinion, extended, in proportion to their work, to all the war-work agencies and the men and women who endured, suffered, and were killed in their service.

CHAPTER XXXV

AT THE BATTLE–FRONTS IN THE GREAT WAR

I⊤ was in the summer of 1918 that Edward Bok received from the British Government, through its department of public information, of which Lord Beaverbrook was the minister, an invitation to join a party of thirteen American editors to visit Great Britain and France. The British Government, not versed in publicity methods, was anxious that selected parties of American publicists should see, personally, what Great Britain had done, and was doing in the war; and it had decided to ask a few individuals to pay personal visits to its munition factories, its great aerodromes, its Great Fleet, which then lay in the Firth of Forth, and to the battle-fields. It was understood that no specific obligation rested upon any member of the party to write of what he saw: he was asked simply to observe and then, with discretion, use his observations for his own guidance and information in future writing. In fact, each member was explicitly told that much of what he would see could not be revealed either personally or in print.

The party embarked in August amid all the attendant secrecy of war conditions. The steamer was known only by a number, although later it turned out to be the White Star liner, *Adriatic*. Preceded by a powerful United States cruiser, flanked by destroyers, guided overhead by observation balloons, the *Adriatic* was found to be the first ship in a convoy of sixteen other ships with thirty thousand United States troops on board.

It was a veritable Armada that steamed out of lower New York harbor on that early August morning, headed straight into the rising sun. But it was a voyage of unpleasant war reminders, with life-savers carried every moment of the day, with every light out at night, with every window and door as if hermetically sealed so that the stuffy cabins deprived of sleep those accustomed to fresh air, with over sixty army men and civilians on watch at night, with life-drills each day, with lessons as to behavior in life-boats; and with a fleet of eighteen British destroyers meeting the convoy upon its approach to the Irish Coast after a thirteen days' voyage of constant anxiety. No one could say he travelled across the Atlantic Ocean in war days for pleasure, and no one did.

Once ashore, the party began a series of inspections of munition plants, ship-yards, aeroplane factories and of meetings with the different members of the English War Cabinet. Luncheons and dinners were the order of each day until broken by a journey to Edinburgh to see the amazing Great Fleet, with the addition of six of the foremost fighting machines of the United States Navy, all straining like dogs at leash, awaiting an expected dash from the bottled-up German fleet. It was a formidable sight, perhaps never equalled: those lines of huge, menacing, and yet protecting fighting machines stretching down the river for miles, all conveying the single thought of the power and extent of the British Navy and its formidable character as a fighting unit.

It was upon his return to London that Bok learned, through the confidence of a member of the British "inner circle," the amazing news that the war was practically over: that Bulgaria had capitulated and was suing for peace; that two of the Central Power provinces had indicated their strong desire that the war should end; and that the first peace intimations had gone to the President of the United States. All diplomatic eyes were turned toward Washington. Yet not a hint of the impending events had reached the public. The Germans were being beaten back, that was known; it was evident that the morale of the German army was broken; that Foch had turned the tide toward victory; but even the best-informed military authorities, outside of the inner diplomatic circles, predicted that the war would last until the spring of 1919, when a final "drive" would end it. Yet, at that very moment, the end of the war was in sight!

Next Bok went to France to visit the battle-fields. It was arranged that the party should first, under guidance of British officers, visit back of the British lines; and then, successively, be turned over to the American and French Governments, and visit the operations back of their armies.

It is an amusing fact that although each detail of officers delegated to escort the party "to the front" received the most explicit instructions from their superior officers to take the party only to the quiet sectors where there was no fighting going on, each detail from the three governments successively brought the party directly under shell-fire, and each on the first day of the "inspection." It was unconsciously done: the officers were as much amazed to find themselves under fire as were the members of the party, except that the latter did not feel the responsibility to an equal degree. The officers, in each case, were plainly worried: the editors were intensely interested.

They were depressing trips through miles and miles of devastated villages and small cities. From two to three days each were spent in front-line posts on the Amiens-Bethune, Albert-Peronne, Bapaume-Soissons, St. Mihiel, and back of the Argonne sectors. Often, the party was the first civilian group to enter a town evacuated only a week before, and all the horrible evidence of bloody warfare was fresh and plain. Bodies of German soldiers lay in the trenches where they had fallen; wired bombs were on every hand, so that no object could be touched that lay on the battle-fields; the streets of some of the towns were still mined, so that no automobiles could enter; the towns were deserted, the streets desolate. It was an appalling panorama of the most frightful results of war.

The picturesqueness and romance of the war of picture books were missing. To stand beside an English battery of thirty guns laying a barrage as they fired their shells to a point ten miles distant, made one feel as if one were an actual part of real warfare, and yet far removed from it, until the battery was located from the enemy's "sausage observation"; then the shells from the enemy fired a return salvo, and the better part of valor was discretion a few miles farther back.

The amazing part of the "show," however, was the American doughboy. Never was there a more cheerful, laughing, good-natured set of boys in the world; never a more homesick, lonely, and complaining set. But good nature predominated, and the smile was always uppermost, even when the moment looked the blackest, the privations were worst, and the longing for home the deepest.

Bok had been talking to a boy who lived near his own home, who was on his way to the front and "over the top" in the Argonne mess. Three days afterward, at a hospital base where a hospital train was just discharging its load of wounded, Bok walked among the boys as they lay on their stretchers on the railroad platform waiting for bearers to carry them into the huts. As he approached one stretcher, a cheery voice called, "Hello, Mr. Bok. Here I am again."

It was the boy he had left just seventy-two hours before hearty and well.

"Well, my boy, you weren't in it long, were you?"

"No, sir," answered the boy; "Fritzie sure got me first thing. Hadn't gone a hundred yards over the top. Got a cigarette?" (the invariable question).

Bok handed a cigarette to the boy, who then said: "Mind sticking it in my mouth?" Bok did so and then offered him a light; the boy continued, all with his wonderful smile: "If you don't mind, would you just light it? You see, Fritzie kept both of my hooks as souvenirs."

With both arms amputated, the boy could still jest and smile!

It was the same boy who on his hospital cot the next day said: "Don't you think you could do something for the chap next to me, there on my left? He's really suffering: cried like hell all last night. It would be a God-send if you could get Doc to do something."

A promise was given that the surgeon should be seen at once, but the boy was asked: "How about you?"

"Oh," came the cheerful answer, "I'm all right. I haven't anything to hurt. My wounded members are gone—just plain gone. But that chap has got something —he got the real thing!"

What was the real thing according to such a boy's idea?

There were beautiful stories that one heard "over there." One of the most beautiful acts of consideration was told, later, of a lovable boy whose throat had been practically shot away. During his convalescence he had learned the art of making beaded bags. It kept him from talking, the main prescription. But one day he sold the bag which he had first made to a visitor, and with his face radiant with glee he sought the nurse-mother to tell her all about his good fortune. Of course, nothing but a series of the most horrible guttural sounds came from the boy: not a word could be understood. It was his first venture into the world with the loss of his member, and the nurse-mother could not find it in her heart to tell the boy that not a word which he spoke was understandable. With eyes full of tears she placed both of her hands on the boy's shoulders and said to him: "I am so sorry, my boy. I cannot understand a word you say to me. You evidently do not know that I am totally deaf. Won't you write what you want to tell me?"

A look of deepest compassion swept the face of the

boy. To think that one could be so afflicted, and yet so beautifully tender and always so radiantly cheerful, he wrote her.

Pathos and humor followed rapidly one upon the other "at the front" in those gruesome days, and Bok was to have his spirits lightened somewhat by an incident of the next day. He found himself in one of the numerous little towns where our doughboys were billeted, some in the homes of the peasants, others in stables, barns, outhouses, lean-tos, and what not. These were the troops on their way to the front where the fighting in the Argonne Forest was at that time going on. As Bok was walking with an American officer, the latter pointed to a doughboy crossing the road, followed by as disreputable a specimen of a pig as he had ever seen. Catching Bok's smile, the officer said: "That's Pinney and his porker. Where you see the one you see the other."

Bok caught up with the boy, and said: "Found a friend, I see, Buddy?"

"I sure have," grinned the doughboy, "and it sticks closer than a poor relation, too."

"Where did you pick it up?"

"Oh, in there," said the soldier, pointing to a dilapidated barn.

"Why in there?"

"My home," grinned the boy.

"Let me see," said Bok, and the doughboy took him in with the pig following close behind. "Billeted here—been here six days. The pig was here when we came, and the first night I lay down and slept, it came up to me and stuck its snout in my face and woke me up. Kind enough, all right, but not very comfortable: it stinks so."

"Yes; it certainly does.   What did you do?"

"Oh, I got some grub I had and gave it to eat: thought it might be hungry, you know.   I guess that sort of settled it, for the next night it came again and stuck its snout right in my mug.   I turned around, but it just climbed over me and there it was."

"Well, what did you do then?   Chase it out?"

"Chase it out?" said the doughboy, looking into Bok's face with the most unaffected astonishment.   "Why, mister, that's a mother-pig, that is.   She's going to have young ones in a few days.   How could I chase her out?"

"You're quite right, Buddy," said Bok.   "You couldn't do that."

"Oh, no," said the boy.   "The worst of it is, what am I going to do with her when we move up within a day or two?   I can't take her along to the front, and I hate to leave her here.   Some one might treat her rough."

"Captain," said Bok, hailing the officer, "you can attend to that, can't you, when the time comes?"

"I sure can, and I sure will," answered the Captain. And with a quick salute, Pinney and his porker went off across the road !

Bok was standing talking to the commandant of one of the great French army supply depots one morning. He was a man of forty; a colonel in the regular French army.   An erect, sturdy-looking man with white hair and mustache, and who wore the single star of a subaltern on his sleeve, came up, saluted, delivered a message, and then asked:

"Are there any more orders, sir?"

"No," was the reply.

He brought his heels together with a click, saluted again, and went away.

The commandant turned to Bok with a peculiar smile on his face and asked:

"Do you know who that man is?"

"No," was the reply.

"That is my father," was the answer.

The father was then exactly seventy-two years old. He was a retired business man when the war broke out. After two years of the heroic struggle he decided that he couldn't keep out of it. He was too old to fight, but after long insistence he secured a commission. By one of the many curious coincidences of the war he was assigned to serve under his own son.

When under the most trying conditions, the Americans never lost their sense of fun. On the staff of a prison hospital in Germany, where a number of captured American soldiers were being treated, a German sergeant became quite friendly with the prisoners under his care. One day he told them that he had been ordered to active service on the front. He felt convinced that he would be captured by the English, and asked the Americans if they would not give him some sort of testimonial which he could show if he were taken prisoner, so that he would not be ill-treated.

The Americans were much amused at this idea, and concocted a note of introduction, written in English. The German sergeant knew no English and could not understand his testimonial, but he tucked it in his pocket, well satisfied.

In due time, he was sent to the front and was captured by "the ladies from hell," as the Germans called the Scotch kilties. He at once presented his introduction, and his captors laughed heartily when they read:

"This is L——. He is not a bad sort of chap. Don't shoot him; torture him slowly to death."

One evening as Bok was strolling out after dinner a Red Cross nurse came to him, explained that she had two severely wounded boys in what remained of an old hut: that they were both from Pennsylvania, and had expressed a great desire to see him as a resident of their State.

"Neither can possibly survive the night," said the nurse.

"They know that?" asked Bok.

"Oh, yes, but like all our boys they are lying there joking with each other."

Bok was taken into what remained of a room in a badly shelled farmhouse, and there, on two roughly constructed cots, lay the two boys. Their faces had been bandaged so that nothing was visible except the eyes of each boy. A candle in a bottle standing on a box gave out the only light. But the eyes of the boys were smiling as Bok came in and sat down on the box on which the nurse had been sitting. He talked with the boys, got as much of their stories from them as he could, and told them such home news as he thought might interest them.

After half an hour he arose to leave, when the nurse said: "There is no one here, Mr. Bok, to say the last words to these boys. Will you do it?" Bok stood transfixed. In sending men over in the service of the Y. M. C. A. he had several times told them to be ready for any act that they might be asked to render, even the most sacred one. And here he stood himself before that duty. He felt as if he stood stripped before his Maker. Through the glassless window the sky lit up constantly with the flashes of the guns, and then followed the booming of a shell as it landed.

"Yes, won't you, sir?" asked the boy on the right cot as he held out his hand. Bok took it, and then the hand of the other boy reached out.

What to say, he did not know. Then, to his surprise, he heard himself repeating extract after extract from a book by Lyman Abbott called *The Other Room*, a message to the bereaved declaring the non-existence of death, but that we merely move from this earth to another: from one room to another, as it were. Bok had not read the book for years, but here was the subconscious self supplying the material for him in his moment of greatest need. Then he remembered that just before leaving home he had heard sung at matins, after the prayer for the President, a beautiful song called "Passing Souls." He had asked the rector for a copy of it; and, wondering why, he had put it in his wallet that he carried with him. He took it out now and holding the hand of the boy at his right, he read to them:

> For the passing souls we pray,
> Saviour, meet them on their way;
> Let their trust lay hold on Thee
> Ere they touch eternity.

Holy counsels long forgot
Breathe again 'mid shell and shot;
Through the mist of life's last pain
None shall look to Thee in vain.

To the hearts that know Thee, Lord,
Thou wilt speak through flood or sword;
Just beyond the cannon's roar,
Thou art on the farther shore.

For the passing souls we pray,
Saviour, meet them on the way;
Thou wilt hear our yearning call,
Who hast loved and died for all.

Absolute stillness reigned in the room save for the half-suppressed sob from the nurse and the distant booming of the cannon. As Bok finished, he heard the boy at his right say slowly: "Saviour—meet—me—on—my—way": with a little emphasis on the word "my." The hand in his relaxed slowly, and then fell on the cot; and he saw that the soul of another brave American boy had "gone West."

Bok glanced at the other boy, reached for his hand, shook it, and looking deep into his eyes, he left the little hut.

He little knew where and how he was to look into those eyes again!

Feeling the need of air in order to get hold of himself after one of the most solemn moments of his visit to the front, Bok strolled out, and soon found himself on what only a few days before had been a field of carnage where the American boys had driven back the Germans. Walking in the trenches and looking out, in the clear moonlight, over the field of desolation and ruin, and thinking of the inferno that had been enacted there only so recently, he suddenly felt his foot rest on what seemed to be a soft object. Taking his "ever-ready" flash from his pocket, he shot a ray at his feet, only to realize that his foot was resting on the face of a dead German!

Bok had had enough for one evening! In fact, he had had enough of war in all its aspects; and he felt a sigh of relief when, a few days thereafter, he boarded *The Empress of Asia* for home, after a ten-weeks absence.

He hoped never again to see, at first hand, what war meant!

CHAPTER XXXVI

THE END OF THIRTY YEARS' EDITORSHIP

On the voyage home, Edward Bok decided that, now the war was over, he would ask his company to release him from the editorship of *The Ladies' Home Journal*. His original plan had been to retire at the end of a quarter of a century of editorship, when in his fiftieth year. He was, therefore, six years behind his schedule. In October, 1919, he would reach his thirtieth anniversary as editor, and he fixed upon this as an appropriate time for the relinquishment of his duties.

He felt he had carried out the conditions under which the editorship of the magazine had been transferred to him by Mrs. Curtis, that he had brought them to fruition, and that any further carrying on of the periodical by him would be of a supplementary character. He had, too, realized his hope of helping to create a national institution of service to the American woman, and he felt that his part in the work was done.

He considered carefully where he would leave an institution which the public had so thoroughly associated with his personality, and he felt that at no point in its history could he so safely transfer it to other hands. The position of the magazine in the public estimation was unquestioned; it had never been so strong. Its circulation not only had outstripped that of any other monthly periodical, but it was still growing so rapidly that it was only a question of a few months when it would reach the almost incredible mark of two million copies per month. With its advertising patronage exceeding that of any other monthly, the periodical had become, probably, the most valuable and profitable piece of magazine property in the world.

The time might never come again when all conditions would be equally favorable to a change of editorship. The position of the magazine was so thoroughly assured that its progress could hardly be affected by the retirement of one editor, and the accession of another. There was a competent editorial staff, the members of which had been with the periodical from ten to thirty years each. This staff had been a very large factor in the success of the magazine. While Bok had furnished the initiative and supplied the directing power, a large part of the editorial success of the magazine was due to the staff. It could carry on the magazine without his guidance.

Moreover, Bok wished to say good-bye to his public before it decided, for some reason or other, to say good-bye to him. He had no desire to outstay his welcome. That public had been wonderfully indulgent toward his shortcomings, lenient with his errors, and tremendously inspiring to his best endeavor. He would not ask too much of it. Thirty years was a long tenure of office, one of the longest, in point of consecutively active editorship, in the history of American magazines.

He had helped to create and to put into the life of the American home a magazine of peculiar distinction. From its beginning it had been unlike any other periodical; it had always retained its individuality as a magazine apart from the others.   It had sought to be something more than a mere assemblage of stories and articles. It had consistently stood for ideals; and, save in one or two instances, it had carried through what it undertook to achieve.   It had a record of worthy accomplishment; a more fruitful record than many imagined.   It had become a national institution such as no other magazine had ever been.   It was indisputably accepted by the public and by business interests alike as the recognized avenue of approach to the intelligent homes of America.

Edward Bok was content to leave it at this point.

He explained all this in December, 1918, to the Board of Directors, and asked that his resignation be considered.   It was understood that he was to serve out his thirty years, thus remaining with the magazine for the best part of another year.

In the material which *The Journal* now included in its contents, it began to point the way to the problems which would face women during the reconstruction period. Bok scanned the rather crowded field of thought very carefully, and selected for discussion in the magazine such questions as seemed to him most important for the public to understand in order to face and solve its impending problems.   The outstanding question he saw which would immediately face men and women of the country was the problem of Americanization.   The war and its after-effects had clearly demonstrated this to be the most vital need in the life of the nation, not only for the foreign-born but for the American as well.

The more one studied the problem the clearer it became that the vast majority of American-born needed
a refreshing, and, in many cases, a new conception of
American ideals as much as did the foreign-born, and
that the latter could never be taught what America and
its institutions stood for until they were more clearly
defined in the mind of the men and women of American
birth.

Bok went to Washington, consulted with Franklin
K. Lane, secretary of the interior, of whose department
the Government Bureau of Americanization was a part.
A comprehensive series of articles was outlined; the most
expert writer, Esther Everett Lape, who had several
years of actual experience in Americanization work, was
selected; Secretary Lane agreed personally to read and
pass upon the material, and to assume the responsibility
for its publication.

With the full and direct co-operation of the Federal
Bureau of Americanization, the material was assembled
and worked up with the result that, in the opinion of
the director of the Federal Bureau, the series proved to
be the most comprehensive exposition of practical Americanization adapted to city, town, and village, thus far
published.

The work on this series was one of the last acts of
Edward Bok's editorship; and it was peculiarly grati-
fying to him that his editorial work should end with the
exposition of that Americanization of which he himself
was a product. It seemed a fitting close to the career
of a foreign-born Americanized editor.

The scope of the reconstruction articles now published, and the clarity of vision shown in the selection of the subjects, gave a fresh impetus to the circulation of the magazine; and now that the government's embargo on the use of paper had been removed, the full editions of the periodical could again be printed. The public responded instantly.

The result reached phenomenal figures. The last number under Bok's full editorial control was the issue of October, 1919. This number was oversold with a printed edition of two million copies—a record never before achieved by any magazine. This same issue presented another record unattained in any single number of any periodical in the world. It carried between its covers the amazing total of over one million dollars in advertisements.

This was the psychological point at which to stop. And Edward Bok did. Although his official relation as editor did not terminate until January, 1920, when the number which contained his valedictory editorial was issued, his actual editorship ceased on September 22, 1919. On that day he handed over the reins to his successor.

As Bok was, on that day, about to leave his desk for the last time, it was announced that a young soldier whom he "had met and befriended in France" was waiting to see him. When the soldier walked into the office he was to Bok only one of the many whom he had met on the other side. But as the boy shook hands with him and said: "I guess you do not remember me, Mr. Bok," there was something in the eyes into which he looked that startled him. And then, in a flash, the circumstances under which he had last seen those eyes came to him.

"Good heavens, my boy, you are not one of those two boys in the little hut that I——"

"To whom you read the poem 'Passing Souls,' that evening. Yes, sir, I'm the boy who had hold of your left hand. My bunkie, Ben, went West that same evening, you remember."

"Yes," replied the editor, "I remember; I remember only too well," and again Bok felt the hand in his relax, drop from his own, and heard the words: "Saviour—meet—me—on—my way."

The boy's voice brought Bok back to the moment.

"It's wonderful you should remember me; my face was all bound up—I guess you couldn't see anything but my eyes."

"Just the eyes, that's right," said Bok. "But they burned into me all right, my boy."

"I don't think I get you, sir," said the boy.

"No, you wouldn't," Bok replied. "You couldn't, boy, not until you're older. But, tell me, how in the world did you ever get out of it?"

"Well, sir," answered the boy, with that shyness which we all have come to know in the boys who actually did, "I guess it was a close call, all right. But just as you left us, a hospital corps happened to come along on its way to the back and Miss Nelson—the nurse, you remember?—she asked them to take me along. They took me to a wonderful hospital, gave me fine care, and then after a few weeks they sent me back to the States, and I've been in a hospital over here ever since. Now, except for this thickness of my voice that you notice, which Doc says will be all right soon, I'm fit again. The government has given me a job, and I came here on leave just to see my parents up-State, and I thought I'd like you to know that I didn't go West after all."

Fifteen minutes later, Edward Bok left his editorial office for the last time.

But as he went home his thoughts were not of his last day at the office, nor of his last acts as editor, but of his last caller—the soldier-boy whom he had left seemingly so surely on his way "West," and whose eyes had burned into his memory on that fearful night a year before!

Strange that this boy should have been his last visitor!

As John Drinkwater, in his play, makes Abraham Lincoln say to General Grant:

"It's a queer world!"

CHAPTER XXXVII

THE THIRD PERIOD

THE announcement of Edward Bok's retirement came as a great surprise to his friends. Save for one here and there, who had a clearer vision, the feeling was general that he had made a mistake. He was fifty-six, in the prime of life, never in better health, with "success lying easily upon him"—said one; "at the very summit of his career," said another—and all agreed it was "queer," "strange,"—unless, they argued, he was really ill. Even the most acute students of human affairs among his friends wondered. It seemed incomprehensible that any man should want to give up before he was, for some reason, compelled to do so. A man should go on until he "dropped in the harness," they argued.

Bok agreed that any man had a perfect right to work until he *did* "drop in the harness." But, he argued, if he conceded this right to others, why should they not concede to him the privilege of dropping with the blinders off?

"But," continued the argument, "a man degenerates when he retires from active affairs." And then, instances were pointed out as notable examples. "A year of retirement and he was through," was the picture given of one retired man. "In two years, he was glad to come back," and so the examples ran on. "No big man ever retired from active business and did great work afterwards," Bok was told.

"No?" he answered. "Not even Cyrus W. Field or Herbert Hoover?"

And all this time Edward Bok's failure to be entirely Americanized was brought home to his consciousness. After fifty years, he was still not an American! He had deliberately planned, and then had carried out his plan, to retire while he still had the mental and physical capacity to enjoy the fruits of his years of labor! For foreign to the American way of thinking it certainly was: the protestations and arguments of his friends proved that to him. After all, he was still Dutch; he had held on to the lesson which his people had learned years ago; that the people of other European countries had learned; that the English had discovered: that the Great Adventure of Life was something more than material work, and that the time to go is while the going is good!

For it cannot be denied that the pathetic picture we so often see is found in American business life more frequently than in that of any other land: men unable to let go—not only for their own good, but to give the younger men behind them an opportunity. Not that a man should stop work, for man was born to work, and in work he should find his greatest refreshment. But so often it does not occur to the man in a pivotal position to question the possibility that at sixty or seventy he can keep steadily in touch with a generation whose ideas are controlled by men twenty years younger. Unconsciously he hangs on beyond his greatest usefulness and efficiency: he convinces himself that he is indispensable to his business, while, in scores of cases, the business would be distinctly benefited by his retirement and the consequent coming to the front of the younger blood.

Such a man in a position of importance seems often not to see that he has it within his power to advance the fortunes of younger men by stepping out when he has served his time, while by refusing to let go he often works dire injustice and even disaster to his younger associates.

The sad fact is that in all too many instances the average American business man is actually afraid to let go because he realizes that out of business he should not know what to do. For years he has so excluded all other interests that at fifty or sixty or seventy he finds himself a slave to his business, with positively no inner resources. Retirement from the one thing he does know would naturally leave such a man useless to himself and his family, and his community: worse than useless, as a matter of fact, for he would become a burden to himself, a nuisance to his family, and, when he would begin to write "letters" to the newspapers, a bore to the community.

It is significant that a European or English business man rarely reaches middle age devoid of acquaintance with other matters; he always lets the breezes from other worlds of thought blow through his ideas, with the result that when he is ready to retire from business he has other interests to fall back upon. Fortunately it is becoming less uncommon for American men to retire from business and devote themselves to other pursuits; and their number will undoubtedly increase as time goes on, and we learn the lessons of life with a richer background. But one cannot help feeling regretful that the custom is not growing more rapidly.

A man must unquestionably prepare years ahead for his retirement, not alone financially, but mentally as well. Bok noticed as a curious fact that nearly every business man who told him he had made a mistake in his retirement, and that the proper life for a man is to stick to the game and see it through—"hold her nozzle agin the bank" as Jim Bludso would say—was a man with no resources outside his business. Naturally, a retirement is a mistake in the eyes of such a man; but oh, the pathos of such a position: that in a world of so much interest, in an age so fascinatingly full of things worth doing, a man should have allowed himself to become a slave to his business, and should imagine no other man happy without the same claims!

It is this lesson that the American business man has still to learn: that no man can be wholly efficient in his life, that he is not living a four-squared existence, if he concentrates every waking thought on his material affairs. He has still to learn that man cannot live by bread alone. The making of money, the accumulation of material power, is not all there is to living. Life is something more than these, and the man who misses this truth misses the greatest joy and satisfaction that can come into his life—service for others.

Some men argue that they can give this service and be in business, too. But service with such men generally means drawing a check for some worthy cause, and nothing more. Edward Bok never belittled the giving of contributions—he solicited too much money himself for the causes in which he was interested—but it is a poor nature that can satisfy itself that it is serving humanity by merely signing checks. There is no form of service more comfortable or so cheap. Real service, however, demands that a man give himself with his check. And that the average man cannot do if he remains in affairs.

Particularly true is this to-day, when every problem of business is so engrossing, demanding a man's full time and thought. It is the rare man who can devote himself to business and be fresh for the service of others afterward. No man can, with efficiency, serve two masters so exacting as are these. Besides, if his business has seemed important enough to demand his entire attention, are not the great uplift questions equally worth his exclusive thought? Are they easier of solution than the material problems?

A man can live a life full-square only when he divides it into three periods:

First: that of education, acquiring the fullest and best within his reach and power;

Second: that of achievement: achieving for himself and his family, and discharging the first duty of any man, that in case of his incapacity those who are closest to him are provided for. But such provision does not mean an accumulation that becomes to those he leaves behind him an embarrassment rather than a protection. To prevent this, the next period confronts him:

Third: Service for others. That is the acid test where many a man falls short: to know when he has enough, and to be willing not only to let well enough alone, but to give a helping hand to the other fellow; to recognize, in a practical way, that we are our brother's keeper; that a brotherhood of man does exist outside after-dinner speeches. Too many men make the mistake, when they reach the point of enough, of going on pursuing the same old game: accumulating more money, grasping for more power until either a nervous breakdown overtakes them and a sad incapacity results, or they drop "in the harness," which is, of course, only calling an early grave by another name. They cannot seem to get the truth into their heads that as they have been helped by others so should they now help others: as their means have come from the public, so now they owe something in turn to that public.

No man has a right to leave the world no better than he found it. He must add something to it: either he must make its people better and happier, or he must make the face of the world fairer to look at. And the one really means the other.

"Idealism," immediately say some. Of course, it is. But what is the matter with idealism? What really is idealism? Do one-tenth of those who use the phrase so glibly know its true meaning, the part it has played in the world? The worthy interpretation of an ideal is that it embodies an idea—a conception of the imagination. All ideas are at first ideals. They must be. The producer brings forth an idea, but some dreamer has dreamed it before him either in whole or in part.

Where would the human race be were it not for the ideals of men? It is idealists, in a large sense, that this old world needs to-day. Its soil is sadly in need of new seed. Washington, in his day, was decried as an ideal-ist. So was Jefferson. It was commonly remarked of Lincoln that he was a "rank idealist." Morse, Watt, Marconi, Edison—all were, at first, adjudged idealists. We say of the League of Nations that it is ideal, and we use the term in a derogatory sense. But that was exactly what was said of the Constitution of the United States. "Insanely ideal" was the term used of it.

The idealist, particularly to-day when there is so great need of him, is not to be scoffed at. It is through him and only through him that the world will see a new and clear vision of what is right. It is he who has the power of going out of himself—that self in which too many are nowadays so deeply imbedded; it is he who, in seeking the ideal, will, through his own clearer percep-tion or that of others, transform the ideal into the real. "Where there is no vision, the people perish."

It was his remark that he retired because he wanted "to play" that Edward Bok's friends most completely misunderstood. "Play" in their minds meant tennis, golf, horseback, polo, travel, etc.—(curious that scarcely one mentioned reading!). It so happens that no one enjoys some of these play-forms more than Bok; but "God forbid," he said, "that I should spend the rest of my days in a bunker or in the saddle. In moderation," he added, "yes; most decidedly." But the phrase of "play" meant more to him than all this. Play is diver-sion: exertion of the mind as well as of the body. There is such a thing as mental play as well as physical play. We ask of play that it shall rest, refresh, exhilarate. Is there any form of mental activity that secures all these ends so thoroughly and so directly as doing something that a man really likes to do, doing it with all his heart, all the time conscious that he is helping to make the world better for some one else?

A man's "play" can take many forms. If his life has been barren of books or travel, let him read or see the world. But he reaches his high estate by either of these roads only when he reads or travels to enrich himself in order to give out what he gets to enrich the lives of others. He owes it to himself to get his own refreshment, his own pleasure, but he need not make that pure self-indulgence.

Other men, more active in body and mind, feel drawn to the modern arena of the great questions that puzzle. It matters not in which direction a man goes in these matters any more than the length of a step matters so much as does the direction in which the step is taken. He should seek those questions which engross his deepest interest, whether literary, musical, artistic, civic, economic, or what not.

Our cities, towns, communities of all sizes and kinds, urban and rural, cry out for men to solve their problems. There is room and to spare for the man of any bent. The old Romans looked forward, on coming to the age of retirement, which was definitely fixed by rule, to a rural life, when they hied themselves to a little home in the country, had open house for their friends, and "kept bees." While bee-keeping is unquestionably interesting, there are to-day other and more vital occupations awaiting the retired American.

The main thing is to secure that freedom of movement that lets a man go where he will and do what he
thinks he can do best, and prove to himself and to others
that the acquirement of the dollar is not all there is to
life. No man can realize, until on awakening some
morning he feels the exhilaration, the sense of freedom
that comes from knowing he can choose his own doings
and control his own goings. Time is of more value than
money, and it is that which the man who retires feels
that he possesses. Hamilton Mabie once said, after
his retirement from an active editorial position: "I am
so happy that the time has come when I elect what I
shall do," which is true; but then he added: "I have
rubbed out the word 'must' from my vocabulary,"
which was not true. No man ever reaches that point.
Duty of some sort confronts a man in business or out of
business, and duty spells "must." But there is less
"must" in the vocabulary of the retired man; and it is
this lessened quantity that gives the tang of joy to the
new day.

It is a wonderful inner personal satisfaction to reach
the point when a man can say: "I have enough." His
soul and character are refreshed by it: he is made over
by it. He begins a new life! he gets a sense of a new
joy; he feels, for the first time, what a priceless possession is that thing that he never knew before, freedom.
And if he seeks that freedom at the right time, when he
is at the summit of his years and powers and at the most
opportune moment in his affairs, he has that supreme
satisfaction denied to so many men, the opposite of
which comes home with such cruel force to them: that

they have overstayed their time: they have worn out their welcome.

There is no satisfaction that so thoroughly satisfies as that of going while the going is good.

Still——

The friends of Edward Bok may be right when they said he made a mistake in his retirement.

However——

As Mr. Dooley says: "It's a good thing, sometimes, to have people size ye up wrong, Hinnessey: it's whin they've got ye'er measure ye're in danger."

Edward Bok's friends have failed to get his measure, —yet!

They still have to learn what he has learned and is learning every day: "the joy," as Charles Lamb so aptly put it upon his retirement, "of walking about and around instead of to and fro."

The question now naturally arises, having read this record thus far: To what extent, with his unusual opportunities of fifty years, has the Americanization of Edward Bok gone? How far is he, to-day, an American? These questions, so direct and personal in their nature, are perhaps best answered in a way more direct and personal than the method thus far adopted in this chronicle. We will, therefore, let Edward Bok answer these questions for himself, in closing this record of his Americanization.

CHAPTER XXXVIII

WHERE AMERICA FELL SHORT WITH ME

WHEN I came to the United States as a lad of six, the most needful lesson for me, as a boy, was the necessity for thrift. I had been taught in my home across the sea that thrift was one of the fundamentals in a successful life. My family had come from a land (the Netherlands) noted for its thrift; but we had been in the United States only a few days before the realization came home strongly to my father and mother that they had brought their children to a land of waste.

Where the Dutchman saved, the American wasted. There was waste, and the most prodigal waste, on every hand. In every street-car and on every ferry-boat the floors and seats were littered with newspapers that had been read and thrown away or left behind. If I went to a grocery store to buy a peck of potatoes, and a potato rolled off the heaping measure, the groceryman, instead of picking it up, kicked it into the gutter for the wheels of his wagon to run over. The butcher's waste filled my mother's soul with dismay. If I bought a scuttle of coal at the corner grocery, the coal that missed the scuttle, instead of being shovelled up and put back into the bin, was swept into the street. My young eyes quickly saw this; in the evening I gathered up the coal thus swept away, and during the course of a week I collected a scuttleful. The first time my mother saw the garbage pail of a family almost as poor as our own, with the wife and husband constantly complaining that they could not get along, she could scarcely believe her eyes. A half pan of hominy of the preceding day's breakfast lay in the pail next to a third of a loaf of bread. In later years, when I saw, daily, a scow loaded with the garbage of Brooklyn householders being towed through New York harbor out to sea, it was an easy calculation that what was thrown away in a week's time from Brooklyn homes would feed the poor of the Netherlands.

At school, I quickly learned that to "save money" was to be "stingy"; as a young man, I soon found that the American disliked the word "economy," and on every hand as plenty grew spending grew. There was literally nothing in American life to teach me thrift or economy; everything to teach me to spend and to waste.

I saw men who had earned good salaries in their prime, reach the years of incapacity as dependents. I saw families on every hand either living quite up to their means or beyond them; rarely within them. The more a man earned, the more he—or his wife—spent. I saw fathers and mothers and their children dressed beyond their incomes. The proportion of families who ran into debt was far greater than those who saved. When a panic came, the families "pulled in"; when the panic was over, they "let out." But the end of one year found them precisely where they were at the close of the previous year, unless they were deeper in debt.

It was in this atmosphere of prodigal expenditure and culpable waste that I was to practise thrift: a fundamental in life! And it is into this atmosphere that the foreign-born comes now, with every inducement to spend and no encouragement to save. For as it was in the days of my boyhood, so it is to-day—only worse. One need only go over the experiences of the past two years, to compare the receipts of merchants who cater to the working-classes and the statements of savings-banks throughout the country, to read the story of how the foreign-born are learning the habit of criminal waste-fulness as taught them by the American.

Is it any wonder, then, that in this, one of the essentials in life and in all success, America fell short with me, as it is continuing to fall short with every foreign-born who comes to its shores?

As a Dutch boy, one of the cardinal truths taught me was that whatever was worth doing was worth doing well: that next to honesty came thoroughness as a factor in success. It was not enough that anything should be done: it was not done at all if it was not done well. I came to America to be taught exactly the opposite. The two infernal Americanisms "That's good enough" and "That will do" were early taught me, to-gether with the maxim of quantity rather than quality.

It was not the boy at school who could write the words in his copy-book best who received the praise of the teacher; it was the boy who could write the largest number of words in a given time. The acid test in arithmetic was not the mastery of the method, but the number of minutes required to work out an example. If a boy abbreviated the month January to "Jan."

and the word Company to "Co." he received a hundred per cent mark, as did the boy who spelled out the words and who could not make the teacher see that "Co." did not spell "Company."

As I grew into young manhood, and went into business, I found on every hand that quantity counted for more than quality. The emphasis was almost always placed on how much work one could do in a day, rather than upon how well the work was done. Thoroughness was at a discount on every hand; production at a premium. It made no difference in what direction I went, the result was the same: the cry was always for quantity, quantity! And into this atmosphere of almost utter disregard for quality I brought my ideas of Dutch thoroughness and my conviction that doing well whatever I did was to count as a cardinal principle in life.

During my years of editorship, save in one or two conspicuous instances, I was never able to assign to an American writer, work which called for painstaking research. In every instance, the work came back to me either incorrect in statement, or otherwise obviously lacking in careful preparation.

One of the most successful departments I ever conducted in *The Ladies' Home Journal* called for infinite reading and patient digging, with the actual results sometimes almost negligible. I made a study of my associates by turning the department over to one after another, and always with the same result: absolute lack of a capacity for patient research. As one of my editors, typically American, said to me: "It isn't worth all the trouble that you put into it." Yet no single department ever repaid the searcher more for his pains. Save for assistance derived from a single person, I had to do the work myself for all the years that the department continued. It was apparently impossible for the American to work with sufficient patience and care to achieve a result.

We all have our pet notions as to the particular evil which is "the curse of America," but I always think that Theodore Roosevelt came closest to the real curse when he classed it as a lack of thoroughness.

Here again, in one of the most important matters in life, did America fall short with me; and, what is more important, she is falling short with every foreigner that comes to her shores.

In the matter of education, America fell far short in what should be the strongest of all her institutions: the public school. A more inadequate, incompetent method of teaching, as I look back over my seven years of attendance at three different public schools, it is difficult to conceive. If there is one thing that I, as a foreign-born child, should have been carefully taught, it is the English language. The individual effort to teach this, if effort there was, and I remember none, was negligible. It was left for my father to teach me, or for me to dig it out for myself. There was absolutely no indication on the part of teacher or principal of responsibility for seeing that a foreign-born boy should acquire the English language correctly. I was taught as if I were American-born, and, of course, I was left dangling

in the air, with no conception of what I was trying
to do.

My father worked with me evening after evening;
I plunged my young mind deep into the bewildering
confusions of the language—and no one realizes the confusions of the English language as does the foreign-born
—and got what I could through these joint efforts. But
I gained nothing from the much-vaunted public-school
system which the United States had borrowed from my
own country, and then had rendered incompetent—either
by a sheer disregard for the thoroughness that makes
the Dutch public schools the admiration of the world,
or by too close a regard for politics.

Thus, in her most important institution to the foreign-born, America fell short. And while I am ready to
believe that the public school may have increased in
efficiency since that day, it is, indeed, a question for
the American to ponder, just how far the system is
efficient for the education of the child who comes to
its school without a knowledge of the first word in the
English language. Without a detailed knowledge of
the subject, I know enough of conditions in the average
public school to-day to warrant at least the suspicion
that Americans would not be particularly proud of the
system, and of what it gives for which annually they
pay millions of dollars in taxes.

I am aware in making this statement that I shall be
met with convincing instances of intelligent effort being made with the foreign-born children in special classes.
No one has a higher respect for those efforts than I have
—few, other than educators, know of them better than

I do, since I did not make my five-year study of the American public school system for naught. But I am not referring to the exceptional instance here and there. I merely ask of the American, interested as he is or should be in the Americanization of the strangers within his gates, how far the public school system, as a whole, urban and rural, adapts itself, with any true efficiency, to the foreign-born child. I venture to color his opinion in no wise; I simply ask that he will inquire and ascertain for himself, as he should do if he is interested in the future welfare of his country and his institutions; for what happens in America in the years to come depends, in large measure, on what is happening to-day in the public schools of this country.

As a Dutch boy I was taught a wholesome respect for law and for authority. The fact was impressed upon me that laws of themselves were futile unless the people for whom they were made respected them, and obeyed them in spirit more even than in the letter. I came to America to feel, on every hand, that exactly the opposite was true. Laws were passed, but were not enforced; the spirit to enforce them was lacking in the people. There was little respect for the law; there was scarcely any for those appointed to enforce it.

The nearest that a boy gets to the law is through the policeman. In the Netherlands a boy is taught that a policeman is for the protection of life and property; that he is the natural friend of every boy and man who behaves himself. The Dutch boy and the policeman are, naturally, friendly in their relations. I came to America to be told that a policeman is a boy's natural enemy; that he is eager to arrest him if he can find the slightest reason for doing so. A policeman, I was informed, was a being to hold in fear, not in respect. He was to be avoided, not to be made friends with. The result was that, as did all boys, I came to regard the policeman on our beat as a distinct enemy. His presence meant that we should "stiffen up"; his disappearance was the signal for us to "let loose."

So long as one was not caught, it did not matter. I heard mothers tell their little children that if they did not behave themselves, the policeman would put them into a bag and carry them off, or cut their ears off. Of course, the policeman became to them an object of terror; the law he represented, a cruel thing that stood for punishment. Not a note of respect did I ever hear for the law in my boyhood days. A law was something to be broken, to be evaded, to call down upon others as a source of punishment, but never to be regarded in the light of a safeguard.

And as I grew into manhood, the newspapers rang on every side with disrespect for those in authority. Under the special dispensation of the liberty of the press, which was construed into the license of the press, no man was too high to escape editorial vituperation if his politics did not happen to suit the management, or if his action ran counter to what the proprietors believed it should be. It was not criticism of his acts, it was personal attack upon the official; whether supervisor, mayor, governor, or president, it mattered not.

It is a very unfortunate impression that this American

lack of respect for those in authority makes upon the foreign-born mind. It is difficult for the foreigner to square up the arrest and deportation of a man who, through an incendiary address, seeks to overthrow governmental authority, with the ignoring of an expression of exactly the same sentiments by the editor of his next morning's newspaper. In other words, the man who writes is immune, but the man who reads, imbibes, and translates the editor's words into action is immediately marked as a culprit, and America will not harbor him. But why harbor the original cause? Is the man who speaks with type less dangerous than he who speaks with his mouth or with a bomb?

At the most vital part of my life, when I was to become an American citizen and exercise the right of suffrage, America fell entirely short. It reached out not even the suggestion of a hand.

When the Presidential Conventions had been held in the year I reached my legal majority, and I knew I could vote, I endeavored to find out whether, being foreign-born, I was entitled to the suffrage. No one could tell me; and not until I had visited six different municipal departments, being referred from one to another, was it explained that, through my father's naturalization, I became, automatically, as his son, an American citizen. I decided to read up on the platforms of the Republican and Democratic parties, but I could not secure copies anywhere, although a week had passed since they had been adopted in convention.

I was told the newspapers had printed them. It

occurred to me there must be many others besides myself who were anxious to secure the platforms of the two
parties in some more convenient form. With the eye of
necessity ever upon a chance to earn an honest penny,
I went to a newspaper office, cut out from its files the
two platforms, had them printed in a small pocket edition, sold one edition to the American News Company
and another to the News Company controlling the
Elevated Railroad bookstands in New York City, where
they sold at ten cents each. So great was the demand
which I had only partially guessed, that within three
weeks I had sold such huge editions of the little books
that I had cleared over a thousand dollars.

But it seemed to me strange that it should depend
on a foreign-born American to supply an eager public
with what should have been supplied through the agency
of the political parties or through some educational
source.

I now tried to find out what a vote actually meant.
It must be recalled that I was only twenty-one years old,
with scant education, and with no civic agency offering
me the information I was seeking. I went to the headquarters of each of the political parties and put my
query. I was regarded with puzzled looks.

"What does it mean to vote?" asked one chairman.
"Why, on Election Day you go up to the ballot-box and
put your ballot in, and that's all there is to it."

But I knew very well that that was not all there was
to it, and was determined to find out the significance of
the franchise. I met with dense ignorance on every
hand. I went to the Brooklyn Library, and was frankly

told by the librarian that he did not know of a book that would tell me what I wanted to know. This was in 1884.

As the campaign increased in intensity, I found myself a desired person in the eyes of the local campaign managers, but not one of them could tell me the significance and meaning of the privilege I was for the first time to exercise.

Finally, I spent an evening with Seth Low, and, of course, got the desired information.

But fancy the quest I had been compelled to make to acquire the simple information that should have been placed in my hands or made readily accessible to me. And how many foreign-born would take equal pains to ascertain what I was determined to find out?

Surely America fell short here at the moment most sacred to me: that of my first vote!

Is it any easier to-day for the foreign citizen to acquire this information when he approaches his first vote? I wonder! Not that I do not believe there are agencies for this purpose. You know there are, and so do I. But how about the foreign-born? Does he know it? Is it not perhaps like the owner of the bulldog who assured the friend calling on him that it never attacked friends of the family? "Yes," said the friend, "that's all right. You know and I know that I am a friend of the family; but does the dog know?"

Is it to-day made known to the foreign-born, about to exercise his privilege of suffrage for the first time, where he can be told what that privilege means: is the means to know made readily accessible to him: is it, in fact, as it should be, brought to him?

It was not to me; is it to him?

One fundamental trouble with the present desire for Americanization is that the American is anxious to Americanize two classes—if he is a reformer, the foreign-born; if he is an employer, his employees. It never occurs to him that he himself may be in need of Americanization. He seems to take it for granted that because he is American-born, he is an American in spirit and has a right understanding of American ideals. But that, by no means, always follows. There are thousands of the American-born who need Americanization just as much as do the foreign-born. There are hundreds of American employers who know far less of American ideals than do some of their employees. In fact, there are those actually engaged to-day in the work of Americanization, men at the top of the movement, who sadly need a better conception of true Americanism.

An excellent illustration of this came to my knowledge when I attended a large Americanization Conference in Washington. One of the principal speakers was an educator of high standing and considerable influence in one of the most important sections of the United States. In a speech setting forth his ideas of Americanization, he dwelt with much emphasis and at considerable length upon instilling into the mind of the foreign-born the highest respect for American institutions.

After the Conference he asked me whether he could see me that afternoon at my hotel; he wanted to talk about contributing to the magazine. When he came, before approaching the object of his talk, he launched out on a tirade against the President of the United States; the weakness of the Cabinet, the inefficiency of the Congress, and the stupidity of the Senate. If words could have killed, there would have not remained a single living member of the Administration at Washington.

After fifteen minutes of this, I reminded him of his speech and the emphasis which he had placed upon the necessity of inculcating in the foreign-born respect for American institutions.

Yet this man was a power in his community, a strong influence upon others; he believed he could Americanize others, when he himself, according to his own statements, lacked the fundamental principle of Americanization. What is true of this man is, in lesser or greater degree, true of hundreds of others. Their Americanization consists of lip-service; the real spirit, the only factor which counts in the successful teaching of any doctrine, is absolutely missing. We certainly cannot teach anything approaching a true Americanism until we ourselves feel and believe and practise in our own lives what we are teaching to others. No law, no lip-service, no effort, however well-intentioned, will amount to anything worth while in inculcating the true American spirit in our foreign-born citizens until we are sure that the American spirit is understood by ourselves and is warp and woof of our own being.

To the American, part and parcel of his country, these particulars in which his country falls short with the foreign-born are, perhaps, not so evident; they may even seem not so very important. But to the foreign-born they seem distinct lacks; they loom large; they form serious handicaps which, in many cases, are never surmounted; they are a menace to that Americanization which is, to-day, more than ever our fondest dream, and which we now realize more keenly than before is our most vital need.

It is for this reason that I have put them down here as a concrete instance of where and how America fell short in my own Americanization, and, what is far more serious to me, where she is falling short in her Americanization of thousands of other foreign-born.

"Yet you succeeded," it will be argued.

That may be; but you, on the other hand, must admit that I did not succeed by reason of these shortcomings: it was in spite of them, by overcoming them—a result that all might not achieve.

CHAPTER XXXIX

WHAT I OWE TO AMERICA

WHATEVER shortcomings I may have found during my fifty-year period of Americanization; however America may have failed to help my transition from a foreigner into an American, I owe to her the most priceless gift that any nation can offer, and that is opportunity.

As the world stands to-day, no nation offers opportunity in the degree that America does to the foreign-born. Russia may, in the future, as I like to believe she will, prove a second United States of America in this respect. She has the same limitless area; her people the same potentialities. But, as things are to-day, the United States offers, as does no other nation, a limitless opportunity: here a man can go as far as his abilities will carry him. It may be that the foreign-born, as in my own case, must hold on to some of the ideals and ideas of the land of his birth; it may be that he must develop and mould his character by overcoming the habits resulting from national shortcomings. But into the best that the foreign-born can retain, America can graft such a wealth of inspiration, so high a national idealism, so great an opportunity for the highest endeavor, as to make him the fortunate man of the earth to-day.

He can go where he will: no traditions hamper him; no limitations are set except those within himself. The larger the area he chooses in which to work, the larger the vision he demonstrates, the more eager the people are to give support to his undertakings if they are convinced that he has their best welfare as his goal. There is no public confidence equal to that of the American public, once it is obtained. It is fickle, of course, as are all publics, but fickle only toward the man who cannot maintain an achieved success.

A man in America cannot complacently lean back upon victories won, as he can in the older European countries, and depend upon the glamour of the past to sustain him or the momentum of success to carry him. Probably the most alert public in the world, it requires of its leaders that they be alert. Its appetite for variety is insatiable, but its appreciation, when given, is full-handed and whole-hearted. The American public never holds back from the man to whom it gives; it never bestows in a niggardly way; it gives all or nothing.

What is not generally understood of the American people is their wonderful idealism. Nothing so completely surprises the foreign-born as the discovery of this trait in the American character. The impression is current in European countries—perhaps less generally since the war—that America is given over solely to a worship of the American dollar. While between nations as between individuals, comparisons are valueless, it may not be amiss to say, from personal knowledge, that the Dutch worship the gulden infinitely more than do the Americans the dollar.

I do not claim that the American is always conscious of this idealism; often he is not. But let a great convulsion touching moral questions occur, and the result always shows how close to the surface is his idealism. And the fact that so frequently he puts over it a thick veneer of materialism does not affect its quality. The truest approach, the only approach in fact, to the American character is, as Sir James Bryce has so well said, through its idealism.

It is this quality which gives the truest inspiration to the foreign-born in his endeavor to serve the people of his adopted country. He is mentally sluggish, indeed, who does not discover that America will make good with him if he makes good with her.

But he must play fair. It is essentially the straight game that the true American plays, and he insists that you shall play it too. Evidence there is, of course, to the contrary in American life, experiences that seem to give ground for the belief that the man succeeds who is not scrupulous in playing his cards. But never is this true in the long run. Sooner or later—sometimes, unfortunately, later than sooner—the public discovers the trickery. In no other country in the world is the moral conception so clear and true as in America, and no people will give a larger and more permanent reward to the man whose effort for that public has its roots in honor and truth.

"The sky is the limit" to the foreign-born who comes to America endowed with honest endeavor, ceaseless industry, and the ability to carry through. In any honest endeavor, the way is wide open to the will to succeed. Every path beckons, every vista invites, every talent is called forth, and every efficient effort finds its due reward. In no land is the way so clear and so free.

How good an American has the process of Americanization made me? That I cannot say. Who *can* say that of himself? But when I look around me at the American-born I have come to know as my close friends, I wonder whether, after all, the foreign-born does not make in some sense a better American—whether he is not able to get a truer perspective; whether his is not the deeper desire to see America greater; whether he is not less content to let its faulty institutions be as they are; whether in seeing faults more clearly he does not make a more decided effort to have America reach those ideals or those fundamentals of his own land which he feels are in his nature, and the best of which he is anxious to graft into the character of his adopted land?

It is naturally with a feeling of deep satisfaction that I remember two Presidents of the United States considered me a sufficiently typical American to wish to send me to my native land as the accredited minister of my adopted country. And yet when I analyze the reasons for my choice in both these instances, I derive a deeper satisfaction from the fact that my strong desire to work in America for America led me to ask to be permitted to remain here.

It is this strong impulse that my Americanization has made the driving power of my life. And I ask no greater privilege than to be allowed to live to see my potential America become actual: the America that I like to think of as the America of Abraham Lincoln and of Theodore

Roosevelt—not faultless, but less faulty. It is a part in trying to shape that America, and an opportunity to work in that America when it comes, that I ask in return for what I owe to her. A greater privilege no man could have.

EDWARD WILLIAM BOK

BIOGRAPHICAL DATA

1863: Born, October 9, at Helder, Netherlands.

1870: September 20: Arrived in the United States.

1870: Entered public schools of Brooklyn, New York.

1873: Obtained first position in Frost's Bakery, Smith Street, Brooklyn, at 50 cents per week.

1876: August 7: Entered employ of the Western Union Telegraph Company as office-boy.

1882: Entered employ of Henry Holt & Company as stenographer.

1884: Entered employ of Charles Scribner's Sons as stenographer.

1884: Became editor of *The Brooklyn Magazine*.

1886: Founded The Bok Syndicate Press.

1887: Published Henry Ward Beecher Memorial (privately printed).

1889: October 20: Became editor of *The Ladies' Home Journal*.

1890: Published *Successward:* Doubleday, McClure & Company.

1894: Published *Before He Is Twenty:* Fleming H. Revell Company.

1896: October 22: Married Mary Louise Curtis.

1897: September 7: Son born: William Curtis Bok.

1900: Published *The Young Man in Business:* L. C. Page & Company.

1905: January 25: Son born: Cary William Bok.

1906: Published *Her Brother's Letters* (Anonymous): Moffat, Yard & Company.

1907: Degree of LL.D. of Order of Augustinian Fathers conferred by order of Pope Pius X., by the Most Reverend Diomede Falconio, D.D., Apostolic Delegate to the United States at Villanova College.

1910: Degree of LL.D. conferred, in absentia, by Hope College, Holland, Michigan (the only Dutch college in the United States).

1911: Founded, with others, The Child Federation of Philadelphia.

1912: Published: *The Edward Bok Books of Self-Knowledge;* five volumes: Fleming H. Revell Company.

1913: Founded, with others, The Merion Civic Association, at Merion, Pennsylvania.

1915: Published *Why I Believe in Poverty:* Houghton, Mifflin Company.

1916: Published poem, *God's Hand*, set to music by Josef Hofmann: Schirmer & Company.

1917: Vice-president Philadelphia Belgian Relief Commission.

1917: Member of National Y. M. C. A. War Work Council.

1917: State chairman for Pennsylvania of Y. M. C. A. War Work Council.

1918: Member of Executive Committee and chairman of Publicity Committee, Philadelphia War Chest.

1918: Chairman of Philadelphia Y. M. C. A. Recruiting Committee.

1918: State chairman for Pennsylvania of United War Work Campaign.

1918: August–November: visited the battle-fronts in France as guest of the British Government.

1919: September 22: Relinquished editorship of *The Ladies' Home Journal*, completing thirty years of service.

1920: September 20: Upon the 50th anniversary of arrival in the United States, published *The Americanization of Edward Bok*.

1921: Created the Philadelpia Award of $10,000 a year to the citizen of Philadelphia or vicinity who, during the preceding year, shall have performed, or brought to its culmination, an act or contributed a service calculated to advance the best and largest interests of Philadelphia.

1921: Founded the Philadelphia Forum at Philadelphia.

1921: Elected President of the Netherland-American Foundation at New York.

1921: Awarded, by Columbia University, the Joseph Pulitzer Prize for the best American biography for 1920.

1921: Awarded the Gold Medal by the Academy of Political and Social Science at New York.

1922: Published *Two Persons:* Charles Scribner's Sons.

1922: Created the Citizens' Award of $1000 to be awarded, each year, to each of the six policemen, firemen and park guards of the city of Philadelphia who shall have performed an outstanding act of service or contributed to the efficiency of the service during the preceding calendar year.

1923: Published *A Man from Maine:* Charles Scribner's Sons.

1923: Degree of LL.D. conferred by Rutgers College.

1923: Degree of Doctor of Humane Letters conferred by Tufts. College.

1923: Edited series of *Great Hollanders:* Charles Scribner's Sons.

1923: Created the American Peace Award of $100,000 for the best practicable plan by which the United States may co-operate with other nations to achieve and preserve the peace of the world.

1923: Created the Harvard Awards bestowed by Harvard University for raising the standard of advertisements in American periodicals and for the intelligent conception and execution of plans for advertising.

THE EXPRESSION OF A PERSONAL PLEASURE

I cannot close this record of a boy's development without an attempt to suggest the sense of deep personal pleasure which I feel that the imprint on the title-page of this book should be that of the publishing house which, thirty-six years ago, I entered as stenographer. It was there I received my start; it was there I laid the foundation of that future career then so hidden from me. The happiest days of my young manhood were spent in the employ of this house; I there began friendships which have grown closer with each passing year. And one of my deepest sources of satisfaction is, that during all the thirty-one years which have followed my resignation from the Scribner house, it has been my good fortune to hold the friendship, and, as I have been led to believe, the respect of my former employers. That they should now be my publishers demonstrates, in a striking manner, the curious turning of the wheel of time, and gives me a sense of gratification difficult of expression.

Edward W. Bok

INDEX

COSIMO CLASSICS

COSIMO is an innovative publisher of books and publications that inspire, inform and engage readers worldwide. Our titles are drawn from a range of subjects including health, business, philosophy, history, science and sacred texts. We specialize in using print-on-demand technology (POD), making it possible to publish books for both general and specialized audiences and to keep books in print indefinitely. With POD technology new titles can reach their audiences faster and more efficiently than with traditional publishing.

> **Permanent Availability:** Our books & publications never go out-of-print.

> **Global Availability:** Our books are always available online at popular retailers and can be ordered from your favorite local bookstore.

COSIMO CLASSICS brings to life unique, rare, out-of-print classics representing subjects as diverse as *Alternative Health, Business and Economics, Eastern Philosophy, Personal Growth, Mythology, Philosophy, Sacred Texts, Science, Spirituality* and much more!

COSIMO-on-DEMAND publishes your books, publications and reports. If you are an Author, part of an Organization, or a Benefactor with a publishing project and would like to bring books back into print, publish new books fast and effectively, would like your publications, books, training guides, and conference reports to be made available to your members and wider audiences around the world, we can assist you with your publishing needs.

Visit our website at www.cosimobooks.com to learn more about Cosimo, browse our catalog, take part in surveys or campaigns, and sign-up for our newsletter.

And if you wish please drop us a line at info@cosimobooks.com. We look forward to hearing from you.

Printed in the United States
97134LV00003B/133/A

9 781596 050730